The Psychoanalysis of Money

THE PSYCHOANALYSIS OF MONEY

By
Ernest Bornemann

Urizen Books
New York

Library of Congress Cataloging in Publication Data

Borneman, Ernest, 1915-   comp.
The psychoanalysis of money.

Translation of Die Psychoanalyse des Geldes.
Bibliography: p.
Includes index.
1. Money--Psychological aspects--Addresses, essays, lectures. 2. Psychoanalysis--Addresses, essays, lectures. I. Title.
HG221.3.B5813   332.4'01'9   76-8823
ISBN 0-916354-02-4
ISBN 0-916354-03-2 pbk.

ISBN 0-916354-02-4
0-916354-03-2

Contents

Introduction

I
On the Psychoanalysis of Money

This book is the first attempt to bring together some of the major works of the psychoanalytical literature on the origin and nature of money and to provide a critical commentary on them. Some of these writings have been out of print for many years, while others were originally published in journals that are not readily accessible, and have never been reprinted. My selection was not governed by my own beliefs as to what is true or false but rather by the desire to present the principal schools of the psychoanalytical analysis of money. I even included essays I consider questionable from a clinical point of view, for they also are part of the irrevocable history of psychoanalysis. I hope that my effort to be unprejudiced in my selection entitles me to some critical reflections.

The plan of this book is simple. It begins with Freud's pioneering work (1908) on the anal character of money and then presents in more or less chronological sequence some of the most important writings based on that thesis. The second part comprises the ethnological, archaeological, cultural, and historical studies of important psychoanalysts on the origin and effect of money. The third and final part is made up of psychoanalytical studies which do not derive from Freud's theory of the anal origin of money but examine money, property, and ownership from other psychoanalytical points of view. Where the author did so in the original text, I provide a bibliography at the end of each contribution. My own bibliography at the end of these studies is arranged as follows: 1. psychoanalytical and psychological studies on the theory of money. 2. works on the origin and history of money. Some analysts have posited an analogy between the history of money and the pathogenesis of the obsessive-compulsive anal neurosis and have attempted to derive the former from the latter. Since this appears extremely questionable to me, I feel it is especially important to direct the reader's attention to those works which deal in a concrete, historically documented manner with the actual development of money and ownership.

II

In his *Three Essays on the Theory of Sexuality* (1904-1905), Freud argued that the perdurable character traits of the adult can be traced to three infantile tendencies:

1. The unmodified persistence of the original, inherited instinct.
2. sublimation of this instinct due to environmental influence.
3. reaction formation against it.

Because the strength of the various components (i.e., the original one, the sublimated one, and the one due to reaction formation) differs in the resulting synthesis, character structures of individuals vary. In the case of inherited anal erotic instincts, this means:

1. unmodified persistence of anal erotism expresses itself in adults as coprophilia, the desire for anal coitus, homosexuality, and other anal-oriented forms of sexual intercourse.
2. Sublimation of the anal instinct leads to thrift. For just as the child withholds its feces for the sake of more intense anal excitations during defecation, the adult retains his money for the sake of more in-

tense psychic excitation. Similarly, Freud traces the later stubbornness of the sublimated anal erotic to his early refusal to empty his bowels when he is placed on the chamber pot.

3. Reaction formation against the anal instinct expresses itself in the rejection of excrement, filth, and uncleanliness. Interest in the "reverse side" thus leads to a reversal of the original interest in feces, i.e., to an interest in cleanliness.

The crux of psychoanalytical doctrines concerning the anality of money lies in the observation that feces is the child's first autonomous product, its first "possession." If the child retains feces as long as possible, it does so because it sees in it its first "savings." *Thrift derives from the pleasure of retaining the contents of the intestine.* The child's belief in the omnipotence of its desires (when it cries, it is fed; when it wets itself, it is dried) continues into this relatively late developmental phase because in its excrement it sees the first proof that it can produce something. At the same time, its feces gives it power over its parents: if the child defecates when and where the mother wishes (into the pot rather than the diaper), it is praised as an intelligent, good, and clean child. If it wets its bed, it is chided for being stupid, dirty, and backward. The first influence the child exerts on its surroundings is thus due to the regulation of its stool. The child discovers: if I defecate promptly, as soon as mother places me on the chamber pot, I can please her; I can make her fondle me, give me delicacies, and rewards. But if I defy her and either wet my bed or refuse when *she* wants me to, I can provoke anger. So I can do with that great being on whom I was dependent up to now whatever I please.

The child's discovery of the self and of its power over its surroundings are thus concurrent events. It is also true that much of later character development hinges on the relatively early or relatively late time chosen by parents for the toilet training of their child. As is well known, Freud believed that the child passes through four phases which determine its fate up to an advanced age: the first phase is where the entire skin surface of the child is equally receptive to stimuli of pleasure and displeasure, a phase he called *polymorphous*. There follows a phase where the entire sensuous life of the neonate depends on its relation to the mother's breast or the milk bottle: everything is concentrated in the region of the mouth from which the child derives both food and pleasure. Freud called this phase *oral*. Next we have the phase just described where the child is made to feel the power of its surroundings by being taught to be clean, and thus discovers that it is necessary to subordinate itself to others. But we have seen that this phase also makes possible the discovery of its own influence on the surrounding world. It is therefore an important phase of Ego formation. Since here everything depends on the control of the sphincter, Freud called the entire phase *anal*. Finally, during puberty, and in the case of normal development, the excitations of the oral and anal region give way to those of the sexual organs. Freud called this the *genital* phase. This is not the place to discuss Freud's thesis according to which all so-called "perversions" are psychic infantilisms, forms of sexual immaturity where the person concerned was arrested in an early phase or suffered a relapse into such a phase as the result of later experiences. We must point out, however, that the behavior of the adult may take on a lifelong obsessive-compulsive quality when the psychosexual development of the child encounters premature or excessively intense suppression during the anal phase, particularly as the result of toilet training, a process which occurs much earlier in our civilization than in other, more balanced cultures. A child that is subjected to these interventions at a time it is not ready for them may attain to the genital phase only imperfectly, or not at all. Its genital pleasure is confused, weakened or redirected by anal influences. Through regression to this phase, adults easily develop obsessive-compulsive neuroses where the three characteristics of the anal character described by Freud appear in exaggerated fashion or turn into their exaggerated opposite through reaction formation. In what follows, I shall refer to this type of obsessive-compulsive neurotic as anal neurotic.

In such a person, the qualities that cluster around the focus of thrift may take one of two directions. In the first, we find miserliness, envy, mistrust, doubt, a tendency toward brooding, inwardness, a tendency toward complex rationalizing, prudishness, sexual repression. In the other direction, we get conscientiousness, cleanliness, orderliness, thoroughness, rigidity, willfulness, obstinacy. The reaction formation is the opposite of all these qualities: disorderliness, prodigality, unscrupulousness, and so on. In their rudimentary form, all these elements already show aspects of an obsessive-compulsive character, but in their developed and exaggerated form, they represent an unmistakable obsessive-compulsive neurosis.

But it is not only the case that certain cultures encourage certain character formations and produce certain obsessive-compulsive neuroses; it also happens that within a given culture premature or late weaning, premature or late toilet training produce certain neurotic symptoms which are reflected in the class structure and the forms of production. Orthodox Freudians would say that parents exercise a determining influence on the character of the child by conscious or unconscious educational methods. Once the child is grown up, it will bring up its children in its own image or that of its parents. The educational tradition thus creates a social order which perpetuates the character of the first generation. According to Freud, the anal character has a pronounced conservative tendency, and this also expresses itself in the retention of the parents' pedagogic methods.

In certain respects, the oral character which marked the culture of feudalism was more flexible than the anal character which defines the bourgeoisie. But it was unable to implement new, world-changing methods of production and therefore created a culture that was rigid, recalcitrant, and never changed over the centuries. It reflected less the actual oral character of the individuals than the primitiveness of their means of production. This suggests the simultaneous presence of two, reciprocally neutralizing evolutionary processes. There can be no doubt about the correctness of Freud's thesis that relations between parents and children not only significantly influence the further development of the child but also the nature of the social order itself. At the same time, however, an important developmental process occurs which moves in the opposite direction: new means of production create new tasks for mankind, and new tasks demand new pedagogic methods. The children brought up by these new pedagogic methods can deal more adequately with the new means of production than those brought up according to the old pattern. It follows that ultimately the new character traits can be understood only by reference to the development of new means of production.

This logic was worked out primarily by Marxist analysts, but they could build on a pioneering study by Oskar Pfitzer, *Der seelische Aufbau des klassischen Kapitalismus and des Geldgeistes* (Bibliography 47), where capitalism is interpreted for the first time as a mass obsessional neurosis. In the original version of his *Charakteranalyse* (1933), which is not identical with the edition now commercially available (1970), Wilhelm Reich elaborated these suggestions very intelligently, and in Erich Fromm's *Fear of Freedom* (1941) the same ideas constitute the central theme. In an earlier sketch for this book, the essay "Die Bedeutung der psychoanalytischen Charaktersoziologie für die Sozialpsychologie" (1932), Fromm describes the difference between the relatively late toilet training during the age of feudalism and the premature toilet training which characterized capitalism from its very beginning. Fromm believes, and I am convinced he is right, that this permissive toilet training shaped feudal culture, and that it was modified by that culture in turn. It was a culture based on an indolent, hardly changing mode of production. Surplus could not be invested, there was no competition, incentives were few. Wealth was therefore used for display and extravagance and to acquire gold, precious stones, clothing. But when that "association of craftsmen, merchants and money lenders" which led to the rise of capitalism put forward its claim to power and easily destroyed feudalism in the process, thrift, intelligent investment, competition, and incentive became the slogans and also began to shape the education of children. For the men and women who developed these new values also wanted to give their children an early training in cleanliness and frugality. Children were thus cured of soiling their beds much more drastically and at a much earlier time. As a result, they developed precisely those characteristics their parents expected of them: not merely cleanliness and frugality, but conscientiousness, punctuality, orderliness, persistence, thoroughness, and sexual abstinence.

Since we are still living in the bourgeois age, these criteria of value not only shaped the bourgeoisie itself but also the thought of the anti-bourgeois opposition. When they first begin to reflect about these matters, many readers to whom all this is new will wonder what there may be to criticize in such indisputable virtues as cleanliness, conscientiousness, thoroughness, orderliness, and persistence. Doesn't the development of socialism demand these identical values? The irrational, compulsive nature of these "virtues" reveals itself only to those who have analyzed and interpreted their origin in a large number of instances. To the extent that all these characteristics in their exaggerated form are unmistakable symptoms of an obsessional neurosis, the capitalist system does in fact show marks of an obsessive-compulsive neurotic syndrome. And a good deal of what has turned out to be the wrong track in the history of socialism as it groped for new solutions, especially the authoritarian, irrational, self-negating aspect of Stalinism, can also only be interpreted as a psychic symptom which created the same mischief in the USSR and the Peoples' Republics as in capitalist countries.

The economic basis always determines the pedagogic superstructure. If during the period of transition from late capitalism to the dictatorship of the proletariat those economic structures which demand a centralized administrative system that represses and destroys bourgeois residues necessarily continue to exist as part of the basis, they will bring with them a certain degree of authoritarian education with strict and early oral and anal weaning. Such educational methods not only affect the anal but already the oral and indeed the polymorphous phase of the child's libidinal development.

It is therefore impossible to derive the psychogenesis of human attitudes toward property, possessions, and money from libidinal development alone. But since we decided to present the psychoanalytic theory of money before examining it in all its details, we shall merely point out here that later psychoanalytic theories (Abraham, Ferenczi, Jones) endorsed by Freud maintained that it was only the retentive, collecting aspect of the human interest in money that derived from the anal character. The acquisitive, incorporating aspect belongs to the earlier oral phase. Since one of these aspects occurs only rarely without traces of the other, we can understand the interest in money in its totality only if we also investigate the earlier libidinal stages.

In its genesis, the anal character is closely tied to the vicissitudes of oral erotism, and this is hardly surprising since both experience their most intense transformations at the same time. In bourgeois society, weaning and toilet training usually occur at the same time, or at least within the same year. Initially then, the child has two sources of pleasure: the mouth and the anus, the ingestion of food and its elimination, taking and giving. But now a third element is added in which both of these are involved: holding on to things, retaining things, property.

Abraham once expressed this in the following words:

> The original unchecked voiding of bodily excretions was accompanied by stimulation of the apertures of the body

> which was undoubtedly pleasurable. If the child adapts itself to the demands of training and learns to retain its excretions this new activity also gets to be accompanied by pleasure. The pleasurable sensations in the organ connected with this process form the foundation upon which the mental pleasure in retention of every kind of possession is gradually built up. More recent investigations have shown that the possession of an object originally signified to the infantile mind the having incorporated it into its own body. Whereas to begin with, pleasure was only associated with taking in something coming from without or with expelling bodily contents, now there is added the pleasure in retaining bodily contents, which leads to pleasure in all forms of property. The relation in which these three sources of physical and mental gratification stand to one another is of the greatest practical significance for the later social conduct of the individual. If the pleasure in getting or taking is brought into the most favourable relation possible with the pleasure in possession, as well as with that in giving up, then an exceedingly important step has been made in laying the foundations of the individual's social relations. For when such a relationship between the three tendencies is present, the most important preliminary condition for overcoming the ambivalence of the individual's emotional life has been established. (Karl Abraham, "The Influence of Oral Erotism on Character Formation," in *On Character And Libido Development, Six Essays*, New York, 1966, pp. 154-155)

Abraham warns us here about the danger that lies in an inadequate mastery of *ambivalence* and is using that term in the meaning given it by Freud and Bleuler: it refers to the infantile ambiguity of feelings which may lead to schizophrenia and other psychoses in adults unless it is overcome once and for all during the genital phase. Up to that time, it is completely normal for children to have conflicting emotions which appear simultaneously or in very rapid alternation, such as antipathy and affection, for example, but also (as on the secondary level of the anal phase) a wish to gratify a desire and simultaneous disgust or (as on the primary level of the genital phase, the "phallic" phase) a desire for sexual experience and simultaneous feelings of shame. This ambivalence of the child is characterized, in other words, by the fact that a goal is both desired and unconsciously feared. The danger of ambivalence is not only the intense psychic conflict but, more importantly, the sudden transformation of an emotion into its opposite.

But because it is typical of the anal character that it retains certain aspects of infantile ambivalence or regresses to them, we frequently find in such persons contradictory attitudes toward money which can often be interpreted only by the experienced analyst. Exaggerated cleanliness or thrift, or their opposites, for example, hardly ever appear in isolation; we always also find the other extreme as a weaker or stronger component. A second aspect of libidinal development, of decisive influence on man's attitude toward money, is the maturing of *object libido*, the capacity to love others unselfishly and to be tender toward them. The entire apparatus of libidinal development serves the genesis of this capacity, for the neonate perceives the environment merely as an extension of itself and can therefore neither understand nor love it. It is only by the detour of self love that it turns towards others. But this turning toward others remains ambivalent until here also auto-erotism, narcissism, and ambivalence are conquered during the genital phase and subordinated to the primacy of genital love.

The most important tool in the development of the child's object libido is the object libido of the adults under whose care it matures. A child that does not have the example of love will experience the greatest difficulties in attaining the capacity to love. It will never entirely eliminate those impulses which are directed against the object world and therefore easily fall prey to an exploitative, greedy conception of money. Finally, we also have to consider the development of inhibitions as we examine the maturing of human attitudes toward property and money. The earliest developmental phases of the child are free of such inhibitions because no relations of any kind toward the outside world exist as yet. It is only on the secondary level of the oral phase, when the first teeth irrupt, that the first inhibition, fear, appears. The destructive desire to bite that comes into being during these years also creates a second inhibition: a feeling of guilt. A third inhibition is the ambivalent feelings of disgust and sympathy. Both are reactions against the unconscious but extremely strong desire to incorporate or ingest things. The gamut runs all the way from the eating of feces and the swallowing of toys to the unconscious desire to introject the mother so that she may always be there. If, during the phallic phase, the libido begins to turn toward the opposite sex before the individual becomes sexually mature, the next inhibition to develop is shame. Object libido already exists but in bourgeois society it usually excludes the genitalia, even today. If this inhibition is overcome by satisfactory sexual relations, a final inhibition, a sense of social responsibility, takes its place. It is this feeling which is so frequently absent in the conviction of the money neurotic that all property must be private property.

If in any given phase of libidinal development the inhibition appropriate to it is disregarded or not overcome, attainment of the following phase is rarely successful. An inadequate sense of social responsibility or a lack of respect for the economic needs of others frequently can thus be explained by saying that the inhibitions of earlier phases of libidinal development were either disregarded or not overcome. When we encounter a ruthless character type exclusively devoted to appropriation and who considers the concept of communal welfare and communal property a *contradictio in adjecto*, we are justified in believing that there are unresolved inhibitions somewhere in the etiology of his neurosis.

In order to explain the complicated interaction of libidinal development, object libido, ambivalence, and inhibitions, I have tried to provide a synoptic representation of the seven steps of the maturation process of the child in the following table. The information it contains derives from Freud, Abraham, Melanie Klein, and René Spitz. The concepts "partial love" and "genital exclusion" will be explained in the course of the analysis of the phase to which they belong.

1. Polymorphously perverse phase

We already mentioned this phase at the beginning. It represents the earliest phase of libidinal development. Erogenous zones, love objects, and inhibitions have not yet developed, and for this reason there is as yet no emotional ambivalence. The child is neither subject to oral nor to anal or genital instincts, for erogenous zones have not yet localized, the libido being wholly undifferentiated. We may call this a condition of primitive communism in the hierarchy of feelings and instincts.

2. Primary level of oral phase (sucking stage)

Given favorable conditions, the primary level of the oral phase can become the happiest period of life. Never again (except perhaps in the very first, the polymorphous phase) will so many blissful, gratifying elements come together. The child has no cares, need worry neither about work nor the making of money, experiences the world as totally safe, is fed when hungry (at least that's what ought to be the case), consoled when it cries, dried when it wets itself, embraced, kissed, fondled. The ingestion of food will never again be accompanied by so many sensual excitations. The pleasure in stilling hunger and thirst combines with the pleasant sensation of sucking at the nipple. At the same time, the child presses the warm, elastic breast of the mother with its hands. The mother's warm arm holds the child's body. Frequently, it is rocked and cradled. Consequently skin, muscle, oral, and manual stimuli are mediated simultaneously.

Inhibitions and emotional ambivalence are absent. The child is confused neither by love nor by hatred. In its psyche, there is no opposition between the feeding mother and the sucking child. "I" and "thou" do not yet exist. The child attempts to incorporate the world by sucking, yet does not perceive it as a distinct object but considers it part of its own body. This stage, which usually extends over the greater part of the first year in the bourgeois society of Europe, was called "cannibalistic" by Freud because here a differentiation between the ingestion of food and libidinal activity does not yet exist: "The object of the one activity is also that of the other." This primitive form of pleasure is never wholly overcome and survives throughout life under a variety of masks. In the adult's later attitude toward property it is often characterized by intense desire and striving, and in the attitude toward money as the attempt to "suck others dry," to exploit them. Yet a bad conscience does not burden the individual, for the libidinal tendencies which originate during this phase are wholly free of those destructive desires which attach to the impulses of the following phase. The more undisturbed, the more pleasurable the sucking stage of individuals, the stronger their later conviction that things will always turn out for them. They confront life with an unshakable optimism which often does in fact help them become financially successful in bourgeois society.

But in other oral characters who are fixated at this level or have regressed to it, the opposite often happens. Since they live under the illusion that the world is their mother, they do not work or do so only rarely, and expect society to feed them. The sucking stage has spoiled them so thoroughly that they believe the mother's breast will always flow for them. They neither despise nor respect property and possessions because they do not perceive these things as objects in the first place.

The evils of such overindulgence (coddling, pampering) should not be underestimated. For some time now, there has been such a strong opposition to premature weaning among progressive, liberal, and radical parents that some mothers fall into the opposite extreme. But in bourgeois society, late weaning is almost always done by neurotic, frequently frigid mothers who experience marked sensations of pleasure while given suck to their children and who use them as a surrogate for the satisfaction of normal genital desires. When suckling continues longer than necessary, this is not for the sake of the child but for that of the mother. The result may be either a life-long inhibition against work as we just described it, and which may also express itself as a paralysis of the desire to live and to strive, a paralysis of the ability to make one's way, or it may result in the syndrome of ruthless appropriation. A person unfamiliar with the effects of ambivalence may find it difficult to see how two such opposed character types can result from the same cause. But clinical experience establishes beyond a doubt that we are dealing with identical causes in both cases.

3. *Secondary level of the oral phase (biting stage)*

Every phase of libidinal development is divided into two levels through an act of intervention by the external world: the oral phase through weaning or withdrawal of the bottle, the anal phase through toilet training, the genital phase through the prohibition of sexual intercourse. But during the oral phase, no normal mother attempts to begin weaning until the child has grown teeth for biting and chewing. Thus teeth marks the biological entry into the second oral level.

If the child is weaned too early or too late, the harm is almost irreparable. Just as the primary level of the oral phase is the happiest time of their life for many, so the transition to the secondary level can become the unhappiest for others. This may have many reasons, such as the premature loss of contact with the breast and body of the mother, for example, a negative reaction to the milk being offered, or intestinal colic. If the child cries because of hunger or pain in such cases, the mother usually tends to be less loving and patient than when the neonate is content. But if the child is not fondled, consoled, embraced, or cradled enough, uncertainty and unhappiness already make their appearance at this time.

As a result, the child rushes to the following level with an increased intensity, a kind of unquenchable greed for gratification. This carried the ever-present danger of new disappointment to which it will react with an intensified tendency toward regression to the earlier phase. Pleasure can only be renounced when an exchange takes place. If the child surrenders the gratification of the desire to suck, which is the most important characteristic of the primary oral level, it attempts to derive a special satisfaction from biting, the characteristic of the secondary oral level. It takes every object it can get hold of into its mouth and tries to destroy it with considerable vigor and clearly perceivable pleasure. Here, the ambivalence of pleasure emerges for the first time. We have a case of satisfaction through destruction. In the case of the child that was disappointed during the early oral phase (but also in the case of the child whose sucking period was extended unduly due to pampering), the pleasure taken in biting will be particularly marked. The beginnings of character formation thus occur under the influence of an abnormally accented ambivalence.

While the primary level of the oral phase, the sucking period, may be called pre-ambivalent, the secondary level represents the beginning of a conflict due to ambivalence which will govern all of later life unless it is subordinated to object love on the secondary genital level, and reduced thereby. But the obsessional neurotic almost always fails in this task, indeed this failure is the distinguishing characteristic of this kind of neurotic. Only the healthy, mature, balanced individual who has freed himself from the residues of infantile sexuality is also free of ambivalence. His libido has reached a post-ambivalent stage and thus acquired the capacity to master the object world. It is this mastery which the obsessional neurotic usually fails to attain.

The transformation of the desire to suck into the desire to bite attracts certain forms of aggression like a magnet. Freud speaks of a reservoir of free-floating libido which serves oral and anal instincts indifferently. Since they attach themselves to the instincts like particles to a magnet, Freud called them partial or component instincts. He distinguished primarily four varieties: active and passive aggression (sadism and masochism), and looking and being looked at (scopophilia and exhibitionism). During a time when the hands are used for grasping and holding at best, the teeth are the first organ the child can use to destroy the objects of its environment. In this process, it first discovers the outside world as an autonomous and independently existing entity, something that can be ingested but that is also destroyed during the process of ingestion. It is only here that Freud's interpretation of the oral phase as a cannibalistic period takes on its clear meaning.

Money neurotics who have been fixated at this stage of development or regress to it have been characterized as "vampires" by Karl Abraham, and this in both the psychological and the financial meaning of the term: "One might almost say that they 'cling like leeches' to other people. . . . In some cases . . . their behavior has an element of cruelty in it as well, which makes them something like vampires to other people" (op. cit. p. 159). From the point of view of the psychoanalytic theory of money, this stage is important because it is considered the origin of envy.

As early as 1921, Eisler pointed to the oral source of envy (M. J. Eisler, "Uber Schlaflust und gestörte Schlaffähigkeit," *Internationale Zeitschrift für Psychoanalyse*, 7, 1921, 166-178). If a child that bites and chews its food has the opportunity to observe a younger brother or sister as they suck, envy is increased. According to Eisler, the envious not only covets the property of others but also feels spite toward the person envied. This is a case where oral and aggressive (sadistic) tendencies combine.

Kleptomania also almost always represents a regression to the secondary oral level since its unconscious aim is the oral incorporation of the desired object. Abraham cites a case of kleptomania due to rebellion against the father: "Her kleptomanic impulses were in a great measure derived from her active castration tendency directed against her father. The unconscious aim of her thefts was to rob him of his envied possession so as to have it herself or to identify herself with it. That those thefts were connected with the person of her father was made evident in many ways. For instance, she had on one occasion taken an enema tube out of his room and had used it—as a substitute for his male member—for anal-erotic purposes. She used to 'castrate' him in other ways, by taking money[1] out of his purse, and by stealing his pens, pencils, and other male symbols, as is so common in cases of kleptomania" (op. cit. p. 133). A similar case of kleptomania is reported in Smiley Blanton's *The Hidden Faces of Money* (Contribution 12), where a woman, acting out of an unconscious motive to disgrace her family, stole useless objects. In both instances, we see the typical combination of sadistic partial instincts and the motif of ingestion.

4. Primary level of anal phase (stage of elimination)

Weaning divides the oral phase into two levels as toilet training divides the anal phase. Like the primary level of the oral phase, the primary anal level is a happy time for most people, for, as is well known, their excrement appears to them as their first conscious creation, their first creative achievement, and as long as the parents do not intervene, the kneading and massaging, indeed even the ingestion of excrement is one of the most satisfying activities of childhood. The person who keeps a child from this activity deprives it of a great deal of his growing self-confidence, his pride, and his creativity. It is true, of course, that the degree of satisfaction and the intensity of pleasure during elimination vary considerably. Abraham believes that clinical experience led Freud to the view that there were people whose constitution was responsible for the particular libidinal emphasis that attaches to intestinal processes (op. cit. p. 153). As proof, he cites the unquestionably documented fact that there are families where both the positive aspects of anal erotism and anal character traits regularly recur in what are otherwise quite different family members. But this phenomenon can also be interpreted differently. As we have already seen, every character type, but especially the anal character, tends unconsciously to perpetuate the abnormalities of his parents (which are usually his abnormalities as well). Parents continue their life in their children. This is also true of anal characteristics, and happens to almost the same extent in the case of the anal erotic, the anal character, and the anal neurotic. Usually, the anal erotic is permissive and forgiving about dirt, disorder, and other weaknesses of children. Only the anal erotic who has been turned into an anal character through repression or become an anal neurotic through regression and reaction formation is repressive toward his children and thus perpetuates the tragic escalation of anal neurosis from one generation to the next. While the anal erotic trains his children to cleanliness without particular severity and hurry and thereby prolongs and supports the stage of pleasurable defecation, the anal character trains his children quite drastically and at a particularly early time to be "clean." He thus drives them prematurely to the secondary anal level. In this way, conservatism, avarice, pedantry, and the desire to discipline others as one was disciplined oneself are passed on from generation to generation. Each of these two types thus turns out children who have his own abnormalities, though this is due to education, not heredity.

Since the uninhibited, unsublimated, unrepressed anal erotic individual has no place in bourgeois society (whether he be a "dirty slob," a "disorderly character," or a homosexual, coprophagist, or coprophiliac), exceptionally severe social restraints are imposed on him to induce him to repress his inclinations. Usually, it is too late for sublimation. Even when he has become a mature person, bourgeois society therefore tends to transform the anal neurotic into an obsessional neurotic by mobilizing all available social controls. Other anal erotics are driven into hypochondria by displacing unsublimated coprophilic interests to other parts of the body. But when repression is successful, coprophilia often turns into a pleasure in modelling (i.e., art) or in manipulation (including the manipulation of persons and money). Through reaction formation, coprophilia may become a desire for cleanliness and order, as we have seen, or turn into the pleasure taken in indexing, classifying, organizing. Through sublimation or regression, the pleasure in defecation may lead to wasteful expenditures, the waste of money, and even the "forgetting" of debts. Since the most important inhibitions during this phase of libidinal development are feelings of guilt, it is certainly no accident that money, as a feces symbol, always has guilt attached to it. It is well known that money taken in is listed as a debit, and capital, "reserves," and profits are liabilities. "He who receives, owes," is the basic tenet of finance, and this certainly corresponds to the ambivalence between the libido goal of this level and the feelings of guilt resisting its attainment. Capital accumulation and indebtedness are as closely related as feces accumulation and feelings of guilt. Those who owe nothing to others owe something to themselves. André Amar (Contribution 14) speaks of "eternal debts" and "impossible salvation," a vocabulary which derives from the theological concept of original sin but not out of place here.

In defining the limited object libido which governs the relationship of the child to other human beings during the anal phase, I have adopted the concept of "partial love" coined by Abraham. It is meant to characterize both the unfinished stage of the capacity to love and also the fact that the child's affective interest in others is directed first toward certain parts of the human body and is not yet capable of encompassing the entire person. In the concepts of the psychoanalytic theory of money, this means that the anal neurotic who regresses to this phase sees only one aspect of his fellow human beings, i.e., what they own. The hierarchy of the world presents itself to him as a series of numbers: the large numbers, the rich and the powerful, are worthy of love; the small numbers, the poor and the powerless, are not.

Therapy promises only limited success where anal

neurosis is already fully developed. As in the case of almost all psychoneuroses (I exclude here the "Actual" neuroses as that term is used by Freud in the 1890s), the only effective therapy is prophylaxis, preventive therapy, which should begin with the treatment of the parents. As we have seen, anal neurotics are almost always the children of at least one parent with anal tendencies. Through premature and excessively drastic toilet training, the mother usually merely abreacts her own anal complexes. Under the pretext of merely wanting what is best and of helping the child accustom itself to the demands of the world at the earliest possible moment, she employs "discipline" and "strictness." She only does her "duty as a mother." But when strictness becomes a substitute for love, it has to be feared that as it matures the child itself will only be able to bestow a surrogate love, strictness, in turn.

5. *Secondary anal level (period of retention)*

As is well known, Freud discovered (and child psychologists have clinically confirmed) that the anus is much more intensely erotized among children than among adults. As it expels its feces, the child experiences an excitation which is not dissimilar to the coital pleasure of adults. It would seem that nature arranged things in this way to make bearable the pain the child suffers when it empties its bowels after having taken its first solid nourishment, and to facilitate the training of the sphincter by positive cathexis.

While the primary anal level was characterized by the pleasure taken in expelling excrement, the secondary level is marked by the control of the function of elimination, and that in two contradictory forms which really demand a subdivision of this level into two. To begin with, toilet training forcibly strips the small person of the illusion of omnipotence he had created on the primary anal level. Secondly, this illusion is restored in a sense when he discovers that he can dominate his educators. He learns that he can entice them into complimenting and rewarding him if he discharges when and where he is supposed to, or that he can make them mad by either soiling his bed or stubbornly retaining his feces. Because of the reward, the pleasure taken in emptying his bowels is increased, and by retaining feces and their subsequent violent expulsion the anal zone becomes even more highly erotized.

Thus the child makes four important discoveries during the anal phase:

> 1. The discovery that defecation is a kind of autoerotism. He learns this on the primary anal level.
> 2. The discovery that one can obtain rewards for a prompt discharge of feces. This already takes us from the primary to the secondary anal level.
> 3. The discovery that greater pleasure may be obtained by expelling retained feces than by immediate defecation. This discovery opens up the secondary anal level.
> 4. The discovery that by retaining feces (i.e., through stubbornness, willfulness, spite) one can induce negative affects (anger, fury, indignation) in others. This coming together of anal pleasure and the satisfaction of aggression led Freud to call the entire phase "anal sadistic." But this characterization applies only to this fourth discovery of the child.

While the first two discoveries bring it about that getting rid of objects of value will have libidinal emphasis attached to it at a later time (selling with a profit, but also pleasurable wastefulness), the latter two discoveries lead to a pleasurable retention of objects of value (pleasure taken in collecting things, but also avarice) and a pleasurable resistance to the demands of others (resistance to wage and tax demands, unions, co-determination). In part, this resistance derives from sadistic sources. For just as on the secondary oral level strong, sadistic partial instincts combined with the desire for incorporating the external world and thus led to the destructive aspects of biting, now strong sadistic desires combine on the secondary anal level with partial love, the precursor of object libido, and transform the desire to "retain" into a desire to "dominate."

This explains the proverbial avarice of some anal neurotics by tracing it to the infantile "desire to retain," the withholding of feces. But sadistic partial instincts are always present in such conduct, for the avaricious individual makes the world his slave and brings psychological coercion to bear on his friends, family members, employees, and business partners. In a careful analysis, one therefore always discovers elements of a thirst for power in avarice.

As on the primary anal level, the child is not yet able to love another person in the true meaning of that term on the secondary level of the anal phase. As yet, its libido only directs itself to part of another person. But the tendency toward the incorporation of others which we still found on the primary anal level has been given up. It is replaced by the desire for possession. Although the libido on this level is still far from having attained the goal of object libido, progress has been made in the sense that property now has become something external. What the child takes in by ingestion is no longer property. Instead, property now exists outside the body. This implies the recognition of the existence of objects (of the external world, other persons, the love object) and constitutes an important step in the development of a sense of reality.

This change has enormous practical significance in the social sense, for it makes it possible for two children to own things in common while ingestion only insures possession for one child. At the same time, it is the mechanism by which the child's love of feces, the tendency to eat it, which belongs to the primary anal level, is sublimated and transformed into a sense for cleanliness. Disgust helps to bring about this result. Only when the desire for ingestion has been wholly eliminated does the contempt for feces indispensable for all normal members of the community make its appearance. In some highly sublimated adults, it may manifest itself as a contempt for money. The maturing of a sense for communal well-being and communal ownership very clearly can be traced to both the maturing of the sense of reality just described and the subsequent maturing of the doubt that money is omnipotent.

Freud described the anal character in these terms: during his childhood, he requires a relatively long period to master the infantile incontinentia alvi and suffers even later in his childhood from isolated cases of malfunctioning in this area. During the period of toilet training, he refuses to empty his intestines when he is placed on the pot (Contribution 1). This sounds as if the problem of the later years were entirely due to the inherited structure of the instincts. But actually it is the particular form of toilet training that is at least equally responsible for the later symptoms of anal neurosis. Because the person bringing up the child not only demands cleanliness but strict regularity of excretion, the narcissism of the oral phase is put to a severe test. Sooner or later, the majority of children adapts to these demands. In the most favorable case, the child manages to identify with the demands of the educator and to take pride in what has been achieved. We then have a compensation for the primary injury done to narcissism. The original feeling of power is replaced by the satisfaction taken in the accomplishment, the "good behavior," the praise of the parents. But it often happens during this phase that the parents impose a habit on the child for which it does not have the requisite psychological maturity, which does not develop until the child begins to transfer what are originally narcissist feelings to other persons (father, mother). If the child is already capable of this, it becomes clean "for the sake of" that person. But if cleanliness is demanded prematurely, as almost always happens in bourgeois civilization, the child accustoms itself only because it is afraid. The inner resistance remains, and the libido persists stubbornly in its narcissist fixation. What results is a permanent impairment of the capacity to love.

The true meaning of premature toilet training only becomes really clear when one examines the disappearance of narcissist pleasure in some detail. If we see in the pride the child takes in emptying its bowels a justified feeling of power, we can understand the curious sense of powerlessness we encounter in neurotically constipated victims of premature toilet training. Their libido has been displaced from the genital to the anal zone, and now they mourn the inhibition of the intestinal function as if it were a form of impotence. Characteristically, habitual constipation can sometimes be overcome by revealing and making conscious the money complex of such neurotics.

The regressive change of character that can be observed in such anal neurotics is almost always one to the secondary anal level. If the regressive tendencies become more pronounced, the regression may move one or two levels further into the past and combine with elements of the oral phase. As this happens, obsessional characteristics develop which contain oral and anal regression in equal proportions (and influences due to partial instincts, particularly of the sadistic and voyeuristic variety besides).

A regression from the secondary anal to the secondary oral level is encountered among those obsessional neurotics who eat as little as possible because they want to cut back on expenditures which will not buy permanent possessions. And bodily weight is not necessarily a permanent possession, Abraham thinks, from whom I have taken this case (Bibliography 1). Conversely, Abraham believes that there are those obsessional neurotics who carefully watch their intake, check their weight every day, and direct all their interest toward the question of what remains as permanent possession of the food they eat. In both cases, Abraham believes, we are dealing with a combination of the desire for ingestion typical of the oral stage and the desire to save of the secondary anal level. I consider these cases as particularly important, but do not agree with Abraham's interpretation and will therefore return to this point later.

Those regressions where elements of the secondary anal level combine with those of the primary oral level go back even further into the early past of the child. This oral phase is characterized by the sucking of the child, as is well known. If it combines with the wish characteristic of the secondary anal level, the desire to retain, there often develop obsessional neuroses of a particularly stubborn sort. Such individuals carry the marks of an unsatisfied sucking period throughout their life. Abraham calls special attention to the type of neurotic official "who is only able to exist when all the circumstances of his life have been prescribed for him once and for all. To him the necessary condition of life is that his means of sustenance should be guaranteed to him up to the day of his death. He renounces all ideals of personal success in favour of receiving an assured and regular income" (op. cit. p. 158).

Those cases where sadistic partial instincts combine with the sucking of the primary oral level and the retention of the secondary anal level are even more difficult. "In their social behaviour these people always seem to be asking for something, either in the form of a modest request or of an aggressive demand. . . . They are as little to be put off by hard facts as by reasonable arguments, but continue to plead and to insist" (op. cit. pp. 158-159).

Abraham describes the following case:

> At the same time as he reacted in this way with aversion and hatred towards human beings, he centred his desires in an unmeasured degree on inanimate objects. His whole interest was absorbed in buying things. In this way he set up as much as possible a relationship of *possession* between himself and his environment. During this time he was filled with fear that something belonging to him might get lost or stolen. His whole attitude to the external world was thus dominated by ideas of possession, acquisition, and possible loss. Directly his resistance began to diminish, his oral character-trait of covetousness and his anal one of avarice in regard to objects retreated into the background, and he began once more to enter-

tain personal relationships towards other people and normal feelings about them which continued to develop and establish themselves ("Character-Formation On The Genital Level Of Libido-Development," in *Six Essays*, p. 195).

All these regressions have their common denominator in the fact that the aberrations of anal erotism result from signals which were already incorrectly given during the oral phase. Such wrong signals, which almost always result from incorrect education, can also derail the psychic life of the child between the primary and the secondary anal level. This occurs with particular frequency when the narcissist illusion of infantile omnipotence is not overcome at the end of the primary anal level and then combines with the stubbornness and defiance of the secondary anal level. As early as 1910, Sadger observed this belief in their omnipotence on the part of infantile anal erotics and traced to it the later conviction of many anal neurotics that they could perform all tasks better than anyone else (Bibliography 54). "According to my experience, this conviction is often exaggerated until the patient believes he is a unique person. He will become pretentious and arrogant and tend to underestimate everyone else. One patient expressed this as follows: 'Everything that is not me is dirt.' These neurotics only take pleasure in possessing a thing that no one else has and will despise any activity which they have to share with other people" (Abraham, "Contributions to the Theory of the Anal Character," in *Six Essays*, p. 171).

This is really an exemplary description of the classical entrepreneur at the time of the accumulation of capital during the eighteenth and nineteenth centuries. One only has to remember the touchiness with which the mine- and steel barons of the *Gründerzeit* (period of rapid industrial expansion in Germany during the 1870s. Transl. note) reacted to all criticism, any intervention of the legislative or executive branch, every legitimate demand of their workers and employees.

"It is as though the motto of many of these people were: 'Whoever gives me something is my friend; whoever desires something from me is my enemy.' One patient said that he could not have any friendly feelings towards me during his treatment, and added in explanation: 'So long as I have to pay anybody anything I cannot be friendly towards him' " (*Six Essays*, p. 177). Down to the present day, the capitalist mentality is characterized by the infantile illusion that money is all-powerful (equals feces is all-powerful). Just as the child believes it could do anything it wanted with its excreta, the capitalist also thinks quite seriously that his property gives him the power and the right to use it for whatever purposes he chooses.

Abraham writes: "Jones emphasizes the fact that many neurotics of this class hold fast obstinately to their own system of doing things. They refuse altogether to accommodate themselves to any arrangement imposed from without, but expect compliance from other people as soon as they have worked out a definite arrangement of their own. As an example, I might mention the introduction of strict regulations for use in the office, or possibly the writing of a book which contains binding rules or recommendations for the organization of all offices of a certain kind." Such neurotics "show the same self-will in regard to any demand or request made to them by some other person. We are reminded of the conduct of those children who become constipated when defaecation is demanded of them but afterwards yield to the need at a time that is agreeable to themselves" (Abraham, *Six Essays*, pp. 171, 172). Since the surrender of excrement is the earliest form of giving known to the child, the later neurotic will retain the willfulness just described where giving is involved. In many cases, he will reject a request or demand but then give twice the amount out of pure vanity. He is concerned with retaining his right to decide. "We frequently find in our psycho-analyses that a husband opposes any expenditure proposed by his wife, while he afterwards hands her of his 'own free will' more than what she first asked for. These men delight in keeping their wives permanently dependent on them financially. Assigning money in portions which they themselves determine is a source of pleasure to them. We come across similar behaviour in some neurotics regarding defaecation, which they only allow to take place *in refracta dosi*" (Abraham, *Six Essays*, p. 172). Neurotics intent on introducing their own system into everything tend toward an exaggerated criticism of others, and this may easily degenerate into mere carping. In social life, they make up the bulk of the malcontents. But Jones has convincingly shown (Bibliography 34) that the original anal willfulness may develop in two different directions. What may result are inadequacy and stubbornness, that is, asocial and unproductive qualities. But there are other cases where we find thoroughness and persistence, and these are both qualities which the revolutionary bourgeoisie valued highly during its centuries-long class struggle against feudalism. Yet we must not forget that all systems of order, especially bourgeois conceptions of order, not only arise from the self-inflicted illusion that stable conditions are desirable, but that they are also prompted by the wish that others submit to the person doing the ordering. This means that we are dealing here with the thirst for power, that sadistic component of anality which we have encountered so frequently.

6. *Primary genital level (phallic phase)*

The first phase of sexual maturity involves erotic interest in the opposite sex but also—at least initially—a peculiar revulsion from its genital parts. Freud speaks of a "partial repression," while Abraham uses the more precise designation "object libido with genital exclusion." The two most important neurotic symptoms resulting from a regression to this phase are therefore impotence and frigidity, for it is true of everyone that the genital organ is more strongly cathected with narcissist libido than any other part of the body. As long as the psyche continues to be cathected by narcissist impulses, everything except the genital organ may be loved in the opposite sex. In this phase, polymorphous, oral, and anal instincts have become largely subordinate to the primacy of genitality, but the final step toward sexual maturity, the capacity for object libido where the genital organ of the opposite sex is no longer the object of ambivalent affects but already part of a person loved in its totality, has not yet been taken.

7. Secondary genital level (genital phase)

The final step in character formation consists principally in transferring a positive feeling to the object, which is the sexual partner in a narrow sense and human society in a broader one. Thus the termination of libidinal development goes hand in hand with a final developmental step in the area of object libido. The individual can only find his place within the sphere of interests of society if the phallic level has been overcome and the genital level reached. The contribution of this final developmental level consists primarily in getting rid "of the remaining traces of the more primitive stages of development, in so far as they are unfavourable to the social behaviour of the individual. For he will not, for instance, be able to achieve a tolerant and fair-minded attitude to other people and to interests outside his own, until he has got the better of his destructive and hostile impulses springing from sadistic sources, or of his avarice and mistrust derived from anal ones" (Abraham, "Character-Formation on the Genital Level of Libido-Development," in *Six Essays*, p. 189).

If these difficulties can be negotiated, direct erotic desire for the love object is supplemented by "aim-inhibited" expressions of the libido: tenderness, devotion, readiness to help, compassion, kindness. As friendly impulses, they gradually become directed toward a wider group and finally toward all mankind. Thus love of mankind derives from sexual love, and a sense of community from sexual tenderness. Everywhere, this process shows connections with preceding phases, taking from them what is required for a responsible attitude toward objects. From the primary oral level it takes a forward-moving energy, from the anal source persistence, tenacity, and other traits, from the aggressive partial instincts the energies necessary for the life struggle. Concerning the subduing of narcissism and ambivalence, I can do no better than to paraphrase Abraham once again, for he has understood this process better than any other analyst: The earlier levels of character formation are still largely governed by narcissist impulses. It is true that the fully formed human character still incorporates such components, for experience teaches us that no phase of organic development is ever overcome, nor does it ever disappear without a trace. On the contrary, every new product of development carries marks which derive from earlier stages. Yet although the primitive phenomena of self love survive to some extent, we can say nonetheless that the fully matured character is relatively nonnarcissist. It must be emphasized here that certain contributions to character formation from the polymorphous-perverse and primary oral level coincide with those of the final genital phase, since the libido is free of ambivalence on all three levels.

On all other levels, however, ambivalence rules and subjects the psyche to ever-new schizoid threats. The continued existence of a marked ambivalence in the character thus means that there is the constant danger of a switch from one extreme to the other, for both the individual and his environment. Only when narcissism and ambivalence have been overcome, object libido has been attained, and the partial instincts have yielded to social responsibility can we expect a mature attitude of the individual toward money, an attitude which will renounce private property and affirm a sense of community and communal well-being.

But if this process fails on any given level, the libido rushes into the next stage with the greed we described previously. There, it usually also does not succeed in adapting itself to society. Almost all maladjustments vis-à-vis money, property, and possessions result from regressions which manifest themselves among adults as the result of infantile maladjustments. The etiological characteristic that every new phase of libidinal development rests on the ruins of the preceding one is part of the symptoms of the regressive money neurosis which we will discuss below.

Those cases of anally oriented interest in money which Freud himself described (Contribution 1 and Bibliography 23) also show without exception admixtures of repressed oral instincts, not to mention the activity of partial instincts. Even the basic form of an anal interest in money, the clinging to it, is impossible if one has none, and therefore presupposes the orally conditioned desire for acquisition. André Amar (Contribution 14) expresses this matter as follows: to remain poor, one need do nothing. But those who want to become rich must do something, i.e., something aggressive: they have to take money from someone else. For all money already belongs to someone and therefore the earning of money is a form of aggression. Etiologically, it belongs to the secondary oral level, the period of biting, where sadistic component instincts always combine with the desire for incorporation.

III

To derive all of economics from somatic economy seems an obvious thing to do, for there can be no doubt that the human body is a kind of biological household. But, in the first place, such biological metaphors are deceptive by their very nature, for they encourage simplifications and attribute an autonomy to social processes which they do not have. In the second place, such an analogy disregards the effect of partial instincts, ambivalence, and reaction formation. Yet, it is worthwhile to work out such a theoretical model and to compare it with the Freudian model of erogenous zones.

At least four metabolic stages would have to correspond to the nucleus of such a model:

1. ingesting or incorporation (acquiring, buying)
2. digesting (investing)
3. withholding of excreta (saving, parsimony)
4. expelling of excreta (spending, selling).

1. Ingesting (acquiring, buying)

The oral nature of financial acquisition is hardly open to doubt. We speak of "picking up," "getting between finger and thumb," "making one's own," or "annexing" to describe the acquisition of property. We use the term "money hunger" for the motive and "winning one's bread" to designate the activity of financial acquisition. The ingesting, acquisitive type of money neurotic derives his satisfaction not so much from property as from acquisition, for pleasure in what has been acquired is the mark of the anal, not that of the oral money neurosis.

The type of bargain hunter described by Edmund Bergler (Contribution 13) therefore belongs in the oral rather than the anal category, as Bergler rightly maintains, since he gets his pleasure not so much from what he has bought but from the act of buying itself. He thinks he's really smart when he pays less than others and enjoys his "victory" over the salesman. This is particularly common among individuals that have been weaned too early and suffer from strong inferiority complexes. Through these "savings," they recover their self respect. Actually, such an oral neurotic cheats himself, for he often puts up with large expenditures to buy things he does not need. He may, for example, spend $20 for a taxi in order to get at the earliest possible moment to the largest number of places where sales take place. He may save $15 to $18 while purchasing goods that would normally cost $80, but this means that he will have spent more than necessary to buy things he will never use.

Since this type was not suckled long enough as a child, he tries to suck others dry, now that he is an adult. Thus he is the born exploiter, and this not because he takes any special pleasure in his acquisitions but only because the act of acquisition itself is a source of pleasure. He is the most dangerous of all entrepreneurs because the enjoyment of money interests him less than the making of it. He thus conveys the impression of selflessness to those exploited by him and thereby hides the motives underlying his activity. Actually, he unconsciously attacks his surrogate mother because his real mother did not satisfy him when he was a suckling, and takes his revenge on his fellow men for the suffering she inflicted on him.

With this type, a high degree of aggression is often turned inward. This means that he unconsciously creates his interpersonal relationships in such a way that he will be rejected more and more as his financial successes increase. His unconsciously formulated conviction, of which he is hardly ever aware himself and which tells him that taking is more blessed than giving, makes others suspicious even if he does not himself consume what he has taken, and promptly confirms him in his belief that no one loves him. This in turn makes him more and more of a recluse.

His strength, his nose for the acquisition of money, is also his Achilles' heel, for he is the born victim of money hunters even shrewder than himself, persons who promise him the one kind of love he understands: money. His clever money sense notwithstanding, he therefore easily falls prey to embezzlers, confidence men, and exploitative women. Every one of his marriages ends in divorce, and every one of his wives takes with her a considerable portion of his wealth in the form of a settlement.

But there also exists a more highly sublimated type with the identical tendency toward incorporation who looks upon all of life as a "process of production." For such an individual, acquisitions (money, property, possessions) represent a kind of "import" into the "production system" of the body. Food is merely raw material serving daily requirements. What interests him are the household and production costs of the somatic enterprise. While the first type represents the capitalist of the *Gründerjahre*, the second is the manager of late capitalism.

2. *Digesting (investing)*

With the character just described, we already encounter a curious aspect of the psychoanalytical libido theory and its somatic base: the absence of a psychic analogue to the act of digestion. Libidinal theory knows of an oral stage (with distinct phases for sucking and biting) and then jumps without transition to the anal stage (with distinct phases for the expulsion and the retention of excreta). What is missing is the actual process of digestion, the metabolism which feeds the body, a significant omission which characterizes the idealist apparatus of psychoanalysis which is nowhere clearly localizable in a bodily substance.

This is the reason libidinal theory always makes such laborious attempts to explain psychic processes with the help of complicated combinations of an oral and anal nature in their varying proportions (and by adding partial instincts, reaction formations, factors of ambivalence, displacements, repressions, sublimations, etc.), although such processes clearly belong to a different stage of the psychic economy. It would take us too far afield were we to present the implications of this idea in all their detail. I therefore confine myself to some effects of this hypothesis in the area of money neuroses. How, for example, is one going to classify those neurotics who view food as an "investment," digestion as "turnover," as "profit," with the object of "increasing their wealth"? In the unconscious of such individuals, feces always represents a sort of "annuity": the yield of the psychosomatic process which has earned interest due to a healthy digestion. They let their capital work in the stomach and gain a "profit," namely increased weight.

We have already quoted two cases mentioned by Abraham but interpreted differently by him: those neurotics who constantly and carefully watch their body, check their weight, and direct all their interest to the question of how much of the food they eat remains the permanent possession of the body. "It is evident that they identify the content of the body with money" (Abraham, *Six Essays*, p. 179). This is absolutely correct, but the purpose of the food intake is the *interest* the bodily content yields, i.e., the endeavor to extract from food a "profit," a "yield," an "increase in value." This cannot be explained by the desire to withhold feces. It is a syndrome we frequently encounter among certain athletes, particularly wrestlers and weight lifters. Always thinking about investment, every steak they eat becomes a placement which will bring them that much closer to winning the Olympic gold.

Of course, such a type can be interpreted very simply as a mixture of oral and anal influences. But we deceive ourselves if we formulate the definitions of orality and anality so loosely as to allow them to cover all that eats and defecates. To clarify this matter, I remind the reader of the type who may be understood as a reaction formation to the syndrome just described: "There is a class of patient who avoids spending any money on "passing" things. . . . Some of these neurotics avoid spending money on food, because it is not retained as a permanent possession" (Abraham, *Six Essays*, pp. 178-179). Considerable research remains to be done on this type.

3. *Withholding of excreta (saving, parsimony, collecting)*

The "collecting" of feces in the intestine represents the first form of collecting property. Ferenczi (Contribution 2) has very carefully described all of the steps of the ontogeny of the interest in money. Fixation at or regression to this retentive phase of anality arouses the desire to collect *something. What* is collected is not decided by the anal character but by the external world. The child collects buttons, pits, June bugs, glass beads, comic books, stamps; the adult books, pictures, antiques, coins. The neurotic collects useless things and fills basements, attics, garages, and even entire houses with them. The libidinously irrational character of collecting becomes evident in all cases where it turns into a mania and no attention is paid to the value of what is being collected. As in the case of the voiding of intestinal contents which have been accumulating over a long period of time, so in that of almost every collector. One day, a great "emptying," a great "clean-up" takes place and the entire collection or part of it is sold, given away, or even thrown out. Conversely, the disinclination to throw anything away often becomes "a compulsive tendency to make use of even the most trifling thing. A rich man used to cut his empty matchboxes into small strips and give them to his servants to light the fires with" (Abraham, *Six Essays*, p. 181). This form of neurotic parsimony becomes particularly apparent where the amount saved is insignificant: a well-to-do neurotic continues using the same razor blade until he has completely scratched up his face. Another invents the most complicated maneuvers and tricks to avoid leaving a tip after an expensive meal in a restaurant. A third would rather run in the pouring rain for ten minutes than leave his car in a garage. A fourth risks a ticket before he will put a dime in the meter. Frequently, the focus of saving shifts from money to time. "Time is money." The individual lives in perpetual fear of losing time, and only the time he spends working is well used. He hates 'restlessness,' but becomes restless during holidays, spends his vacation with a bad conscience and only recovers when he returns to his work. Ferenczi calls this syndrome "Sunday neuroses" (Bibliography 20). Others attempt to save time by simultaneously taking off their shirt and sweater, or pants and underpants, and by putting them on at the same time when they dress in the morning.

Such symptoms may seem to be taking us a long way away from the causative factors, the anal privations of childhood, yet they derive from the same etiology as other forms of saving. In all these cases, the anal neurotic looks on the contents of his intestine as "property," as "something he has worked for," in which he has "vested rights" because he "produced" and "took care of" them. Having these things inside himself, he is their owner and believes he must not let them go. Such an individual always makes the impression of being "buttoned up," "reserved," for he is psychically constipated. His thrift may become avarice, but avarice need not necessarily express itself in money or possessions. Abraham (*Six Essays*) mentions a farmer who fed his goat by giving it each blade of grass separately, a mirror image of defecation in refracta dosi. The pleasure taken in property, which frequently manifests itself in looking at money or possessions, derives from the pleasure the child takes in looking at its intestinal products. When such a person pulls bundles of banknotes out of his pocket whenever he pays small amounts, we can be certain that we see here the regressed pleasure in manipulating one's own feces. If every expense makes him mournful as if it were a beloved who had left him, it is the mourning over the incapacity of retaining his feces forever.

Since he believes everyone wants to take his money away from him just as his mother once took away his excreta, he looks upon his fellow men with extreme suspicion. This is the type which everywhere and always proclaims that man is bad by "nature," that the desire for possessions is man's nature, and that the idea of communal property is "against nature."

In contrast to the digestive type, he takes no real pleasure in using his property. He therefore often lives badly, stints on his food, but feels a secret satisfaction when he observes others consuming what they own, for then he tells himself: "if you, who publicly and shortsightedly blow your money, only knew how much richer I am, a person you despise because I seem poorer to you."

He handles everything he owns with care and only delights in his possessions as long as they are unused or stored in his house or the bank, unseen by others. He experiences a certain masochistic pleasure in the sacrifices he makes to his avarice, and this is undoubtedly in part an inward-directed aggression which is endogenous to this form of anal neurosis. Should this partial instinct turn outward, it manifests itself in the "punishment" inflicted on all relatives and subordinates who infract his principles of parsimony. If one of his employees buys a house or a car which his employer believes he cannot afford, he will dismiss him but rationalize his act by deluding himself into believing that the employee in question must have acquired the necessary funds in a questionable manner. He disinherits his children because they spend too much money and makes life hell for himself and his family by denying to all others what he does not need himself. Charles Odier quotes the case of a wealthy man who heaped reproaches on his wife because she put a twenty—instead of a ten—centime stamp on a letter (Bibliography 45). This is an unconscious expression of his belief that "you are not worth ten centimes." Blanton (Contribution 12) describes the case of a self-made man who worked his way out of impoverished conditions although he had had no schooling. All his money was invested so that his wife and children were more than generously provided for. But he lived very poorly and refused to permit his wife and children to visit their Scottish relatives. During treatment, it became apparent that he suffered because he came from eastern Jews and had had inadequate schooling, considered the Scottish ancestor worship of his educated wife and children justified but hateworthy, and therefore saw Scotland as the symbol of his wife's and children's superiority. In avarice, the hatred of a surrogate mother is almost always involved. The real mother trained the miserly individual to control his movements at too early a time in his childhood.

Among such anal neurotics there are many tax evaders, because they view the state as a surrogate mother on whom they seek revenge by refusing to pay. Righteousness and defiance of this kind stem from the behavior of the child that pretends being constipated when the mother puts it on the pot and then takes special pleasure in soiling its pants or the rug the moment the mother has left. Abraham ("Contributions to the Theory of the Anal Character") is right in saying that this is not merely a rebellion against what the child "shall" do, but also against what it "must" do. The "individualist," so highly touted in bourgeois ideology and always praised as a "free" person, is almost always a stubborn anal neurotic of this type, who presents the incapacity of working with others as a virtue, and insists on the "free, unhampered development of the personality" as his fundamental right. The landlord who would rather have his house remain empty than turn it over to students and the owner who will shut down his factory before allowing his workers to unionize belong in the same category which Freud already described in 1908 as "orderly, parsimonious and obstinate" (Contribution 1). In such people, the anal erotic interest is hidden in a tendency toward the "reverse side," the opposite of the communal weal. They look upon all those who endeavor to improve the living conditions of the majority as "enemies of society," for they see only themselves as society. When one reminds them that only a few are wealthy and a great many poor, that consequently the poor have a stronger claim to the representation of their interests, a money neurotic of this type will brand such an argument treason, for in his opinion the state must primarily serve the big taxpayer. If during any public event a poor person is given preferential treatment, he takes it as a personal affront and complains. Property, in his opinion, gives him special rights. Putting the world on its head in this manner is characteristic of the anal neurotic. The entire world is out of step except himself. He considers it his sacred mission to save it from the majority. If the major part of the globe is ruled by a political system other than his, force must be used to save "freedom," *his* freedom.

Since the anal character wishes to retain, keep, guard, protect his excreta, he also "conserves" his property, maintains traditions, clings to what has been "tested," upholds what is traditional and of long standing. He is "conservative," which means he is so keen on property that he even wishes to "conserve" his excreta.

He is very "precise" in the handling of his money, and that is the reason everything around him has to be "exactly right." His desk is "orderly," "clean," "neat." His furniture and office utensils are symmetrically arranged. He cannot bear "disorder," he perceives it as a mixture of incompetence and recalcitrance. He is the apostle of "order and stability." But what he really has in mind when he uses these terms are the well-to-do: people who have a permanent residence, a dependable income, who own houses and land. In short, he can only consider those as stable, as "one of us" who suffer from the same neurosis as himself. There is only a short distance from this mania for order to those psychotics who count their steps because they want to reach their destination with an "orderly number of paces" (Abraham, op. cit. p. 184).

Individuals who once suffered a traumatic money crisis and afterwards always carry large sums with them in order never to have to repeat the experience of being unable to pay their bills are another variant of the neurotic anal character. Such persons also frequently suffer from the obsessional neurosis of having to count and recount their money during psychic crises. When the crisis has been resolved, the compulsion to count subsides. But its cause is always traceable to childhood experiences during the anal phase, to toilet training in most instances, which imbue the child with the lifelong feeling of having been deprived of its rightful possessions.

Frequently, such individuals become money fetishists and ascribe to money in general, or to individual coins and bills, quasi magical power. Self confidence and peace of mind can be assured only if the person has such a talisman with him. Often, they rationally explain their dependency by saying that the talisman was found or given to them in a situation of critical importance. But, actually, it is never anything but a substitute for the libido that was withdrawn in childhood. The money fetishist thinks the coin loves him because it once brought him good luck. It thus expresses the object libido he did not receive as a child and therefore cannot bestow as an adult.

4. Expelling of feces (spending, selling, producing)

Depending on earlier libidinal development, the act of expelling feces is interpreted quite differently by the unconscious. There are those who see it as a *loss*. All evacuation is a decrease of property, a losing proposition, an irremediably, irreplaceably lost happiness. This results in a profoundly pessimistic, frequently melancholic world view which operates with such concepts as "dissipating," "squandering," "renouncing," and always believes that others have no "backbone." One only has to think of those reproaching others for a "politics of surrender," a cry always raised by people who have already unconsciously given up and directed against those who refuse to do so.

But there are those who view the identical process in an optimistic, indeed often actually ecstatic manner as a *gain*. Each act of evacuation is a creative achievement, a "big deal," a rain of gold, a large item. Such people rid themselves of the contents of their intestines as if they were throwing goods on the market. Every evacuation is a clearance sale where they make huge profits. In such cases, the intestinal contents become quite literally "silvered" or "gilded." They view themselves and all others as productive, which is sometimes justifiable but also may be merely due to euphoria. In almost every respect, they are the most agreeable fellow human beings, for they are not concerned with possessions but with creativity. Their optimism is contagious even when unjustified, and its consequences are more frequently positive than negative. They are people whose toilet training began neither too early nor too late and who, as adults, retain without negative results their enthusiasm about their first "creation." Just as the most evident vice of the other anal type is miserliness, this type suffers from being spendthrift. But here also, we have to distinguish between two fundamentally different forms of wastefulness. One of them goes back to the primary anal level, the time where pleasure is taken in feces. As we have just described it, it represents a kind of *evacuation from joy*. The other goes back to the secondary anal level, the time of toilet training, and is a form of opposition against the mother and therefore an evacuation out of spite, in most cases an evacuation into the diaper, on the floor, or into bed—into the "wrong" place, in any event. Just as avarice is a neurotic obstipation, this second form of waste represents a neurotic diarrhea, a surrogate for the longed-for but neurotically inhibited expenditure of libido. The character type suffering from neurotic wastefulness usually attempts to compensate for libido by money. Since this is a case where either a displacement from the genital to the anal zone has occurred, or the anal zone continues to insist on its rights even after puberty, he spends money instead of love to rid himself of the painful feeling of sexual inadequacy. He can often be identified because, irrespective of income, he ostentatiously seeks to spend more than all the other members of his group.

But the more genital activity is restricted, the more libido turns toward possessions. Even giving them often takes on the quality of owning, for the generosity of the giving person and his ability to have acquired what is being given away must be documented. This narcissist tinge is perceptible in the charitable acts of many anal neurotics of this type. They like to pose as maecenases and give away large sums, but only to institutions which will advertise their name as donors. Grants, gifts, endowments, legacies contribute toward assuaging unconscious feelings of guilt which are typical of this anal phase. But, in all this, their libido remains remote from the objects of their beneficence. In extreme, nearly psychotic cases of this kind, such individuals sometimes send gifts and flowers to themselves in order to show others how abundantly the world bestows its love on them. But frequently, there is also a sadistic component present so that the gifts such neurotics make themselves or others betray the unconscious intent of hurting a third person. Surprisingly often, such behavior is found among grandparents whose affection omits one generation and who revenge themselves on their own children for their alleged lack of love by alienating the love of their grandchildren. Not infrequently, this is done by financial means. They may, for example, disinherit their children and make their grandchildren their heirs.

In the following three cases, the sadistic element, the desire to hurt someone by one's own wastefulness, is clearly in evidence. Abraham mentions a female patient who squandered money because she wanted to impoverish her husband (*Six Essays*, p. 182). Kaufman describes the case of a female patient who wasted money to ruin her father (Contribution 11). Blanton writes of a female patient who squandered money to force her parents to recognize that they had acted unjustly toward her (Contribution 12).

The compulsive prodigal only feels good when he can spend money. If he is forced to save, he becomes ill. What he unconsciously strives for is a return to a passive and dependent status similar to that of the small child. Unconsciously, he seeks a parent surrogate to whom he can surrender his entire fortune and hopes that this will be reciprocated by dispensing him of all obligations so that he will be cared for and pampered like a child. This applies to many men who marry older women, and also to some prostitutes who turn their entire income over to their pimp so that he might "protect" them.

In even more extreme cases, wastefulness becomes self-destruction. Either the squanderer ruins himself by unconsciously but systematically engineering his own bankruptcy, or he attempts to win the love of people about whom his rational consciousness clearly tells him that they do not love but merely exploit him. This psychically immature type therefore has a marked tendency to turn his money over to money hyenas of the opposite sex that have as little capacity for love as he himself.

The chronic gambler is a form of this self-destructive type of squanderer. His rational explanation that he gambles to win is refuted by his irrational behavior which ultimately and invariably deprives him of his winnings. For this reason, gamblers are almost always anal erotics with a weak ego. By winning, they seek to prove that fate loves and prefers them.

IV

Some, but not all of the questions touched upon here are dealt with in the fifteen contributions of major analysts which have been brought together in the following three parts of the book.

Part I

The contributions of the first part deal exclusively with the connections between anal erotism, anal character, anal neurosis, anal symbolism on the one hand, and property, possessions, money, and money symbolism on the other. Although there necessarily has to be some mention of oral and genital elements, they are not investigated with reference to their implications for money and its uses. It is only in the second part, and especially in the third, that we turn to the oral and genital implications of money.

Contribution 1. The idea of the anality of money first emerged in Freud's pioneering study of this theme in 1908 and was completely developed in his essay on the same subject in 1927 (Bibliography 23). When the first of these contributions appeared, lay criticism objected, among other things, that the genealogy of obstinacy also allowed the opposite conclusion, i.e., that the character traits of the stubborn adult already manifested themselves during childhood instead of being caused by childhood experiences. Although Freud might be right when he described the coming together of certain character traits in a certain character type, these critics went on to say, he had not proved causality. It was not known whether obstinacy during childhood toilet training later led to obstinacy in adults, or whether the obstinacy of the later adult did not already manifest itself during toilet training.

This objection has proven absurd, but the derivation of obstinacy from sublimated anal libido continues to be doubtful. For the sublimation of an instinct is only what can actually be derived from the instinct, not from its inhibition or its reaction to that inhibition. Consequently, sublimation of anality is only what derives from anal excitation, as, for example, the withholding of excreta if it increases the pleasure taken in expelling them. But if the child sublimates the *refusal*, it does not sublimate a primary instinct but the blocking of that instinct by the external world, and that is a secondary phenomenon. It would therefore seem to me that spite and obstinacy do in fact have their origin in the anal stage, but Freud went too far in his first interpretation of this phenomenon when he thought that this character quality could be derived from sublimations of or reaction formations to anality, as avarice and cleanliness can.

Contribution 2. Ferenczi's essay on the ontogeny of the interest in money is one of those pioneering studies to which we owe our understanding of the anal character. He was the first to call attention to the object libido of the anal erotic. To the anal characteristics posited by Freud, he added the conjecture that art might have its origin in the child's manipulation of feces. Meanwhile, this has become a commonplace of psychoanalytic esthetics via the detour intestinal evacuation = creation, and feces = work of art. Since I mistrust this equation somewhat, I mention it here only in passing.

Ferenczi also considers hypochondria as a "fermentation product of anal erotism." I have adopted this thesis. I also owe him the insight that in cases of successful and satisfactory sublimation of anal instincts, some part of unsublimated anal erotism is always carried into adult life as a consolation. The super-clean individual only makes an exception when it comes to his shorts, and does not have them laundered as regularly as his shirts and undershirts. He thus unconsciously combines sublimated anal erotism (saving of money for laundry) with unsublimated anal erotism (pleasure taken in feces stains in his shorts).

Contribution 3. It is from Ferenczi that Coriat took the unfortunate terminus technicus "capitalistic instinct." He then proceeds to document it by some observations from the biography of a well-known millionaire. The observations are exact, but Coriat is mistaken in his belief that there is such a thing as an instinct to amass money. What we have instead are libidinal tendencies that have been repressed, or sublimated at most, but that more frequently have merely regressed and find in money a substitute for libidinally cathected feces.

Judging by all the clinical discoveries made by Freud and his disciples, there is no reason to assume that a desire for the private ownership of the means of production would have to persist in a socialist society with appropriate weaning and toilet training. For that, and only that, can be meant by the concept "capitalistic drive" or "capitalistic instinct." The fact that *something* is collected is undoubtedly due to the libidinal development of the anal stage. But *what* is collected is not due to any instinct but the accidents of one's experience of the external world. All psychoanalytical experience suggests that the desire for possessions which exceed requirements (i.e., which go beyond a house, a garden, furniture, pictures, books, etc.) and can only be satisfied by the private ownership of the means of production is neurotic in its origin. This entire book is a cumulative demonstration of this insight.

Contribution 4. The two case studies Ferenczi subsumes under the title "Pecunia olet" convey a good insight into the clinical work this analyst did in the therapy of anal neuroses.

Contribution 5. I conclude the first part of this book with Karl Abraham's short essay on the spending of money during anxiety states, which is as balanced as the rest of the work of this excellent analyst. Those interested in this subject should read Abraham's penetrating study "Melancholia and Obsessional Neurosis," where these insights are documented more fully (Karl Abraham, *Six Essays*, pp. 71-82).

Part II

Although this part of the book goes beyond the anal theory of money and even contradicts it in certain respects, it is also based on the equations money = feces and feces = money. In Róheim's and Posinsky's studies, we have the additional equation feces = body of the father that has been murdered and devoured, and which comes from Freud's *Totem and Tabu*. As early as 1897, Freud wrote to Fliess: "I read one day that the gold which the devil gave his victims regularly turned into excrement; and next day Herr E., who reports that his nurse had money deliria, suddenly told me (by way of Cagliostro-alchemist-Dukatenscheisser) that Louise's money was always excrement. Thus in the witch stories it is only transformed back into the substance of which it originally consisted" (letter dated 1-24-1897). We add this explanation: Mr. E. was Freud's patient in 1897. The Louise who is mentioned here was both the nurse and the first mistress of the patient, who saw her as a witch since that is apparently what she took herself to be, for she reported to her youthful lover that the money the devil had given her had been feces "from the very beginning." Already at that time Freud understood the connection with the exchangeability of money and feces in the delusions of his psychotic patients. In the same letter to Fliess he also wrote: "Another tributary into the main stream is suggested by the consideration that to this day people tell stories similar to those of witches and my patients; nobody believes them, though that does not shake their belief in them. As you will have guessed, I refer to paranoiacs, whose complaints that excrement is put into their food . . . are pure memory content."

Eleven years later, in Contribution 1, Freud returned to the same subject: "We know that the gold which the devil gives his paramours turns into excrement after his departure, and the devil is certainly nothing else than the personification of the repressed unconscious instinctual life" (*Complete Works*, vol. IX, p. 174). At a later point in that same essay, Freud points out that according to old Babylonian doctrine, gold was referred to as the "feces of hell," and Theodor Reik mentions (Bibliography 49) that the Aztecs used to call gold the "feces of the gods." Géza Róheim reminds us that the inhabitants of the Gazelle peninsula in Melanesia called their shell money "excrement of the sea" (Bibliography 51). Thus the equation money = feces seems to be very widespread. How is it to be explained? Freud believed that through polarization or reaction formation, man had everywhere equated the least (feces) with the most (money) valuable. According to the laws of ambivalence which govern our childhood, this would be perfectly logical. Since fairy tales are lodged deep in the unconscious, it would also explain the countless stories of the golden donkey, the goose that lays golden eggs, the "Dukatenscheisser," and similar themes.

The popular dream interpretations where feces always means wealth, the forms of superstition where a bird, for example, that defecates on one's head is considered a lucky omen, belong here. And this is also true of the custom of thieves who leave something at the scene of their crime, that "something" being a pile of excrement which they refer to as an "item."

The metaphors of all languages known to me contain allusions to this equation. During the eleven years I worked on the two parts of my anthology of the scatological vocabulary of colloquial German (*Sex im Volksmund*, Reinbek, 1971), I came across more than one hundred examples, of which only a few can be quoted here. The most telling one has already been mentioned in passing and probably not been noticed by most readers as falling into this category. It is the term used by children: "to do one's business." The person who expels his excrement makes a pile, a person who urinates only produces a dribble. Regional expressions are less well known. Examples would be "a golden deal" or "a silver deal" for defecation, or "to lay golden eggs" for defecating. In other regions, defecating is called "devaluing" or "to lay in a stock," and diarrhea is a "rain of gold."

The anus is a "gold mine." A person with hemorrhoids has a "golden vein." The toilet is called "gold mill," "office," "bank," "stock exchange," or *Juliusturm*. This word refers to the tower of the former citadel at Spandau where the reparations paid by the French after the 1870-1871 war were kept until 1914. The chamber pot is often called "piggy bank." Toilet paper is "securities," "treasury bill," or "invoice." A person who breaks wind is referred to as someone who leaves a "safe" or a "strong-box" behind. The feces stains left in a hotel bed are called "legacies" by chambermaids. The lavatory attendant is a "gold digger," his female counterpart a "gold miner" (cf., the English "gold finder" as a colloquial term for someone who empties public toilets. See Partridge. Transl. note)

In the vocabulary of homosexuals, the individual practicing *paedicatio* is called "gold digger," "gilderer" or "silverer." Anal coitus is referred to as "gilding" or "silvering the tail." To have anal coitus with someone is called "probing a gold mine" or "mining gold." The successful male prostitute has a "golden tail." The male engaging in anilingus is a "gold washer," the female a "gold throat." The individual who is particularly successful in satisfying someone during anilingus is said to have a "golden tongue."

Conversely, the language of the bank and the stock

exchange abounds in expressions where money and feces are equated. A person in financial difficulties is called "constipated" (cf., the American colloquialism "to be up shit-street"). Once again in possession of cash, he becomes "liquid." Someone who refuses to pay "balks" or "blocks." We have the terms "hard" and "soft" currency as if we were talking about bowel movements. The haggler "squeezes" like someone who is constipated. A millionaire "wallows in money" as the child does in its feces. Officials of the Federal Bank are called "Dukatenscheisser" (i.e., excretors of ducats), and of someone who no longer knows how to pay his debts it is said that "he is up to his neck in shit." To repay debts may be referred to as "unloosening the purse-strings" or "satisfying" one's creditors. A newcomer to the stock exchange is called a "shit-breech," and when he treats his older colleagues to a drink, he "puts on his spending britches." (Cf., such English terms as "tight-arsed" [reluctant to spend money] or "tight bargain" = hard bargain. Transl. note) As early as 1908, Freud called attention to the fact that popular language calls a wealthy miser "filthy" or "matted." In England, the rich are said to be "filthy with money." In Germany, they are "so rich, they stink." The phrase "money doesn't smell" was coined by the Roman emperor Vespasian (A.D. 9-79) who had taxed the collection of urine because the ammonia it contained was used by the Romans to do their laundry. When his son Titus reproached him with enriching himself through filth, Vespasian held a coin under his nose and asked him if it smelled. When Titus denied this, Vespasian said: "You see, money doesn't stink." In this connection, a discovery I made while working on my *Sexualgeschichte des Altertums* (2 volumes, Munich, 1973-1974) may have some interest. Emperor Tiberius had an anal obsession which caused him to fear that he was made of feces and was considered feces by others. He therefore forbade the Romans ever to enter public toilets with rings or gold coins showing his portrait. Before Romans defecated, they had to "rid themselves" of all portraits of the emperor.

The most persuasive proofs for the validity of the equation feces = money come from the analysis and therapy of neurotics and psychotics. During the manic phase, excreta are often collected and quite seriously offered as means of payment, while during the depressive stage entire sheaves of bills are taken for feces and thrown into the toilet. The therapy of melancholia taught us long ago that the reason for mourning is almost always a lost love object which is experienced by the subconscious as an anal loss. To compensate for it, the melancholiac attempts to re-ingest the expelled love object in the form of money (resembling the anal neurotic in this respect). Conversely, the destruction of an object is often experienced by the unconscious as the anal process of expulsion.

Often, the anal neurotic reacts to a disorderly room, a messy drawer or closet as if they were intestines filled with feces and takes pleasure in allowing the disorder to grow until he eliminates it by suddenly tidying up as if he were finally voiding his long constipated bowels. The analogy to the previously described "dispersal" (or dissolution) of a collection accumulated over a lifetime is obvious.

Ferenczi mentions a female patient who always suffered from violent diarrhea toward the end of the month when she was obliged to send her parents a certain sum of money for their support. Another patient compensated for the fee he had to pay the analyst by farting copiously (both examples from Contribution 2). Abraham mentions a wealthy banker who urged his children to retain the contents of their intestines as long as possible so that they might extract the last ounce of nourishment from the expensive food ("Contributions to the Theory of the Anal Character"). Codet quotes a patient who was not miserly in other ways but insisted that there should be no light in the toilet since it was unnecessary and cost too much money besides (Contribution 14). The sparing use of toilet paper undoubtedly derives from the same unconscious equation of feces and money or represents a reaction formation to it.

The habit of reading or learning while sitting on the toilet so that no time may be wasted belongs to the same syndrome. At the same time, it furnishes a good pretext for remaining there as long as possible. Abraham (op. cit.) mentions a patient who strongly resisted free association during his psychoanalytic sessions but held his own at home on the toilet and then brought his ideas all worked out to his analysis. For such neurotics, the toilet is not only the place where real "production" goes on but also the place one does "big business": where one earns or saves money by ruminating. In all the cases described here, the equations feces = money and money = feces are unconsciously present.

Contribution 6. To document this equation, Harnik here quotes three examples of the nexus between anal erotism and debts from the folklore of Italy and the Netherlands.

Contribution 7. William H. Desmonde goes back to early history to show the origin of Egyptian coinage in the symbol of the scarab.

Contribution 8. In a complicated, frequently contradictory essay, the same author attempts to show that Greek coins originated in archaic animal sacrifice. This very bold, frequently speculative thesis is largely based on analogies between pathogenesis and phylogenesis, a technique about which I have considerable doubts. It is not my intention here either to criticize or correct the steps by which Desmonde arrives at his conclusions. (In a study I am now preparing on the history of matrilocal, matrilineal clans in the Aegean, I deal with the same subject.) Here, I simply wish to point out the danger which always results from the attempt to interpret historical, let alone prehistorical, events as projections of individual case histories.

Desmonde believes that during the early Greek period money developed as a token that entitled a person to certain parts of a totemic animal that was eaten by the group. To the extent that this rite represented a common subordination to a communally worshipped and communally introjected ancestor figure, money promoted "an enhanced feeling of noble commitment. Early money . . . thus revivified the spirit of creative cooperation . . . reintensified the bonds of loyalty and love . . . established a loving union, or contract, among the participants, each individual committing himself to the renunciation and efforts involved in the mutual aid (rights and correlative duties) which are at the basis of all law and social organization." If that were true, the future of human society would be in serious danger. Fortunately, however, Desmonde is mistaken, and this in spite of some really excellent observations. When an ingenious, highly intelligent contribution arrives at such mistaken conclusions, there must be something wrong with its methodology. Where the error may lie can be seen in the following comments on three studies of my former teacher Géza Róheim (On Desmonde, see my bibliographical references 66, 67, 110, 115).

Contribution 9. The problem lies in the temptation to give a clinical interpretation of the facts gathered from history, early history, and prehistory as if they were the associations of a patient on the analyst's couch. Conversely, it may also lie in the attempt to reconstruct the history of an entire social system from the analysis of two or three members of that society.

Géza Róheim (born in Hungary in 1891, died in America in 1953) had his training analysis with Ferenczi (1915-1916), worked in the ethnographic section of the Hungarian National Museum in Budapest from 1917 to 1919, and from 1928 to 1931 did important field work (financed by Marie Bonaparte) in East Africa, Central Australia, Melanesia, and among the Yuma Indians of Arizona. This accounts for his interest in the United States, where he later took up residence. Although William H. Desmonde and S. H. Posinsky, whose essay is the final contribution in this part of the book, were not Róheim disciples, their thought can hardly be understood without Róheim's influence. It is true that significant psychoanalytic efforts have been made by English and

American ethnologists (such as Bronislaw Malinowski, Margaret Mead, Alexander Goldenweiser, Edward Sapir, A. L. Kroeber, and Abram Kardiner), but the work of other psychoanalytically oriented ethnologists (George Devereux, Weston La Barre, Warner Muensterberger, and Sidney Axelrad) cannot be appreciated without Róheim's influence. Yet among these analysts we nowhere find the tendency to underestimate the influence of the social reality on ego formation, or even to ascribe an inhibiting effect to it as we do so markedly in Róheim. He often writes as if the Ego had developed from the Id by its own unaided efforts. When he mentions the Super-Ego at all, it plays a curiously static and negative role. He seems to conceive of the "freedom" of the inherited structure of instincts as if it were a kind of lost paradise where the snake committed the deadly sin of prompting man to develop his Super-Ego. He therefore traces the exchange of goods in human society to the original exchange between mother and child. The child demands milk from its mother, the mother demands feces from the child. At least that's what it looks like to the latter, because the mother sees to it that the child neither dirties itself nor becomes constipated, and she demands bowel movements at fixed times. Róheim points out that in many societies the dead are worshipped by defecation on their graves. At a later time, feces are replaced by stone- or shell money or coins which are given to the dead for his journey to the Beyond. Basing himself on the Freudian myth of the primal horde whose leader is killed, eaten, and excreted by his sons, Róheim establishes the equation: body of the father = feces = money. He explains the poor logic of this equation by claiming that pregenital thinking simply is not logical. But even if we assume that the equation is both logical and valid, it still does not prove what Róheim wants it to: the anal source of money. For the thesis that it was invented in order to obtain a symbol for both feces and the body of the father cannot convince according to Freudian logic if only because the human character is not wholly shaped by inherited instincts but also by the limitations imposed on it by society, and especially the influence it exerts on society in turn. When Róheim thus confines himself to an analysis of the structure of our instincts and their symbolism, he gives us less than half of the total Freudian picture of our psyche. Just as our id has its history, so do our ego and super ego, which in turn were molded by historical, autonomously developing material conditions. Like anal erotism, money is the result of the interaction between internal and external reality. Both of them can only be understood historically. The desire to amass wealth has only arisen in specific social systems and specific phases of development. It neither has nor will exist forever.

In the course of our analysis of the anal character, we already pointed out that the anal neurotic thinks of the desired object as the child does during the anal phase: it is property, i.e., the most primitive form of property—the bodily content or feces. Since the ambivalence of partial instincts is still total during this phase, the positive attitude toward the object expresses itself as retention of his property (avarice), and the negative one as its rejection (wastefulness). The anal neurotic often unconsciously experiences the loss of the object (expenditures, losses on the stock market, bankruptcy) as its expulsion, just as feces are expelled. For that reason, some anal neurotics react to financial losses with diarrhea, others with constipation. The loss is thus confirmed or resisted according to Freudian "organ speech."

Róheim tells us that while we should not overlook the overdetermination of such a reaction, we must also see it as an archaic form of mourning that the unconscious clings to and which has been preserved among some primitive peoples in the custom of defecating on the grave of a dear departed. At the Psychoanalytical Congress of 1922, Róheim first enunciated his thesis that mourning in its archaic form found expression in the devouring of the person that had died. Later, Abraham furnished an explanation of this phenomenon. He derived it from the analysis of melancholia where the impulse toward coprophagy emerges time and again. He interpreted it as a cannibalistic impulse toward the introjection of a "murdered" love object, i.e., as a self-imposed punishment for a grave offense.

In his essay "After the Death of the Primal Father" (*Imago*, 1923, vol. 1), Róheim attempted to show that the end of mourning consists in a symbolic killing and devouring of the deceased, but that this act is accompanied by unmistakable pleasure. The homeopathic repetition of the Oedipus act ends mourning, in other words. Here also Abraham discovered an analogy in the behavior of melancholiacs who always experience increased sexual desire during mourning ("A Short Study in the Development of the Libido, Viewed in the Light of Mental Disorders," in *Six Essays*). The best critique of Róheim's theses and perhaps the best that was written prior to the studies by Parin, Morgenthaler, and Matthey in the area of psychoanalytical ethnology was a work we could not use in this book for copyright reasons: Wilhelm Reich's first (1932) and second (1935) version of his most important anthropological work, *Der Einbruch der Sexualmoral* (*The Imposition of Sexual Morality*) which was intended as a reply to the Róheim essay "Original Forms and Origin of Property" contained in this book. Here, Reich describes a meeting with Róheim in the winter of 1926:

> We discussed the interpretation of symbols and in connection with that the analytic interpretation of the origin of tools. I put forward the view that an axe is first a rational creation, and intended to facilitate the splitting of wood. Secondly, it could take on symbolic significance, but this did not necessarily occur. In a dream, a tree or a stick may but need not necessarily mean a phallus. . . . Airplanes are constructed to advance the mastery over time and space. That they become phallic symbols in dreams is of importance only for the psychology of individuals, but not sociologically. Róheim, on the other hand, was of the opinion that an axe is a penis symbol and is created as such, and that its rational purpose is

> secondary, that in reality all creation of the means of production is nothing more than the projection of unconscious symbolism.

Róheim answered as follows in a review of this book (*Imago*, 19, 1933, 552-561): "Reich is incorrect when he says that civilization arises from some sort of economic motives and then causes neurosis; what happens is the reverse: collective neurosis explains, determines, creates social organizations, religion, economy, law and everything else." In answer to which, Reich asked: "And where does the collective neurosis come from? From eternity, apparently." Here, I clearly and definitely side with Reich. And in spite of the bitter conflict which ultimately arose between Freud and Reich, I cannot imagine that the father of psychoanalysis would not have agreed with Reich on this point. For Freud always saw neurosis as the result of social influences on the individual. If neuroses were prior, as Róheim believes, that would negate the entire structure of psychoanalysis, and especially its therapeutic significance. If there is any aspect of psychoanalysis that can be considered established today, it is the fact that the structure of instincts does not of itself lead to neuroses but only through interaction with the external world. Nor is it true that there are entire tribes where a libidinously, particularly strongly cathected anal zone constitutes the hereditary basis for the development of an obsessional interest in collecting and the amassing of wealth, as Róheim, Desmonde, Posinsky, and their school appear to believe. For what is true of the individual is equally true of the group: it is not the disposition in and of itself which determines whether the group shall be healthy or ill, but the interaction of disposition and experience. Disposition, infantile experience, and day-to-day experience are absolute magnitudes which complement each other, as Freud suggested. In cases of strongly neurotic instinctual structure, an insignificant pathogenic experience suffices to trigger a neurosis. But if the former is weak, more intense and frequent pedagogic influences are necessary. It is my impression that these complementary magnitudes are not absolute but relative and that their relationship is dialectical. Under favorable external conditions, individuals with a marked pregenital disposition do not develop neuroses, while others with less pregenital cathexis become neurotics if parents or society exert unfavorable influences. The various erotogenic sources are not only dependent on each other but also on the milieu. A disposition which impresses one as being strongly anal may disappear if the stimuli affecting it cease, once genital repression has been overcome. Excitations communicate with each other and depend primarily on the order of the entire sexual household.

A good deal of what Róheim and his disciples attribute to anal "disposition" may thus be the product of external influences which have nothing to do with any sexually determined syndrome. If a group brings up its children by allowing them to suck the mother's breast up to the time the genital phase begins, it is perfectly conceivable that neither an anal phase nor anal reaction formation will occur. This does not mean that I wish to deny the influence of hereditary elements; I simply wish to call attention to the fact that much of the work of Róheim, Desmonde, and Posinsky does not go beyond tracing the overestimation of money to an instinctual basis, and fails to explore the sociological reasons why a given society introduces inhibitions. A sociologically more searching analysis may show that "inhibitions" not only have negative effects but also stimulate creativity. But in the simplistic analysis of certain epigones of Freud, the external world is wholly viewed and interpreted in its inhibiting aspect.

In her review of Róheim's most important book, *The Riddle of the Sphinx*, Margaret Mead formulated a fundamental critique of this method:

> So while Róheim reiterates that the system is self-perpetuating, he suffers from the handicap which is apparent in so much work which stems from the life-history

> approach; he sees the plot of human life as beginning, in every sense, with the birth of a new generation, and in his final argument ignores the society into which the first group of children who suffer from this trauma are born. . . . His argument is not so much that ontogeny recapitulates phylogeny as that the development of the human race and its cultural institutions can be derived from a study of the development of the character of a given human individual. He has left out of consideration the nature of society. . . . If one neglects to consider that societies are after all aggregations of individuals which have their own laws of integration, laws which may possibly be paralleled with the laws of integration of an organism, but which are not comparable to the laws which govern the psyche alone, the result is Róheim's theoretical statement (*Character and Personality*, 4, 1935, 85-90).

I have nothing to add to this except for a brief comment concerning a factual matter. Róheim is mistaken in his belief that money is an invention of the matriarchy. As proof, he quotes the payment of sacred money in the cult of the Great Mother in Asia Minor. (Desmonde makes the same error, Bibliography 14.) The so-called temple prostitution was a symptom of decay of the matriarchy and arose under the influence of the patriarchy. There is nothing more antithetical than the mother religions of the prehistorical clan societies with their basis in communal property and the money cultures of the patriarchy founded on private property where we see the first appearance of that alienation and reification which were altogether unknown to the matriarchate of the proto-Greek and proto-Roman gentes.

Contribution 10. Posinsky's study of the shell money of the Yurok is undoubtedly one of the most intelligent analyses of primitive societies ever written by a psychoanalyst. But even this fascinating study has its limitations because the author refuses to investigate the historical, concrete development of Yurok society before turning to the special area of the analytical interpretation of the psychic aspects of money. What results is something of hair-raising complexity which makes considerable demands even on an experienced, clinically schooled analyst (and even ethnologist), yet finally fails to provide an answer to the principal questions concerning the psychoanalytical investigation of ethnological problems: How did the Yurok come to invent this incredibly complicated system? What is the relationship between the external world, the production of food, the hierarchical structure of the tribe on the one hand, and the somatic disposition of the individual on the other which resulted in the phenomena described and analyzed by Posinsky? As long as these questions are not answered satisfactorily, the reader has no yardstick by which to measure the validity of the analysis.

Part III

The third and final part of the book deals with psychoanalytical theories of money which are not (or at least not exclusively) based on the Freudian thesis of the anal origin of money. To illustrate these theories, I chose the work of analysts that belong to the English, French, and American school. While it is true that both Bergler and Schilder are Austrians by birth their work was done in America and bears the stamp of American attitudes toward analysis. I chose the contribution by Kaufman because it illustrates the premise that it is the function of the physician to adapt the patients to whatever economic system prevails (American capitalism, in this case), and I used the essays of Schilder and Amar because they question this premise.

Contribution 11. In what is otherwise a perfectly respectable study of the neurotic misuse of money (but with the typically "positive" title: "Some Emotional Uses of Money"), Kaufman seriously suggests that curing a patient means getting him to consent, to adapt to the theory and practice of the ruling class, since failure to do so leads to psychic isolation and thus to neurosis. In other words, the criterion for human maturity is the degree to which the individual can accept as binding what exists. The notion that apparent neurotics may be healthy and society sick does not even emerge as a hypothesis. Nor does he consider that a given social system may be less mature than certain individuals. This is also the reason he completely fails to understand the most important insight of modern social therapy, namely that society has to adapt to the progressive individual, not man to an anachronistic social order.

Everything is a question of adapting oneself to the existing order since its right to rule is already proven by the fact that it does. Whether the society deserves that one adapt to it is a question that is not raised. The mature, balanced individual is characterized by his acceptance of the wealth of others as if such were the divine will: "The child may have to accept as a reality the fact that he cannot have as much money as others," Kaufman states apodictically. Why does he have to? What authority does the analyst have to tell me that I am condemned to lifelong inferiority? Would it not be more appropriate to tell me that I will have to use my intelligence, my willpower, all the resources of my libido to build a world where people who have committed no wrong are not condemned to inequality? "Even at this early age, a child may try to buy love and friendship by giving his money to others in his play group." Really? Everywhere? In all cultures? In all classes? As in Freud's own writings, we here observe the delusion that the bourgeois patients from whom the analyst derives his diagnostic and therapeutic experience are not a select group but represent all of mankind. Proletarian children who have learned to question the value of money from earliest youth seldom try to buy the love and friendship of their playmates. They have nothing they can use for payment and consequently cannot test the proposition or answer the question whether love can be bought.

Like most analysts, Kaufman lives almost exclusively off upper-middle-class patients. He therefore unquestioningly assumes that the patient is well-to-do. "What this agitated child needs most is . . . understanding that there is enough money to take care of all its basic needs, and even for some luxuries; and that there is no real cause for worry." But what if there is not enough money? Is a child incurable in such a case? Suppose it has perfectly good economic reasons for concern? Do we then give up on it? Perhaps we have to, but if that should be true, Kaufman should tell us loudly and clearly.

On the other hand, his description of the corruption of the child by its bribing parents is so wholly lacking in perspective that we must assume that he is not aware of what is going on: "He learns to his pleasure that he can buy certain reward foods such as ice cream, candy, and cookies. Later he realizes that money can obtain for him toys, comic books, special clothes and admission to the movies or circus. Because money becomes associated with pleasure in the child's mind, parents can now use it as a reward to reinforce habit development of various desirable forms of behavior." This reification and alienation of love is so serious that one has to be profoundly committed to the "morality" of capitalism not to notice that what happens here is precisely the opposite of what Kaufman thinks. Such a child is not brought up to accept reality but is having its libido corrupted. If, as a result, the child sooner or later gets to the point where it says to its parents, "you don't love me," Kaufman advances the absurd explanation that this is due to its illusion that the parents have unlimited resources and therefore turn it down for reasons of their own. But that interpretation is false: the child protests because it has been prostituted; because the parents inculcated the illusion that love can be bought. This is so serious a mistake in pedagogy that it can never be made good. Almost all the other syndromes Kaufman describes in his extended and carefully documented article stem from this initial and fundamental pedagogic sin.

"The possessor of money can manipulate the behavior of other human beings for constructive or destructive purposes through the use of monetary reward." A tragic illusion which has dragged capitalism from one crisis to the next and should reveal its moral inadequacy to the trained eye of the analyst. "When used constructively, monetary rewards encourage socially desirable activities in individuals and groups." Among what persons? Among what groups? What is "constructive" use? What is being "constructed" here? Who is served by what is being constructed? What are "socially desirable" activities? *What* society desires here? If it were possible to get rid of such questions by categorical assertions, we could have saved ourselves a few centuries of the most bitter wars and civil wars, and all of psychoanalysis besides.

Contribution 12. This is part of a book by Smiley Blanton, an American guidance counsellor who tells his patients how they may become wealthy and happy through psychoanalysis. It seems to me that this is the nadir of psychoanalysis, for here the consumer society has taken hold of a clinical technique and turned it into the instrument of the ruling class and its progeny. But it is also one of the most characteristic examples of the temptation into which one falls so easily when one adopts the premises of the society one serves uncritically and without perspective. It is widespread not only in American popular psychoanalytical literature but especially evident in the popular literature dealing with the analysis of money. To omit such examples would amount to providing a censored presentation of psychoanalysis.

Although Blanton repeatedly refers to himself as an analyst, he reports exclusively about his activity in a guidance clinic for well-to-do seekers of advice. He uses rational argument instead of interpreting whatever material may be relevant. The following presuppositions are accepted as matters of course:

1. One has employees rather than being one.
2. One tends to have too much rather than too little money.
3. If one gives one's wife and children too little money, this is for reasons of stinginess and not because one doesn't have enough.

The entire chapter rests on the following central tenet: "We Americans, by and large, are good at making money, and there's nothing wrong with that, a man should be proud to be productive, and *earning capacity is a reflection of productivity*." (*Now or Never, The promise of the middle years*, by Smiley Blanton, M.D., with Arthur Gordon. Prentice Hall, Inc. 1959, p. 133). But this is precisely what it doesn't do. The illusion that it does implies profounder thoughts about the Ego than all the superficial corrections of self knowledge which Blanton attempts to teach his patients as they strive to develop a "healthy" attitude toward money.

Contribution 13. Edmund Bergler is an analyst who has said many good and intelligent things, but also some that are not wholly thought through, and others that are false. During his formative years, as the collaborator of Wilhelm Reich, he was one of the best analysts of his time and especially well known for his preliminary work on a prophylactic youth therapy. After his emigration to the United States, his thought underwent a certain coarsening and simplification which we also encounter in his brief study on the psychopathology of the "bargain hunter." For reasons of style and content, this contribution should really have appeared in the first part of this book. But Bergler believes that individuals of this type are motivated by oral rather than anal regressions. What I consider important and correct in his essay is the distinction between the "buyer" (who is interested in his purchase), the "collector" (who is interested less in the object itself than in amassing a number of objects of the same kind), and the "haggler" (who is interested neither in the article nor in collecting objects but finds his pleasure only in outwitting the salesman). "Bargain hunters behave as if evil reality, which is a mother surrogate, wanted to reject them. It therefore has to be outsmarted aggressively, and this expresses itself in the persistence with which some people bargain."

Contribution 14. André Amar's study deals with a question which either is not dealt with or considered irrelevant in the other contributions in this third part: *If the therapy for a neurosis consists in adaptation to reality, how do we define the reality to which we want to adapt the neurotic*? Or, in terms of the money complex: *To what monetary system are we to adapt the money neurotic so that he can find his way out of it and return to the solid ground of reality*?

These are the questions which caused me to put this book together. But in spite of the courage of his questions and the elegance of his dialectical method, Amar shies away from advancing the answer that stares him in the face. He is right when he says: "It is the social structures which explain individual phenomena, not the other way around." But then he confines himself to furnishing proofs for the irrational nature of money and of the bourgeois belief in it so that the central problem remains unanswered: *If the capitalist system does not provide the rational ground of reality, what social system should furnish the guideposts by which to orient the neurotic if we propose to lead him back to reality*?

It is my conviction that such a reality can only be found gropingly and in the act of resistance against the corruption and degradation of man in bourgeois society. No analyst can tell his patients with a good conscience: this is the right and this the wrong political, economic, financial system. But he cannot only reconcile it with his conscience but *owes* it to that conscience to call his patient's attention to the significance of active resistance against the things that have made him a neurotic. There is no effective therapy which leaves the patient in a state of passive acceptance, for that would be tantamount to allowing him to once again become the plaything of those forces which brought on his illness. When the patient leaves the analyst at the end of a successful analysis and returns without his support to the hard life in a society torn by internal contradictions, the physician can only suggest how he might help himself: by mobilizing all his strength, and by discovering in his active resistance against all those aspects of society which made him ill the self-confidence, the certainty, and the satisfaction which no one else can give him. Only he can liberate himself. Only if he learns to free himself from the narcissistic absorption in his own self and directs all his strength toward the object love of his fellow beings can he recover from the self-destructive preoccupation with the symptoms of his illness and use the entire power of his libido in all its forms in an attempt to help others. Only this actively given help frees us from those neurotic symptoms of which no one, including the physician, can ever be wholly free unless he fights for the improvement of human society.

Contribution 15. The final contribution, Paul Schilder's "The Psychoanalysis of Economics," deals with these questions. Although Schilder was a young Hegelian and studied Marxism, he does not belong to that tiny group of Marxist psychoanalysts who have made this field their own. Like Wilhelm Reich and Otto Fenichel, Schilder emigrated to the United States during the Hitler period and gradually adapted to the forms of thought and perception current there. In contrast to Reich, who degenerated completely in America, and to Fenichel, who became discouraged because of his lack of success, Schilder, an especially competent clinician, soon became famous and successful.

Considering that he was not a professional philosopher, he had an exceptional knowledge of philosophical problems. Already at age twenty-seven, he discovered a disease (later named after him and called "encephalitis periaxialis diffusa," "Schilder's disease") and its cure, and was therefore considered a kind of child prodigy by his colleagues. Since he was both a doctor of philosophy and of medicine, and had written a philosophical work, *Gedanken zur Naturphilosophie* (Vienna, 1928), his political views were taken more seriously than those of many of his colleagues.

In America, his advancement was rapid. He soon became clinical director of the psychiatric division of Bellevue Hospital in New York and research professor of psychiatry at New York University. His study on the psychoanalysis of economics, dictated in the year of his death (1940) and not revised by him, is written in the laborious, repetitive style of some English-writing Germans and Austrians. Certain unimportant passages therefore had to be cut.

Almost everything Schilder says here has since been said better and more elegantly by others, such as Herbert Marcuse, Reimut Reiche, Klaus Holzkamp, Dietrich Haensch, Hannes Schwenger, Klaus Horn, and others. But his study is important nonetheless, and this for two reasons. In the first place, Schilder's clinical reputation was so considerable that his apolitical colleagues were willing to read a text they would never have looked at had it been written by Reich, for example. In the second place, it was the first half-way Marxist study the conservative professional journal *Psychoanalytic Review* dared print. For almost all of its readers, this article was therefore the first encounter with a form of thought which impresses us as obvious, indeed almost as a cliché today, but which triggered a genuinely revolutionary shock among American readers at the time.

V

To provide a balanced presentation of the psychoanalytic theory of money, this book would of course have had to end with the work of the only analyst who really added something new to Freud's fundamental insights into this subject: Wilhelm Reich. In spite of the unfortunate publicity of the early writings which were censored by the author himself and which he ruined to the point of unrecognizability with his foolish additions when he had become an unhappy and bitter man; in spite of the late writings of his American exile (1938-1957), a period already marked by illness, we must not underestimate the work of the years from 1927 to 1937. My profound respect for Karl Abraham, Freud's loyal disciple, notwithstanding, I do not hesitate to say that Reich's studies during this decade are the only writings of any analyst whose originality, clarity, and profundity can be compared with Freud's own. Even the tragic lapses of his thought during the American diaspora do not invalidate that of the preceding decade, a period that is unique in the history of psychoanalysis.

It would lead too far to sum up Reich's contributions to psychoanalysis. I simply want to direct the interest of young analysts to the question whether and to what extent the anal theory of money can survive, should Reich be correct in his belief that neuroses do not have their source in the pregenital but in a disturbed genital libido. In that case, "character" is no more and no less than the result of unsatisfied genitality: a person who cannot find satisfaction in genital intercourse becomes a "character," a "personality."

On the other hand, genital satisfaction is ipso facto impossible in a society which demands that character be "formed." To eliminate neuroses and psychoses, perversions and even "character," it becomes necessary to create a social system which does not *require* repression. But because Reich was convinced that every society where the means of production are privately owned came into being through repression and required repression for its existence, any analytic therapy was ultimately senseless from his point of view. For if the miracle of freeing the patient from his neuroses should really occur, he would become an unworldly outsider, unable to come to terms either with the social reality of the bourgeoisie or that of the proletariat.

Even his youthful conviction that it might perhaps be possible to prevent the inevitable neuroses of the adult in bourgeois society by preventive therapy during childhood was abandoned in 1935. Toward the end of his creative period (1936-1937), he only retained the hope that through prophylactic analysis leaders of the working class might be raised who would no longer succumb to the temptations of the misuse of power and bureaucratization as had been true of their predecessors for generations on end. But because he doubted his own abilities (and those of all analysts raised in bourgeois society) to give the patient something the analyst himself did not already have, i.e., a "classless" libido structure based neither on oral, nor anal, or genital primacy, the analytic theory of society seemed hopeless to him: one could not pull oneself by one's own bootstraps out of the swamp in which society threatened to become engulfed. Analysts with a classless libidinal structure could exist only in a classless society, and only such analysts would be able to cure the illnesses of others, only they would be able to preserve society from the ever-threatening danger of a relapse into the den of cutthroats that is capitalism. But how were such men to be trained in a class society? However justified it may be, I do not share Reich's pessimism here, and will therefore confine myself to a more modest critique of the anal theory. Contrary to the belief of those analysts who once thought that capitalism was a product of sublimated anal erotism, it seems to me that it has become apparent in the meantime that the opposite tends to be true: while capitalism did not create the anal character, it has raised to a degree of prominence unknown elsewhere a character type that is relatively rare in other social systems. The libidinous attitude of certain neurotics toward money, which derives from anal sources, has helped develop a money fetishism in our system which is even adopted by healthy persons because it mediates respect for capital and subjection to its power. But if we make use of the theory of the anal origin of money, we must avoid the snare of believing that the preservation of infantilisms could ever produce creative values. For, clinically speaking, the "invention" of money does not significantly differ from other products of neurotic origin. Anyone who preserves what has been repressed in its repressed state runs the risk of losing command over himself and his world. His sense of reality does not mature completely, his judgment suffers. Dominated by a desire to "collect" money, the anal character can never become a good businessman, for according to the laws of capitalist economics, money must be invested, not hoarded. Those who hoard money don't earn any. Otto Fenichel once compared the neurotic illusion of being able to "make" money with the libidinal excitation certain neurotics experience while walking: "To deduce the function of money from such a misuse of money would be like drawing from the secret sexual meaning of walking in the hysteric, shown by psychoanalysis, the deduction that we walk for the sake of sexual pleasure and not in order to get from one place to another" (Bibliography 17). When children who once found pleasure in retaining their stool later become collectors, this tells us nothing about the origin and development of capitalism, for what such anal erotics collect need not have monetary value. And even if a few anal characters should become bankers, this does not explain why capitalists constantly have to increase their capital if they do not want to be destroyed by competitors with larger capital reserves. Anal erotism has its specific laws, capitalism has others. During certain periods, both need and promote each other. At other times, they conflict. Since the anally oriented desire for possessions does not take its cue from the value of the collected objects but is governed by the compulsive element in collecting, it becomes irrational and, in its extreme form, contradicts the logic of capital and therefore harms it. Besides, there are aspects of anal erotism such as obstinacy and a desire for order which are directed against the ruling class and can in no way be reconciled with the interests of capital. All equations of anality and an interest in money should therefore be studiously avoided.

Translated by Michael Shaw

Part I

Studies on the Anal Theory of Money

Contribution 1

Character and Anal Erotism

Sigmund Freud

Among those whom we try to help by our psychoanalytic efforts we often come across a type of person who is marked by the possession of a certain set of character-traits, while at the same time our attention is drawn to the behaviour in his childhood of one of his bodily functions and the organ concerned in it. I cannot say at this date what particular occasions began to give me an impression that there was some organic connection between this type of character and this behaviour of an organ, but I can assure the reader that no theoretical expectation played any part in that impression.

Accumulated experience has so much strengthened my belief in the existence of such a connection that I am venturing to make it the subject of a communication.

The people I am about to describe are noteworthy for a regular combination of the three following characteristics. They are especially *orderly*, *parsimonious* and *obstinate* Each of these words actually covers a small group or series of interrelated character-traits. "Orderly"[1] covers the notion of bodily cleanliness, as well as of conscientiousness in carrying out small duties and trustworthiness. Its opposite would be "untidy" and "neglectful." Parsimony may appear in the exaggerated form of avarice; and obstinacy can go over into defiance, to which rage and revengefulness are easily joined. The two latter qualities—parsimony and obstinacy—are linked with each other more closely than they are with the first—with orderliness. They are, also, the more constant element of the whole complex. Yet it seems to me incontestable that all three in some way belong together.

It is easy to gather from these people's early childhood history that they took a comparatively long time to overcome their infantile *incontinentia alvi* [faecal incontinence], and that even in later childhood they suffered from isolated failures of this function. As infants, they seem to have belonged to the class who refuse to empty their bowels when they are put on the pot because they derive a subsidiary pleasure from defaecating;[2] for they tell us that even in somewhat later years they enjoyed holding back their stool, and they remember—though more readily about their brothers and sisters than about themselves—doing all sorts of unseemly things with the faeces that had been passed. From these indications we infer that such people are born with a sexual constitution in which the erotogenicity of the anal zone is exceptionally strong. But since none of these weaknesses and idiosyncrasies are to be found in them once their childhood has been passed, we must conclude that the anal zone had lost its erotogenic significance in the course of development; and it is to be suspected that the regularity with which this triad of properties is present in their character may be brought into relation with the disappearance of their anal erotism.

I know that no one is prepared to believe in a state of things so long as it appears to be unintelligible and to offer no angle from which an explanation can be attempted. But we can at least bring the underlying factors nearer to our understanding by the help of the postulates I laid down in my *Three Essays on the Theory of Sexuality* in 1905.[3] I there attempted to show that the sexual instinct of man is highly complex and is put together from contributions made by numerous constituents and component instincts. Important contributions to "sexual excitation" are furnished by the peripheral excitations of certain specially designated parts of the body (the genitals, mouth, anus, urethra), which therefore deserve to be described as "erotogenic zones." But the amounts of excitation coming in from these parts of the body do not all undergo the same vicissitudes, nor is the fate of all of them the same at every period of life. Generally speaking, only a part of them is made use of in sexual life; another part is deflected from sexual aims and directed towards others—a process which deserves the name of "sublimation." During the period of life which may be called the period of "sexual latency"—i.e., from the completion of the fifth year[4] to the first manifestations of puberty (round about the eleventh year)—reaction-formations, or counter-forces, such as shame, disgust and morality, are created in the mind. They are actually formed at the expense of the excitations proceeding from the erotogenic zones, and they rise like dams to oppose the later activity of the sexual instincts. Now anal erotism is one of the components of the [sexual] instinct which, in the course of development and in accordance with the education demanded by our present civilization, have become unserviceable for sexual aims. It is therefore plausible to suppose that these character-traits of orderliness, parsimony and obstinacy, which are so often prominent in people who were formerly anal erotics, are to be regarded as the first and most constant results of the sublimation of anal erotism.[5]

The intrinsic necessity for this connection is not clear, of course, even to myself. But I can make some suggestions which may help towards an understanding of it. Cleanliness, orderliness and trustworthiness give exactly the impression of a reaction-formation against an interest in what is unclean and disturbing and should not be part of the body. ("Dirt is matter in the wrong place.")[6] To relate obstinacy to an interest in defaecation would seem no easy task; but it should be remembered that even babies can show self-will about parting with their stool, as we have seen above, and that it is a general practice in children's upbringing to administer painful stimuli to the skin of the buttocks—which is linked up with the erotogenic anal zone—in order to break their obstinacy and make them submissive. An invitation to a caress of the anal zone is still used today, as it was in ancient times, to express defiance or defiant scorn, and thus in reality signifies an act of tenderness that has been overtaken by repression. An exposure of the buttocks represents a softening down of this spoken invitation into a gesture; in Goethe's *Götz von Berlichingen* both words and gesture are introduced at the most appropriate point as an expression of defiance.[7]

The connections between the complexes of interest in money and of defaecation, which seem so dissimilar, appear to be the most extensive of all. Every doctor who has practised psychoanalysis knows that the most refractory and long-standing cases of what is described as habitual constipation in neurotics can be cured by that form of treatment. This is less surprising if we remember that that function has shown itself similarly amenable to hypnotic suggestion. But in psychoanalysis one only achieves this result if one deals with the patients' money complex and induces them to bring it into consciousness with all its connections. It might be supposed that the neurosis is here only following an indication of common usage in speech, which calls a person who keeps too careful a hold on his money "dirty" or "filthy."[8] But this explanation would be far too superficial. In reality, wherever archaic modes of thought have predominated or persist—in the ancient civilizations, in myths, fairy tales and superstitions, in unconscious thinking, in dreams and in neuroses—money is brought into the most intimate relationship with dirt. We know that the gold which the devil gives his paramours turns into excrement after his departure, and the devil is certainly nothing else than the personification of the repressed unconscious instinctual life.[9] We also know about the superstition which connects the finding of treasure with defaecation,[10] and everyone is familiar with the figure of the "shitter of ducats [*Dukatenscheisser*]."[11] Indeed, even according to ancient Babylonian doctrine gold is "the faeces of Hell" (Mammon = *ilu mamman*[12]). Thus in following the usage of language, neurosis, here as elsewhere, is taking words in their original, significant sense, and where it appears to be using a word figuratively it is usually simply restoring its old meaning.[13]

It is possible that the contrast between the most precious substance known to men and the most worthless, which they reject as waste matter ("refuse"[14]), has led to this specific identification of gold with faeces.

Yet another circumstance facilitates this equation in neurotic thought. The original erotic interest in defaecation is, as we know, destined to be extinguished in later years. In those years the interest in money makes its appearance as a new interest which had been absent in childhood. This makes it easier for the earlier impulsion, which is in process of losing its aim, to be carried over to the newly emerging aim.

If there is any basis in fact for the relation posited here between anal erotism and this triad of character-traits, one may expect to find no very marked degree of "anal character" in people who have retained the anal zone's erotogenic character in adult life, as happens, for instance, with certain homosexuals. Unless I am much mistaken, the evidence of experience tallies quite well on the whole with this inference.

We ought in general to consider whether other character-complexes, too, do not exhibit a connection with the excitations of particular erotogenic zones. At present I only know of the intense "burning" ambition of people who earlier suffered from Enuresis.[15] We can at any rate lay down a formula for the way in which character in its final shape is formed out of the constituent instincts: the permanent character-traits are either unchanged prolongations of the original instincts, or sublimations of those instincts, or reaction-formations against them.[16]

Notes and References

1. ["*Ordentlich*" in German. The original meaning of the word is "orderly"; but it has become greatly extended in use. It can be the equivalent of such English terms as "correct," "tidy," "cleanly," "trustworthy," as well as "regular," "decent" and "proper," in the more colloquial senses of those words.]

2. Cf., Freud, *Three Essays on the Theory of Sexuality* (1905*d*), *Standard Ed.*, 7, 186.

3. [The material in the present paragraph is derived mainly from Section 5 of the first essay and Section 1 of the second (*Standard Ed.*, 7, 167 ff. and 176 ff.).]

4. [In the German editions before 1924 this read "from the completion of the fourth year."]

5. Since it is precisely the remarks in my *Three Essays on the Theory of Sexuality* about the anal erotism of infants that have particularly scandalized uncomprehending readers, I venture at this point to interpolate an observation for which I have to thank a very intelligent patient. "A friend of mine," he told me, "who has read your *Three Essays on the Theory of Sexuality*, was talking about the book. He entirely agreed with it, but there was one passage, which—though of course he accepted and understood its meaning like that of the rest—struck him as so grotesque and comic that he sat down and laughed over it for a quarter of an hour. This passage ran: 'One of the clearest signs of subsequent eccentricity or nervousness is to be seen when a baby obstinately refuses to empty his bowels when he is put on the pot—that is, when his nurse wants him to—and holds back that function till he himself chooses to exercise it. He is naturally not concerned with dirtying the bed, he is only anxious not to miss the subsidiary pleasure attached to defaecating.' [*Standard Ed.*, 7, 186.] The picture of this baby sitting on the pot and deliberating whether he would put up with a restriction of this kind upon his personal freedom of will, and feeling anxious, too, not to miss the pleasure attached to defaecating—this caused my friend the most intense amusement. About twenty minutes afterwards, as we were having some cocoa, he suddenly remarked without any preliminary: 'I say, seeing the cocoa in front of me has suddenly made me think of an idea that I always had when I was a child. I used always to pretend to myself that I was the cocoa-manufacturer Van Houten' (he pronounced the name Van 'Hauten' [i.e., with the first syllable rhyming with the English word "Cow"]) 'and that I possessed a great secret for the manufacture of this cocoa. Everybody was trying to get hold of this secret that was a boon to humanity but I kept it carefully to myself. I don't know why I should have hit specially upon Van Houten. Probably his advertisements impressed me more than any others.' Laughing, and without

thinking at the time that my words had any deep meaning, I said: 'Wann haut'n die Mutter?' ["When does mother smack?" The first two words in the German phrase are pronounced exactly like "Van Houten."] It was only later that I realized that my pun in fact contained the key to the whole of my friend's sudden childhood recollection, and I then recognized it as a brilliant example of a screen-phantasy. My friend's phantasy, while keeping to the situation actually involved (the nutritional process) and making use of phonetic associations ("Kakao" ["cocoa"—"Kaka" is the common German nursery word for "faeces"—cf., a dream at the end of Section IX of Freud, 1923*c*] and 'Wann haut'n'), pacified his sense of guilt by making a complete reversal in the content of his recollection: there was a displacement from the back of the body to the front, excreting food became taking food in, and something that was shameful and had to be concealed became a secret that was a boon to humanity. I was interested to see how, only a quarter of an hour after my friend had fended the phantasy off (though, it is true, in the comparatively mild form of raising an objection on formal grounds), he was, quite involuntarily, presented with the most convincing evidence by his own unconscious."

6. [This sentence is in English in the original.]

7. [The scene occurs in Act III, when Götz is summoned by a Herald to surrender. In the later acting version of the play the words are toned down.]

8. [The English "filthy" as well as the German "*filzig*" appears in the original. Freud had already commented on the usage mentioned here, in a letter to Fliess of December 22, 1897 (Freud, 1950*a* Letter 79) and, later, in the first edition of *The Interpretation of Dreams* (1900*a*), *Standard Ed.*, 4, 200.]

9. Compare hysterical possession and demoniac epidemics. [Freud discussed this at considerable length in Part III of his paper "A Seventeenth Century Demonological Neurosis" (1923*d*). The legendary transformation of witches' gold into faeces and the comparison with the "*Dukatenscheisser*" below had already been mentioned by Freud in a letter to Fliess of January 24, 1897 (1950*a*, Letter 57).]

10. [Numerous examples of this derived from folklore are given in Freud and Oppenheim's paper on "Dreams in Folklore" (1957*a* [1911]), *Standard Ed.*, 12, 187 ff.]

11. [A term vulgarly used for a wealthy spendthrift.]

12. Cf. Jeremias (1904, 115*n*.). " 'Mamon' ('Mammon') is 'Manman' in Babylonian and is another name for Nergal, the God of the Underworld. According to Oriental mythology, which has passed over into popular legends and fairy tales, gold is the excrement of Hell."

13. [For the occurrence of this in dreams, see a passage added in 1909 to *The Interpretation of Dreams, Standard Ed.*, 5, 407.]

14. [In English in the original.]

15. [The connection between urethral erotism and ambition seems to find its first mention here. Freud occasionally returned to the point, e.g., in a sentence added in 1914 to *The Interpretation of Dreams, Standard Ed.*, 4, 216 and in a footnote added in 1920 to the *Three Essays* (1905*d*), ibid., 7, 239. In a long footnote to Section III of *Civilization and its Discontents* (1930*a*) he brought the present finding into connection with his two other main lines of thought concerning enuresis—its symbolic association with fire and its importance as an infantile equivalent of masturbation. See also the still later paper on "The Acquisition and Control of Fire" (1932*a*).]

16. [There are not many accounts by Freud of the nature of "character" and the mechanism of its formation. Among them may be mentioned a passage near the end of the *Three Essays* (1905*d*), *Standard Ed.*, 7, 238-9, some remarks in the paper on "The Disposition to Obsessional Neurosis" (1913*i*), ibid., 12, 323-4, and especially a discussion in the first half of Chapter III of *The Ego and the Id* (1923*b*), the gist of which is repeated in Lecture XXXII of the *New Introductory Lectures* (1933*a*).]

The Ontogenesis of the Interest in Money

Sándor Ferenczi

The deeper psychoanalysis penetrates into the knowledge of social-psychological productions (myths, fairy-tales, folk-lore) the stronger becomes the confirmation of the phylogenetic origin of symbols, which stand out in the mental life of every individual as a precipitate of the experiences of previous generations. Analysis has still to perform the task of separately investigating the phylogenesis and ontogenesis of symbolism, and then establishing their mutual relation. The classical formula of "Daimon kai Tyche" in Freud's application (the coöperation of heredity and experience in the genesis of individual strivings) will finally become applied also to the genesis of the psychical contents of these strivings, and this also brings to the front the old dispute about "congenital ideas," though now no longer in the form of empty speculations. We may already, however, anticipate to this extent, namely, that for the production of a symbol individual experiences are necessary as well as the congenital disposition, these providing the real material for the construction of the symbol, while the congenital basis preceding experience has perhaps only the value of an inherited but not yet functioning mechanism.

I wish here to examine the question of whether, and to what extent, individual experience favours the transformation of anal-erotic interest into interest in money.

Every psychoanalyst is familiar with the symbolic meaning of money that was discovered by Freud. "Wherever the archaic way of thinking has prevailed or still prevails, in the old civilisations, in myths, fairy-tales, superstition, in unconscious thinking, in dreams, and in neuroses, money has been brought into the closest connection with filth."

As an individual-psychological phenomenon parallel with this fact Freud asserts that an intimate association exists between the strongly marked erogenicity of the anal zone in childhood and the character trait of miserliness that develops later. In the case of persons who later on were especially tidy, economical, and obstinate, one learns from the analytic investigation of their early childhood that they were of that class of infants "who refuse to empty the bowel because they obtain an accessory pleasure from defaecation," who even in the later years of childhood "enjoyed holding back the stools," and who recall "having occupied themselves in their childhood in all sorts of unseemly ways with the evacuated material." "The most extensive connections seem to be those existing between the apparently so disparate complexes of defaecation and interest in money."[1]

Observation of the behaviour of children and analytic investigation of neurotics allow us now to establish some single points on the line along which the idea of the most valuable thing that a man possesses (money) is developed in the individual into a symbol "of the most worthless thing, which a man casts aside as dejecta."[2]

Experience gathered from these two sources shews that children originally devote their interest without any inhibition to the process of defaecation, and that it affords them pleasure to hold back their stools. The excrementa thus held back are really the first "savings" of the growing being, and as such remain in a constant, unconscious interrelationship with every bodily activity or mental striving that has anything to do with collecting, hoarding, and saving.

Faeces are also, however, one of the first toys of the child. The purely auto-erotic satisfaction afforded to the child by the pressing and squeezing of the faecal masses and the play of the sphincter muscles soon becomes—in part, at least—transformed into a sort of object-love, in that the interest gets displaced from the neutral sensations of certain organs on to the material itself that caused these feelings. The faeces are thus "introjected," and in this stage of development—which is essentially characterised by sharpening of the sense of smell and an increasingly adroit use of the hands, with at the same time an inability to walk upright (creeping on all fours)—they count as a valuable toy, from which the child is to be weaned only through deterrents and threats of punishment.

The child's interest for dejecta experiences its first distortion through the smell of faeces becoming disagreeable, disgusting. This is probably related to the beginning of the upright gait.[3] The other attributes of this material—moistness, discolouration, stickiness, etc.—do not for the time being offend his sense of cleanliness. He still enjoys, therefore, playing with and manipulating moist street-mud whenever he has the chance, liking to collect it together into larger heaps. Such a heap of mud is already in a sense a symbol, distinguished from the real thing by its absence of smell. For the child, street-mud is, so to speak, deodourised dejecta.

As the child's sense of cleanliness increases—with the help of paedagogic measures—street-mud also becomes objectionable to him. Substances which on account of their stickiness, moistness, and colour are apt to leave traces on the body and clothing become despised and avoided as "dirty things." The symbol of filth must therefore undergo a further distortion, a dehydration. The child turns its interest to sand, a substance which, while the colour of earth, is cleaner and dry. The instinctive joy of children in gathering up, massing together, and shaping sand is subsequently rationalised and sanctioned by the adults, whom it suits to see an otherwise unruly child playing with sand for hours—and they declare this playing to be "healthy," *i.e.*, hygienic.[4] None the less this play-sand also is nothing other than a copro-symbol—deodourised and dehydrated filth.

Already in this stage of development, by the way, there occurs a "return of the repressed." It gives children endless pleasure to fill with water the holes they dig in the sand, and so to bring the material of their play nearer to the original watery stage. Boys not infrequently employ their own urine for this irrigation, as though they wanted in this way to emphasise quite clearly the relationship of the two materials. Even the interest for the specific odour of excrement does not cease at once, but is only displaced on to other odours that in any way resemble this. The children continue to shew a liking for the smell of sticky materials with a characteristic odour, especially the strongly smelling degenerated product of cast off epidermis cells which collects between the toes, nasal secretion, ear-wax, and the dirt of the nails, while many children do not content themselves with the moulding and sniffing of these substances, but also take them into the mouth. The passionate enjoyment of children in moulding putty (colour, consistency, smell), tar, and asphalt is well-known. I knew a boy who had an intense passion for the characteristic smell of rubber materials, and who could sniff for hours at a piece of indiarubber.

The smell of stables and of illuminating gas greatly pleases children at this age—indeed, at much older ages even—and it is not chance that popular belief appreciates places having these smells as being "healthy," even as being a cure for diseases. A special sublimation path of anal-erotism branches off from the smell of gas, asphalt, and turpentine: the fondness of substances with an agreeable odour, for perfumes, by means of which the development of a reaction-formation—representation through the opposite—is concluded. People with whom this kind of sublimation occurs often develop in other respects as well into aesthetes, and there can be no question that aesthetics in general has its principal root in repressed anal-erotism.[5] The aesthetic and playful interest springing from this source not infrequently has a share in the developing pleasure in painting and sculpture.[6]

Already in the mud and sand periods of coprophilic interest it is striking how fond children are of fabricating objects out of this material—so far as their primitive artistic skill allows—or, more correctly, of imitating objects the possession of which has a special value for them. They make out of them different articles of diet, cakes, tarts, sweetmeats, etc. The reinforcement of purely egoistic instincts by coprophilia begins here.

Progress in the sense of cleanliness then gradually makes even sand unacceptable to the child, and the infantile stone age begins: the collecting of pebbles, as prettily shaped and coloured as possible, in which a higher stage in the development of replacement-formation is attained. The attributes of evil odour, moisture, and softness are represented by those of absence of odour, dryness, and now also hardness. We are reminded of the real origin of this hobby by the circumstance that stones—just as mud and sand—are gathered and collected from the *earth*. The capitalistic significance of stones is already quite considerable. (Children are "stone-rich"[7] in the narrow sense of the word).

After stones comes the turn of artificial products, and with these the detachment of the interest from the earth is complete. Glass marbles, buttons,[8] fruit pips, are eagerly collected—this time no longer only for the sake of their intrinsic value, but as measures of value, so to speak as primitive coins, converting the previous barter exchange of children into an enthusiastic money exchange. The character of capitalism, however, not purely practical and utilitarian, but libidinous and irrational, is betrayed in this stage also: the child decidedly enjoys the collecting in itself.[9]

It only needs one more step for the identification of faeces with gold to be complete. Soon even stones begin to wound the child's feeling of cleanliness—he longs for something purer—and this is offered to him in the shining pieces of money, the high appreciation of which is naturally also in part due to the respect in which they are held by adults, as well as to the seductive possibilities of obtaining through them everything that the child's heart can desire. Originally, however, it is not these purely practical considerations that are operative, enjoyment in the playful collecting, heaping up, and gazing at the shining metal pieces being the chief thing, so that they are treasured even less for their economic value than for their own sake as pleasure-giving objects. The eye takes pleasure at the sight of their lustre and colour, the ear at their metallic clink, the sense of touch at play with the round smooth discs, only the sense of smell comes away empty, and the sense of taste also has to be satisfied with the weak, but peculiar taste of the coins. With this the development of the money symbol is in its main outlines complete. Pleasure in the intestinal contents becomes enjoyment of money, which, however, after what has been said is seen to be nothing other than odourless, dehydrated filth that has been made to shine. *Pecunia non olet*.

In correspondence with the development of the organ of thought that in the meanwhile has been proceeding in the direction of logicality, the adult's symbolic interest in money gets extended not only to objects with similar physical attributes, but to all sorts of things that in any way signify value or possession (paper money, shares, bankbook, etc.). But whatever form may be assumed by money, the enjoyment at possessing it has its deepest and amplest source in coprophilia. Every sociologist and national economist who examines the facts without prejudice has to reckon with this irrational element. Social problems can be solved only by discovering the real psychology of human beings; speculations about economic conditions alone will never reach the goal.

A part of anal-erotism is not sublimated at all, but remains in its original form.[10] Even the most cultivated normal being displays an interest in his evacuation functions which stands in a curious contradiction to the abhorrence and disgust that he manifests when he sees or hears about anything of the kind in regard to other people. Foreign people and races as is well-known, cannot "*riechen*"[11] each other. In addition to the retention of the original form, however, there also exists a "return" of what is actually concealed behind the money symbol. The intestinal disorders, first observed by Freud, that follow on a wounding of the money complex are examples of this.[12] A further instance is the curious fact, which I have noticed in countless cases, that people are economical as regards the changing of under-linen in a way quite out of proportion to their standard of living in other respects. Meanness finally, therefore, makes use of the anal character in order to gain once more a piece of anal-erotism (tolerance of dirt). The following is a still more striking example: A patient could not recall any kind of coprophilic manipulations, but soon after related without being asked that he took a special pleasure in brightly shining copper coins, and had invented an original procedure for making them shine; he swallowed the piece of money, and then searched his faeces until he found the piece of money, which during its passage through the alimentary canal had become beautifully shining.[13] Here the pleasure in the clean object became a cover for satisfaction of the most primitive anal-erotism. The curious thing is that the patient was able to deceive himself as to the real significance of his transparent behaviour.

Apart from striking examples of this sort, the erotic enjoyment of heaping in and gathering up gold and other money pieces, the pleasurable "wallowing in money," can be observed countless times in daily life. Many people are ready enough to sign documents that bind them to pay large sums, and can easily expend large amounts in paper money, but are striking tardy in giving out gold coins or even the smallest copper coins. The coins seem to "stick" to their fingers. (Cf., also the expression "current capital," and the reverse of this, "argent sec," which is used in the Franche-Comté).[14]

The ontogenetic path of development of interest in money, as here sketched, while shewing individual differences dependent on the conditions of life, is nevertheless on the whole among civilised people to be regarded as a psychical process which seeks realisation under the most diverse circumstances, in one way or another. It thus seems natural to regard this developmental tendency as a racial attribute, and to suppose that the biogenetic ground principle is also valid for the formation of the money symbol. It is to be expected that phylogenetic and historical comparison of the path of individual development here described will shew a parallelism with the development of the money symbol in the human race in general. Perhaps the coloured stones of primitive men which have been found in cave excavations will then be capable of interpretation; observations concerning the anal-erotism of savages (the primitive men of today, who in many cases still live in the stage of barter exchange and of pebble or shell money) should considerably further this investigation of the history of civilisation.

After what has been communicated, however, it is already not improbable that the capitalistic interest, increasing in correlation with development, stands not only at the disposal of practical, egoistic aims—of the reality-principle, therefore—but also that the delight in gold and in the possession of money represents the symbolic replacement of, and the reaction-formation to, repressed anal-erotism, i.e., that it also satisfies the pleasure-principle.

The capitalistic instinct thus contains, according to our conception, an egoistic and an anal-erotic component.

Notes and References

1. Freud. "Charakter und Analerotik," in his Sammlung kl. Schr. z. Neurosenlehre, Bd. II, S. 132 et seq.

2. Freud. Loc cit.

3. Freud conceives of the repression of anal-erotism and of the pleasure in smell altogether in the human race as a result of the upright posture, the erection from the earth.

4. The habit of euphemistically disguising coprophilic tendencies as "hygienic" is very widespread. The fairly harmless behaviour of stool pedants is well-known, who devote to the regulation of their bowel activities a considerable part of the interest at their disposal; such persons, however, are rather prone to fall into what has been called "stool-hypochondria." A whole series of analyses, by the way, has convinced me that in very many cases hypochondria is really a fermentation-product of anal-erotism, a displacement of unsublimated coprophilic interests from their original objects on to other organs and products of the body with an alteration of the qualifying pleasure. The choice of the organ towards which the hypochondria is directed is determined by special factors (somatic disposition, pronounced erogenicity even in diseased organs, etc).

5. (See on this matter a monograph of mine in the Jahrbuch, Bd. VI. Transl.)

6. I have already in another connection pointed out the probable part played by the childish interest in flatus in later fondness for music. See Ch. IV.

7. (A German idiom. Transl.)

8. Cp. Lou Andreas-Salomé: "Vom frühen Gottesdienst." Imago. II. 1913.

9. The German word "Besitz" (= possession) shews, by the way, that man tries even in his speech to represent by the idea of "sitting on it" that which is valuable to him, which belongs to him. Rationalists evidently content themselves with the explanation of this simile to the effect that the sitting on is meant to express a concealing, protecting and guarding of the valued object. The fact, however, that it is the buttocks and not the hand—which would be more natural with men—that is used to represent protection and defence speaks rather in favour of the word "Besitz" being a copro-symbol. The final decision on the point must be reserved for a philologist who has had a psychoanalytic training.

10. The sum of anal-erotism present in the constitution is thus shared in adults among the most diverse psychical structures. Out of it develop: 1. The anal character traits in Freud's sense. 2. Contributions to aesthetics and to cultural interests. 3. To hypochondria. 4. The rest remains unsublimated. From the different proportion of the sublimated and the original parts, from the preference for this or that form of sublimation, the most variegated character types arise, which must

naturally have their special conditional factors. Anal characteristics are specially suited for rapid characterological orientation concerning an individual, indeed concerning whole races. The anal character, with his cleanliness, love for order, defiance, and miserliness, sharply deviates from the pronounced anal-erotic, who is tolerant on the matter of dirt, extravagant, and easygoing.

11. (A German idiom, meaning "cannot stand." "*Riechen*" literally means to smell. Transl.)

12. See Chapter VII. P. 176. "Temporary rectal troubles," etc.

13. The case reminds one of the coprophilic joke in which the doctor who had had succeeded in expelling by means of a purge a piece of money that a child had swallowed was told he could keep the money as his fee. As to the identification of money and faeces see also the fairy-tale of "*Eslein streck dich.*" The word "*Losung*" (= deliverance) means proceeds of a sale (in business), but in hunting speech it means the faeces of wild animals.

14. (To be "*à sec*" is French vernacular for "hard up." Transl.)

Contribution 3

A Note on the Anal Character Traits of the Capitalistic Instinct

Isador H. Coriat

In his illuminating paper entitled *The Ontogenesis of the Interest in Money*, Ferenczi states: "After what has been communicated, however, it is already not improbable that the capitalistic interest, increasing in correlation with development, stands not only at the disposal of practical, egotistic aims—of the reality principle, therefore—but also that the delight in gold and in the possession of money represents the symbolic replacement of, and the reaction formation to, repressed anal-erotism, i.e., that it satisfies the pleasure principle. The capitalistic instinct thus contains, according to our concept, an egotistic and an anal-erotic component."

This viewpoint is clearly illustrated in a recent newspaper account of the death of a capitalist of international fame, in which the character traits are sketched with skill and profundity worthy of a Lytton Strachey. This account is the more valuable because the character traits which are here delineated agree in nearly every respect with the usual conception of the anal character as revealed by psychoanalytic investigation. They could not have been better described if they had been subjected to analysis. A summary of the principal features of this sketch will show the relationship between anal-erotism, the interest in making money, and the so-called capitalistic instinct.

He found a peculiar pleasure in confiding the size of his fortune and the details of his vast industrial enterprises to all who would listen. He was very careless in his dress and would go about in the clothes of a workingman as sort of a reaction-formation to his vast fortune. In addition to the child-like pleasure in talking about his possessions, he also showed other childhood traits, such as a passion for novelties and toys, and in addition the writer of the newspaper article states that his egotism was no less pronounced than his juvenility and his love of toys. Another almost completely unsublimated anal trait was shown in the manner in which he delighted in producing a huge bank roll, inviting inspection of its size and then restoring it to his pocket, adding that it was "all mine." When he passed one of his great industrial plants or a hotel or a newspaper office which he owned, he would also remark that it was all his, all of which demonstrated the child-like pleasure in possession.

At times he was quite irritable, particularly if the size of his fortune was disputed and as a reaction tendency he would often deliver a tirade against the aristocracy, which he hated with great intensity. Here we see the relationship between hate and anal-erotism. Yet on the other hand, as a reaction-formation against this repressed sadistic hate which is so often associated with the anal character traits, as was previously pointed out in the analysis of Shylock,[1] he showed a domestic tenderness and a great love for children, fashioning new toys for them, mending old ones, or searching the stores for novelties. In spite of his immense fortune, he cared nothing for luxury and had no personal extravagances.

In this description the analyst will easily recognize the fundamental traits of anal-erotism, traits which are possessed by all those whose chief aim in life is the accumulating or acquisition of money, either for the power and possessions that money will bring, in those with more social instincts, or for the mere pleasure of handling the hoarded money itself, as in the anti-social and avaricious miser. The social behavior of anal-erotics is strongly bound up with money and pedantic behavior. Perseverance is also a mark of the anal character, a trait necessary for the accumulation of wealth. Thus in the character sketch of the capitalist above detailed occur all the anal components, such as pedantry, parsimony leading to avarice, hate as an anal-sadistic regression, overtenderness to children as a reaction-formation, and the connection between force and possession. That he had never advanced beyond the narcissistic pleasure of childhood is shown by the delight with which he would produce and show a roll of bank bills, an only partially sublimated reaction proceeding from the time when the child enjoyed and luxuriated in viewing its excretions. Thus the capitalist is an individual whose libido has turned with an almost complete exclusiveness to the acquisition and possession of money for the mere pleasure in possession.[2] All the described traits, if taken separately, would probably have little significance, but when they are all combined in one individual in the type known as the anal character, they then form components of the complete personality.

Notes and References

1. Isador H. Coriat. "Anal-Erotic Character Traits in Shylock." *Int. J. Psycho-Analysis*, II, 3–4, 1921.

2. See also a paper by Karl Abraham, "Contributions to the Theory of the Anal Character." *Int. J. Psycho-Analysis*, IV, 4, Oct. 1923.

Contribution 4

Pecunia Olet

Sándor Ferenczi

A young merchant was under my care for a prolonged period on account of obsessional and anxiety conditions. I could not pursue the case to an end, for the improvement that set in was, as so often, used by the resistance as a motive for breaking off the treatment. As the analysis soon showed, the actual cause of his illness was his relationship to his wife. I had to explain to the patient on the strength of very clear indications that he was coming to grief over the conflict between his love of money (anal erotism) and the rest of his sexuality. He married a more than well-to-do woman with whom he was not in love, while his unconscious dreamt of disinterested devotion; amongst other things he often thought consciously about a quite penniless but most charming woman, by whose side he had perhaps found the happiness for which he longed. I had, of course, to make clear to the patient that this happiness, too, would not have been unclouded, since his other no less powerful passion, the love of money, would have been unsatisfied.

At one of our talks the patient gave me absolute confirmation, according to my views, of the preceding interpretation. He recalled that shortly after his engagement, during an intimate association with his bride, he was alarmed by an unpleasant odour from her mouth. He left her abruptly, hastened to a confidential friend, and wanted to break off the engagement at once. He was soothed, however, and as the bad smell did not occur again he gave up his intention—the marriage took place.

I had to explain this memory as follows: an evidently insignificant odour from the lady's mouth became associated with the patient's primitive anal erotism from which was derived his love of money; he was nigh owning to himself that he was about to marry for money; he wished to escape from this possibility as anxiously as he did from his own badly repressed anal erotic impulses. This was, therefore, a case of *character regression*, the falling back of a character trait (love of money) on to its erotic pre-stage.[1] For a moment the unconscious phantasy succeeded in converting the bride's mouth into the anal orifice.

Anyone who has not had considerable psychoanalytical experience will find this explanation extraordinarily forced and certainly very disagreeable. He will ask, as I hear so often, "Why *must* the so-called 'anal erotism' play a part again here? Is the case not to be explained more simply by the quite comprehensible dislike of any cultured person for an unpleasant smell, which was present in the given case, without dragging in 'character regression'?"

Instead of dealing with this question I shall briefly recount a second case.

II

I suggest to a lady who imagines herself passionately in love with her husband that various of her symptoms indicate that she married mainly from interested motives, and that because she considers anything of the kind irreconcilable with her character she exaggerates her passionate attachment to her husband. After a prolonged resistance, she had to own to herself and me that at the time of her engagement she had really preferred another young man to her future husband, further that she and her family had at that time been in great material want, and, finally, that her husband had been thought a wealthy heir.

As in the above case, I drew her attention to her anal erotism, whereupon the patient at once reacted with the following reminiscence:

"When I saw for the first time after my engagement the young man with whom I was previously in love, the following incident occurred. He greeted me and kissed my hand; at the moment the thought flashed through my mind that I had shortly before been to the closet and had not yet had an opportunity of washing my hands. He will smell faeces on my fingers! My anxiety was so great that I had at once to carry my fingers to my nose and smell them, whereupon it seemed to me as though a girl friend of mine who was present smiled ironically."

Naturally I interpreted this reminiscence as a confirmation of the assumption already indicated, and added that she was really alarmed that the young man might "smell" from her that she was marrying from motives of interest. Behind this scene I had to suppose, moreover, the repetition of infantile faecal games. The patient had dim memories of having carried on games of this kind in the closet with her brother.

I must leave it to the reader to explain the marked resemblance between the two cases as accidental, or to afford it a meaning, ultimately the meaning that psychoanalysis attributes to it. On this occasion, however, I must emphasize that psychoanalysis never founds its theses on speculation, but always on the piling up of such correspondences, therefore on facts. The reply to the question of whence these correspondences originate is another matter, and analysis will not leave it unanswered. But it must not be impatient to give explanations so long as it only commands facts. It is in any case unjustifiable to reject the testing of facts on grounds of logic.

The Latin proverb which, in an alternative wording, I chose for the title of this article appears in a new light after the above explanation. The sentence, money does *not* smell, is a euphemistic reversal. In the unconscious it is certainly: *pecunia olet*, that is money = filth.

Notes and References

1. Compare "*Passagère Symptombildungen während der Analyse*" and "*Mischgebilde von erotischen und Charakterzügen.*" ["On Transient Symptom Formation during Analysis," Chap. VII. of *Contributions to Psycho-Analysis* and "Composite Formations of Erotic and Character Traits," Chap. XXXI. of my *Theory and Technique of Psychoanalysis*.

Contribution 5

The Spending of Money in Anxiety States

Karl Abraham

The attitude of the neurotic to the possession of money has been the subject of much study in psychoanalytic literature. Both Freud and other analysts who have followed him in directing their interest to "anal" character-traits have dealt with neurotic avarice and the anxious retention of money from the point of view of unconscious motives; but the opposite behaviour of many neurotics, the excessive spending of money, has not received the same attention, although the psychoanalyst frequently comes across it. This tendency appears suddenly in many neurotics, like a kind of attack, and stands in conspicuous contrast to their usual parsimony.

From the few cases that I have been able to observe during my psychoanalytic work, it seems to me that this condition is found in a definite group of neurotics—in persons who are in a state of permanent infantile dependence on the parental home and who are attacked with depression or anxiety as soon as they are away from it. The patients themselves say that the spending of money relieves their depression or anxiety; and they produce rational explanations for this, such as that spending money increases their self-confidence, or that it distracts them from their condition. Psychoanalysis takes the unconscious into consideration and adds a deeper explanation to this purely superficial one.

Every psychoanalysis of a case of this kind shows once again that the patient, in consequence of the fixation of his libido, is prevented from removing himself physically from his parents or the persons representing them. Leaving the home signifies to his unconscious a detachment of the libido from its object. Two contrary mental currents can always be found to exist in these patients—a conservative one, in the direction of a permanent fixation, and another one, in the direction of turning toward objects of the external world.

Every attempt to transfer the libido on to new subjects is accompanied by severe anxiety, for the very reason that the unconscious desire is so especially violent and impetuous. It is only necessary to call to mind the fact that female patients who suffer from street anxiety are heavily burdened with unconscious, at times even conscious, phantasies of prostitution. Their unconscious wants to yield without restraint to every person they meet; but their conscious anxiety restricts the transference of their libido within the narrowest bounds, so that they become incapable of making free use of it, and this not only in the strict sense of actual sex-relationships.

A far-reaching limitation of genital sexuality leads to a substitutive and increased emphasis of other erotogenic zones. Anal erotism takes the place of genital erotism to a greater or less degree. In many cases it can be very clearly shown that the morbid fixation of the patient on his father or mother is carried on through the agency of the anal zone. A small abstract from an analysis will illustrate this.

The patient, a woman, who suffered from severe street anxiety, was completely attached to her father. Her repeated attempts to loosen the fixation always miscarried. This fixation had been very much reinforced by the patient's father during her childhood by the fact that he had been excessively careful about the activity of her bowels, and had very frequently administered enemas, etc. This mistaken procedure had contributed in a fatal manner to maintaining her childish dependence. To use a nursery expression, she could "do" nothing without her father, could only "leave the room" under his superintendence. As her analysis showed, her attempts to free herself also demonstrated her anal fixation. To her unconscious, emptying her bowels without paternal superintendence signified independence. If she went out of the house and was overtaken by anxiety she used as a defence against it to spend money on all sides in a quite needless way. She was giving out *money* instead of *libido*. The explanation of this compensatory significance of money is derived from the unconscious equation of money and faeces. It is worth noting that the patient herself suspected that she frequently intensified her anxiety in order to provide herself with a reason for spending money.

In this patient, and also in two other cases, I noticed the tendency to buy many objects at random, articles that were for the most part valueless and only desired at the moment. In this way they could deceive themselves about the free motility of their libido, which in reality was fixed and inhibited to the last degree. Buying objects which have only a momentary value, and passing quickly from one object to another, are symbolic gratifications of a repressed desire—that of transferring the libido in rapid succession to an unlimited number of objects. The allusion to prostitution is unmistakable in this connection; for there, too, money is the means of obtaining transitory and easily changed relationships.

The patients' idea that they spend money in order to increase their self-reliance now receives corroboration in a certain sense; for the spending of money deceives them as to the want of freedom of their libido and thus relieves them for a short time of the painful feeling of sexual insufficiency. In other words, they are under an abnormally strict prohibition, proceeding from the parental imago, against expending their libido freely. A compromise between instinct and repression is made by which the patient, in a spirit of defiance, does expend—not his sexual libido but an anal currency.

We are here reminded of the attitude of certain neurotics whose libido is also bound in an excessive degree. They are, in part or wholly, incapable of sexual love in the mental and physical sense. They give other people not love but pity and become benefactors, and often give money away too freely. They are forever doomed to this form of substitutive gratification; and, in the vague feeling that they are not giving the right gift in a qualitative sense, they exaggerate it in a quantitative one. Nevertheless, their spending of money is altruistic in its effect, while in the previously described cases such an effect is entirely absent. What is common to both groups is that the spending of money forms a substitute for the sexual transference which their neurosis forbids and at the same time serves as a bulwark against neurotic disturbances.

Part II

Cultural-historical, Archeological and Ethnological Studies on Psychoanalytic Theories of Money

Contribution 6

Some Data from Cultural History Relating to the Subject of the Money Complex and Anal Erotism

J. Harnik

In Flögel-Bauer's *Geschichte des Grotesk-Komischen*,[1] we find the following interesting pieces of information under the heading, *Batter il culo sul lastrone*:

> In Naples, in former times, the insolvent debtor mounted a low pillar on the square in front of the Palace of Justice (Palazzo de' Tribunali) where he had to let down his pants, expose his naked bottom, and repeat three times: Let all those whom I owe something come forward and collect! (*chi ha d'avere, si venga a pagare.*) This custom extended as far as Sicily.
>
> In Florence, insolvent debtors used to have to strike a large paving stone with their buttocks. This took place on the Mercato nuovo, with a crowd looking on. Through this act, they were freed of all pressure creditors might bring to bear on them. The custom is the source of the expression "*batter il culo sul lastrone*," i.e., to become bankrupt.
>
> In the Netherlands, insolvent merchants had to sit down on a stone, their bottom bare. In Swabia, in the village of Pfaffenhofen near Güglingen, a similar usage allegedly obtained.

I merely wish to add that I changed the geographic

sequence of the data provided by Flögel-Bauer (Florence, Naples, The Netherlands) because I had the impression that this would underline the effect of a progressive repression of the original instinct. Among the people living in more southern climes, words and gestures seem to have been more vivid and expressive, and even more unembarrassed among Neapolitans than Florentines, whereas in the North we note an attenuation of the gesture. Here, it becomes a mere baring.

Notes and References

1. K. F. Flögel, *Geschichte des Grotesk-Komischen*, revised and edited by Max Bauer, Munich 1914, II, vol., p. 374. Sources ibid.

Contribution 7

On the Anal Origin of Money

William H. Desmonde

In his essay, "Character and Anal Erotism," Freud pointed out the unconscious equation between money and excrement, and called attention to this phenomenon in primitive cultures. Ferenczi also predicted[1] that historical research would reveal a parallelism between the development of money in the growth of civilization and in individual maturational processes. This essay offers a contribution to Ferenczi's hypothesis.

The orthodox numismatic theory of the origin of coinage is that coins originated with the placing of the signet of the issuing agent upon a lump of metal, to guarantee its weight and its genuineness. According to Macdonald,

> Originally, then, coins were simply pieces of sealed metal impressed with the emblem either of the issuing city or of the responsible magistrates. Whatever special influences may have come into play subsequently, types were at the outset no more than signets.[2]

Barclay V. Head took a similar position on the origin of coinage:

> We may take it therefore as certain that the . . . type placed by authority on metal intended to circulate as money was simply the signet or guarantee of the issuer, a solemn affirmation on the part of an individual or of a State, that the coin was of just weight and good metal.[3]

The custom of placing a seal upon property to safeguard the object and to guarantee its value was widespread long prior to the minting of coins, and the above theory presumes that coinage stemmed from this practice. According to Herodotus, money originated in Lydia in the seventh century, B.C. The same author relates, however, that, among the Babylonians, each man carried a signet. Macdonald says that there is every reason to believe that this custom had prevailed from immemorial antiquity. It was undoubtedly familiar to the Lydians and other peoples of Asia Minor in the eighth century, B.C. As we can determine from the laws of Solon, the practice of sealing, at a later period, played a very important part in Athenian commerce. The great jars of pottery which were exported from Hellas were made to regulation sizes, and a seal was placed upon them, to guarantee their capacity. In the words of the nineteenth century numismatist, Burgon:

> As the act of impressing a seal or signet was an understood sign of solemn compact from the most early periods; and as engraved seals and signets were undoubtedly in general use long anterior to the invention of coining, it appears highly probable that the original idea of impressing a stamp on the uncoined lumps of gold or silver, was most probably derived from the common application of a seal to wax. The earliest coins may therefore be looked upon as pieces of *sealed metal*.[4]

According to Newberry, the origin of the seal quite likely goes back to the very institution of the right of private property. In all of the countries of the ancient world, the seal was used as a signature.

> Doubtless in the earliest times only the most powerful persons possessed seals, but as civilization advanced the

officers of the administration came to use, besides their own personal seals, official ones for government purposes. Thus it was that the seal, being the real instrument of the power and authority of an office, came to be used as the symbol of it, and the delivery of an official or State seal to an individual, gave to that individual the authority and power to execute the rights and duties of his office.[5]

There were two types of signets used in antiquity: the scarab and the cylinder seal—the latter having originated from the primitive bead. The signet-ring was probably a later development from the scarab or the cylinder seal. Both of these types of signet devices also had an important magical significance as charms and amulets.

We shall concern ourselves here with the Egyptian scarab, showing that it originated from anal conceptions.

The scarab was extremely popular in ancient Egypt. Millions of them were made, to be worn by *fellahs*, who strung them around their neck to be employed as seals.[6] Indeed, scarabs are found all through the Mediterranean areas that had commercial relations with Egypt.

> Archaeologists frequently find in lands bordering on the shores of the Mediterranean sea, scarabs and scarabeoids, on which are engraved subjects which are Egyptian, Chaldean, Assyrian, Hittite, or Persian; they are intended apparently to be used as signets, and were incised with short inscriptions in Phoenician, and sometimes, in Aramaic or in Hebrew, giving the name of the owner of the signet.[7]

The beetle was venerated in Egypt from prehistoric times. Models of beetles found in prehistoric Egyptian graves were used as amulets, and the earliest form of the seal in Egypt was that of a in scarab.[8]

Our next task is to inquire into why the scarab was venerated, and imbued with a magical significance. Petrie said that the statements of the ancient writer Horapollo throw much light on the reason for the religious significance of the scarab in ancient Egypt:

> To denote an *only begotten*, or, *generation*, or *a father*, or the *world*, or, a *man*, they delineate a scarabaeus. And they symbolize by this, an *only begotten*; because the scarabaeus is a creature self-produced, being unconceived by a female; for the propagation of it is unique and after this manner:—when the male is desirous of procreating, he takes the dung of an ox, and shapes it into a spherical form like the world; he then rolls it from him . . . then having dug a hole, the scarabaeus deposits this ball in the earth for the space of twenty-eight days. . . . By thus remaining under the moon, the race of scarabaeus is endued with life.[9]

A similar statement concerning the religious significance of the beetle in ancient Egypt was made by Plutarch. Percy E. Newberry writes that the *scarabaeus sacer* is remarkable for,

> . . . its habit of rolling up balls of excrementitious matter in which the female encloses her eggs. The balls of dung the insect rolls about the sand until they become coated with a thick layer of dust, and grow to a size often as large as the insect itself. The Egyptians, who were always keen observers of nature, early noticed this remarkable habit.[10]

Thus, the sacred beetle, worn as an amulet-signet by millions of people, was believed by the ancient Egyptians to arise from excrement. Since, in its later development as a seal, the scarab played an important part in the origin of coinage, we may regard the beginning of coined money as associated with the primitive anal erotic fantasies.

Notes and References

1. Ferenczi, Sandor: *The Ontogenesis of the Interest in Money, Sex in Psychoanalysis*, Basic Books Publishing Co., Inc., New York, 1950.

2. Macdonald, George: *Coin Types: Their Origin and Development*, James Maclehose & Sons, Glasgow, 1905, page 52.

3. Head, Barclay V.: *Historia Numorum*, Oxford at the University Press, 1911, page lvi.

4. Quoted in Macdonald, op. cit., page 45.

5. Newberry, Percy E.: *Scarabs*, Archibald Constable & Co., Ltd., London, 1906, page 7.

6. Hastings' *Encyclopedia of Religion and Ethics*, Vol. 11, page 223.

7. Myer, Isaac: *Scarabs*, Edwin W. Dayton, New York, 1894, page 128.

8. Ibid., page 37.

9. Ibid., page 9.

10. Op. cit., page 63.

Contribution 8

The Origin of Money in the Animal Sacrifice

William H. Desmonde

In this paper, we will present the hypothesis that money in Western culture originated in ancient Greece and Rome in the animal sacrifice, or food communion ritual. The meaning of the early forms of money will be interpreted from a psychoanalytic point of view. We will suggest that the animal sacrifice and the monetary forms derived from this ritual symbolized various aspects of the parent-child relation, containing attitudes of ambivalence toward the father and mother, both of an oedipal and pregenital nature. The eating of the sacrificial animal was to a great extent motivated by the quest for union with the mother, and this need for ecstatic communion was carried over into the motivations behind the first forms of coinage. Various mass compulsions stemming from hostility toward the father, or king, were also present in early attitudes toward money. Finally, although this paper stresses the nonrational motivations symbolized by the first forms of money, it is the writer's opinion that there was also a rational, sublime significance inhering in the animal sacrifice, in that this ritual symbolized man's need to revivify the creative forces within himself, as well as man's desire to promote human welfare by maintaining justice through a fair apportionment of economic goods.

The Animal Sacrifice and the Cult of the Dead

The first forms of society in ancient times consisted of the family, or the extended family, the *gens*, or clan; and the motivational factor underlying the existence of the family was the worship of the ancestral souls. It was believed that after a person's death his soul continued to exist and to exert an influence, beneficial or evil, upon the survivors. The family was basically a religious organization held together by the rituals of the ancestor cult. These facts are in accordance with Freud's *Group Psychology* (10), in which he stated that a social group is constituted by the identification of each group member with the parent image.[1] The noted historian of legal origins, Fustel de Coulanges, wrote,

> The father ranks first in presence of the sacred fire. . . . In all religious acts his functions are the highest; he slays the victim, his mouth pronounces the formula of prayer which is to draw upon him and his the protection of the gods. The family and the worship are perpetuated through him; he represents, himself alone, the whold series of ancestors, and from him are to proceed the entire series of descendants. . . . When death shall come, he will be a divine being whom his descendants will invoke [11, p. 112].

The central ritual of the family was a common meal at the altar, in which each person partook of the sacrificial animal, in this way identifying with the parental images:

> . . . the principal ceremony of the domestic worship was a repast, which they called a sacrifice. To eat food prepared upon an altar was, to all appearances, the first form which man gave to the religious act. The need of putting themselves in communion with the divinity was satisfied by this repast, to which they invited him, and of which they gave him his part [11 p. 205].

These practices were carried over in the formation of the larger social units, such as the city; and we shall see that money had its origin in this sacrificial ritual. The king of the city was regarded as the city father, and his main duty was to preside at the communion meal.

> These old customs give us an idea of the close tie which united the members of a city. Human association was a religion; its symbol was a meal, of which they partook together. We must picture to ourselves one of these little primitive societies, all assembled, or the heads of families at least, at the same table, each clothed in white, with a crown upon his head; all make the libation together, recite the same prayer, sing the same hymns, and eat the same food, prepared upon the same altar; in their midst their ancestors are present, and the protecting gods share the meal. Neither interest, nor agreement, nor habit creates the social bond; it is this holy communion piously accomplished in the presence of the gods of the city [11, p. 209].

The Religious Symbolism on Ancient Coins

All social relations, including economic activities, were in ancient times regarded as religious acts, and it is therefore not surprising that the images on the early coins were religious in nature.

The religious significance of the images on early Greek and Roman coins has long been accepted by numismatists. Burgon of the British Museum proposed as early as 1837 that these coin types had a religious motivation. This hypothesis was elaborated by Ernst Curtius, who suggested that coinage had been invented by the priesthoods, who first struck coins in the temples, in order to facilitate the commercial transactions arising from bequests and consecrations made to the temple treasury (6). Coinage was early associated with the cults of the mother-goddesses Astarte, Mylitta, Aphrodite, Artemis, and Hera, who indeed were the protecting patronesses of many ancient commercial enterprises.[2]

Percy Gardner in 1883, accepting Curtius' theory of the religious nature of the ancient Greek coin types, stated that these images stemmed from the city coat-of-arms, which was of a religious nature, or from the image of the city divinity or some symbol representing this deity (12). George Macdonald (22) enlarged upon Gardner's point of view that the coin types were the badge or coat-of-arms of the state. The coin type, he declared, was a form of the seal or signet, which had been used for thousands of years as a magical property mark. Thus, for Macdonald, coinage originated with the affixing of the state seal upon a precious metal to guarantee its weight and quality. Coin types were of a heraldic and commemorative nature, and the religious significance came later. (Since heraldry and commemoration are the main expressions of a group's tradition, or ancestor cult, we should regard Macdonald as incorrect in separating these meanings of ancient coin images from their religious significance.)

Most numismatists have concurred with the hypothesis that religion was the motivation for the ancient coin types. Barclay V. Head, a leading numismatist, stated what may be called the orthodox numismatic attitude. The type was

> . . . a solemn affirmation on the part of the State that the coin was of just weight and good metal, a calling of the gods to witness against fraud. Such being its object, it was of course necessary that the coin type should consist of a generally intelligible device, which might appeal to the eyes of all as a sacred emblem of the god whose dreaded name was thus invoked to vouch for the good faith of the issuer . . . [18].

We shall now turn to the theory that money originated in the ritual killing of the sacrificial bull.

The Sacrificial Bull as a Unit of Value

The bull was a unit of value throughout the cultures of ancient Greece, Rome, and Crete. Indeed, Burns (2) states that the bull was a unit of value in side usage among the Indo-Europeans long before this culture began to employ metals. Ridgeway declares that when gold came into circulation its value was at first based upon the cow. The Homeric poems repeatedly refer to the value of objects in terms of oxen. Philology confirms this evidence: many of our modern terms pertaining to monetary matters are derived from the use of cattle as a unit of value in ancient times. For example, the Latin *pecunia* is derived from *pecus* (cattle), as is the word *peculation*, according to Festus. The term *fee* is believed to be ultimately derived from the Gothic *faihu*, signifying cattle. Similarly, the Indian *rupee* stems from a Sanscrit word meaning cattle. The economist's term *capital* and the legal word *chattel* stem from *capitale*, which originally designated cattle counted by the head. Similar etymologies have been suggested for the Teutonic and Scandinavian languages.

It is also well-known that the ritualistic killing and eating of a sacred bull played an essential part in the religions of classical antiquity, particularly in Greece.[3] The bull was deified in all of the ancient civilizations of the Mediterranean world, being held as sacred in Egypt, Mesopotamia, Persia, Crete, Greece, and India. The hekatombs referred to in Homer's writings consisted of the eating in common of sacrificial bulls.

The Greek god Dionysius, who was frequently identified with Zeus, was often worshiped in the form of a bull. Jane Harrison and other noted scholars have conjectured that a sacred marriage took place every year, at which the Athenian queen was married to a sacred bull representing Dionysius. Art historians have long known that Greek tragedy originated in a religious ceremony of ancient Greece, in which a sacred bull (or goat) was killed and eaten. The Argive Hera was called the "cow-headed" goddess, as was Athene, and the Cretan Zeus was venerated as a bull-god. Frazer (9) wrote:

> A feature in the mythical character of Dionysius . . . is that he was often conceived and represented in animal shape, especially in the form, or at least with the horns, of a bull. Thus he is spoken of as "cowborn," "bull," "horn-shaped," "bull-faced," "bull-browed," "bull-horned," "bull-bearing," "two-horned," "horned." His images were often, as at Cyzicus, made in bull shape, or with bull horns, and he was painted with horns [p. 16].

> . . . the Cretans, when they acted the suffering and death of Dionysius, tore a live bull to pieces with their teeth. Indeed, the rending and devouring of live bulls and calves appear to have been a regular feature of the Dionysiac rites. When we consider the practice of portraying the god as a bull or with some of the features of the animal, the belief that he appeared in bull form to his worshipers at the sacred rites, and the legend that in bull form he had been torn to pieces, we cannot doubt that in rending and devouring a live bull at his festival the worshipers of Dionysius believed themselves to be killing the god, eating his flesh, and drinking his blood [p. 17].

There is ample reason to believe that the king, or city-father, was identified with the bull. This is particularly clear in Egypt where the king-god was often spoken of as the "divine bull." Numerous instances exist in ancient Greece of participants in religious rituals dressing in the guise of the animal deity. Excavations in Crete have revealed that the king was often identified with the bull. The work of Frazer and others indicates that the ancient kings were frequently killed after the end of certain periods of time, or were subject to challenge to a fight for supremacy. Among the Shilluk, whose culture exhibits many similarities to that of the ancient Greco-Roman world, the king could be challenged at any time by one of his sons to a combat for the kingship. The intimate connection between the animal sacrifice and the rituals of the cult of the dead in ancient times, coupled with numerous evidences of ritual cannibalism in early Greece, lead us to conjecture that the bull sacrifices originated in the killing and eating of the father.

The Mithraic rituals are of particular interest in this connection. This cult began to attain tremendous popularity in the Roman Empire toward the end of the first century, A.D., and eventually became the official state religion. One of the central rituals in Mithraism was as follows. The devotee was crowned with gold and wreathed with fillets. He descended into a pit, the top of which was covered by a wooden grating. A bull decorated with flowers and gold leaf was driven on top of the grating, and was there gashed to death with a sacred spear. The hot, reeking blood of the animal poured down upon the worshiper, who let it drench his body completely. He emerged from the pit to receive the adoration and homage of the worshipers, as one who had been purified by the washing away of his sins. The testicles of the bull played an important part in this ceremony. Similar ceremonies were held in all of the cult-centers where Mithra, the sun-god, was worshiped.

It is of great significance for us that the bull sacrifices of early Greece and Rome were performed at altars, and that the altar and the various cult objects connected with these rituals acquired, through contagious magic, the same sanctity, or *mana*, as was possessed by the sacred bull itself. Farnell (8) writes: "It is probable that in the Homeric and early period certain external objects used in ritual were regarded as mysteriously charged with divinity, so that those who handled them were brought into temporary communion with the deity through physical contact."

It is instructive to note that the tripod, a unit of value in Homeric times, originated in the altar, and that the double-axe, a well-known religious symbol in early Greek culture, is believed to have originated in the axe used for killing the sacrificial animal.

The Origin of Money in the Sacrificial Bull Ritual

We will now seek to show that the bull's significance as a unit of value arose from its role as sacrificial animal in the ritual communion meals of ancient times. Our hypothesis is largely based upon the work of Bernhard Laum.[4]

The animal sacrifice, Laum states, exemplifies most clearly the early relation between man and god. The desire to obtain a good harvest, the need for protection against sickness and other dangers caused man to make offerings to the deity. Fear of the god also induced the ancients to seek to propitiate the god. The sacrifice to the god was thus a type of commerce with the deity.

The sacrificial cult was intimately connected with the sacred laws of the early community. The word *nomos*, which in later times signified the laws of the community, originally meant "distribution," referring to the equal division of the sacrificial offering. The sacrificial offering which the individual had to make was fixed by the priests, and thus the bull sacrifice became fixed in value as a means of mediation between man and god. At the same time, participation in the sacred meal was equivalent to receiving compensation for the services an individual had rendered to the group. Here, therefore, the sacrificial offering was fixed as a legal means of payment.

The sacrificial offering thus constituted a fixed good of definite type and quality. These goods, if we conceive of the man-god relationship as a guilt relationship, functioned as means of absolution or payment; at the same time, if we regard the man-god relationship as commercial, they served as objects of trade. Laum suggests that the bull entered into secular trade because the priests used this unit of value in their commercial transactions.

The public meals of the city were state occasions of a religious nature. The god received part of the flesh of the sacrificial victim, the remainder of the bull being distributed among the participants in the ritual. The order of social rank in the community was symbolized in the apportionment of the roasted victim, each person receiving the share that corresponded to his status. These common meals were the first forms of the public finance, and the offering of the bull was the first form of taxation. The king, as the embodiment of the state, presided over the sacrificial repast, carving the flesh and distributing the portions.

The animal victim was roasted on spits called *obelos*, which were a necessary accessory to the public meal. For this reason, the inventory of the temples very often included these spits. In the course of time, the spit of sacrificial meat, Laum states, became known as an *obelos*. The Greek coin called the *obolos* hence originated in the portion of the sacrificial flesh roasted on a spit. A similar origin existed for the tripods and pots which served as units of value in Homeric times: these objects were originally used around the sacrificial altar to hold portions of the sacrificial flesh. The value of these tripods and pots was measured originally in bulls. The iron money of the Spartans, according to Laum, can be traced back to the sickles used to kill the sacrificial animals.

As time went on, various votive objects brought to the gods entered into regular commerce not connected with the cult, their worth being fixed by the cult, in terms of the bull as a unit of value. Thus, gradually, as the norm of value created by the cult was carried over into nonreligious commerce, the bull became the standard unit of value for trading purposes. When metals were first introduced into the Greco-Roman world, their value was reckoned in terms of the bull.

Coins as Religious Medals

Gold and silver in ancient times, indeed all metals, were regarded as possessing magical potencies, and were used as magical amulets with astral affinities. These talismanic powers gave rise to the use of the precious metals as ornaments, which contributed to their commercial value. Because gold was mystically linked with the sun, this metal was regarded as a symbol of royalty, since the king was often identified with the sun.

According to Laum, the first coins were religious medals rather than objects designed to be used in commercial transactions. As medals, they were decorations with magical potencies symbolizing prestige or status.

The word "money," Laum states, stems from the goddess "Moneta," who was identical with the goddess Juno, in whose temple coinage was struck. Moneta was also identical with the goddess "Aequitas," who represented the "just distribution" or "equality" which the state meted out to each citizen. On the basis of this derivation, Laum suggests that coinage originated in the distribution of rights and duties among the members of the community in the sacrifice of the holy bull and the sharing of its flesh among the kinship group. In ancient times, the political unit was identical with the cult congregation: the sharing of the sacrificial flesh was the most sacred right and the most important privilege of the citizen-communicant. The common meal of the flesh and blood of the sacrificial animal was a ritual which established a unity among the participants. In early Greece and Rome, the portion of sacrificial flesh constituted, as has been stated above, a type of fee, reward, or gift, which the state (the temple) distributed to citizens and officials.

The central ritual of the Latin confederacy was a bull sacrifice held every year on Mons Albanus, each participant receiving his share of the sacrificial flesh. The division of the sacrificial victim was of the utmost importance; the ritual had to be repeated if the portions were not equally distributed among the participants. There is reason to believe that the oldest holy place for the worship of Moneta existed on this spot.

According to Laum, the primary functions of the early coin medals were as follows: 1. to serve as a sign of honor; 2. to act as a commemorative monument; 3. to symbolize religious values; 4. and to serve as a sign of the unity of the community. The following are brief explanations of these functions.

1. Medals were given by the king to his subjects as a sign of esteem and honor; they symbolized the citizen's status in the community. The rank held by the person determined the type of medal he received as a gift from the king.

2. The medals also served as a memorial, given out by the king as a souvenir or remembrance. In other words, the coins were symbols of a personal relationship, the images on the medals functioning to immortalize some important, highly regarded person or occurrence.

3. Part of the religious significance of the early coins stemmed from the fact that the stamped metal carried the *mana* of the king. The royal personage is filled with a magic potency which carries over into all of his doings, and each object he comes in contact with overflows with this power. Coins thus were amulets bearing magical potencies. (Consecrated coins, used as charms against disease and danger, were common in the Middle Ages.)

4. Finally, money served as a "community-creating" symbol (*gemeinschaftbildendes* symbol), a symbol which establishes a deep sentimental union among individuals. The ancient city was a union based on the worship of a common god, and the distribution to the citizens of coins bearing the image of the community's protective divinity brought each individual into communion with the deity. The portion of the sacrificial flesh in primitive times established the union with the god; the coin medal in later periods was merely another form of this communion between man and god. The social cohesion of the community was expressed both by the share in the sacrificial flesh and by the distribution of the coin medal bearing the image of the deity.

Thus, the coin medals which were distributed by the king-priest of the temple-state had a significance far greater than simply the commercial value of the metal of which they were comprised. They served the purpose of creating an emotional communion of all of the people who worshiped the same god.

The manner in which the early coin medals entered into commerce as a medium of exchange (money) is not yet fully understood. Laum suggests that public officials were paid at legal proceedings as follows: upon the beginning of the proceedings, each person received an iron spit, or *obelos*, which signified that, at the termination of the session he was to receive a share in the sacrificial flesh. Through practices such as these, according to Laum's conjecture, various objects connected with the common meal became media of exchange.

It is also known that the aristocratic Roman families were accustomed to distribute gifts of money called *sportula*, meaning "basket," and it seems likely that this practice originated in the sharing of the flesh of the sacrificial animal among the entire group, all of whom were regarded as members of the kinship community. Intermediate instances are known in which both money and food were distributed as gifts. The fact that the private treasury of the emperor was called *fiscus* is also significant, for the term *fiscus* is also derived from the word "basket." In the course of time, it is to be presumed that the distribution of food by the ruler or by a noble family was transformed into the distribution of coins.

Tokens signifying that the bearer was a member of a religious brotherhood were common among the people of antiquity. These tokens admitted the bearer to the sacrificial feasts of the cult. It is instructive to note that all industrial organizations in ancient times took the form of religious brotherhoods, whose central ritual was the communion meal. Analogous phenomena existed in the Roman Catholic Church in the Middle Ages, in the form of tokens called *méreaux*, which were given to the clergy as a record of their participation in the mass and other official occasions. The use of tokens in the Protestant Church as certifications admitting the worthy members of the congregation to communion existed in widespread form from the sixteenth century until modern times.

The Roman *tesserae* provide another illustration of symbols intermediary between communion tokens and money. These *tesserae* had the same appearance as regular coinage, and were shaped in the same manner; religious imagery often appeared upon them. They were distributed for several purposes, the most important being to entitle an individual to partake in the public distribution of food (which of course was originally the sacrificial ritual). Other functions of *tesserae* were to admit the bearer to the games or to theatrical presentations, both of which occasions were originally religious ceremonies.

Infantile Motivations in Early Money Symbols

We have very briefly sketched in the above pages the relationship between religion and ancient social organization, as well as some of the evidence for the theory that money originated in the common sacrificial meal. We may now turn to some psychoanalytic interpretations of the early forms of money. We shall assume that the emotions and ideas associated with the food communion rituals were carried over into the coin medals when they eventually became media of circulation used in trade.

It must at the outset be stated that the sacrificial bull was often regarded as a fertility spirit or embodiment of the crops emanating from the goddess Earth. The act of eating the bull, therefore, to some extent represented an eating of the goddess, or mother image. Many of the bull rituals of which we have record were associated with the cult of goddesses. Animal goddesses were common in ancient Greek religion. It is of interest to note that Artemis, an early fertility goddess, was worshiped in the form of a bear, and her priestesses danced around her clad in the skins of bears, thereby identifying themselves with her. Evidence indicates that in early times a sacramental meal of the bear occurred.

From a psychoanalytic standpoint, it seems likely that the eating of the sacrificial bull represented the desire to incorporate the mother, thereby returning to the infantile state of nondifferentiation from the mother. Hence, the acquisition of money represented the finding of a mother substitute which provided an infallible source of emotional security. This is also in accordance with the fact that the early coins were also amulets, i.e., magical devices for retaining the feeling of omnipotence associated with the oral stage of development. In other words, money, which originated in the obtaining and distribution of food, symbolized mother's milk and the various emotions and ideas connected with breast feeding. Thus, to some extent, participation in the communion symbolized by the early monetary forms represented the psychic attaining of an identification with the mother image.

Melanie Klein's point of view suggests that early money may have symbolized oral aggressions toward the mother. The rending and devouring of the live bull with their teeth by the worshipers of Dionysius is certainly suggestive of this very primitive mode of emotional expression. Possibly the guilt feelings toward the mother image resulting from these hostile attitudes may have entered into the motivations for the vast ancient pilgrimages which were made for the purpose of making votive offerings at the shrines of the mother goddesses.

Lewin's study of elation (21) should also be mentioned at this point. The acquisition of money may unconsciously have represented an ecstatic communion with the mother, accompanied by fantasies of attaining immortality through the introjection of the mother's milk (the flesh and blood of the sacrificial bull).

The sacrificial systems of antiquity were certainly motivated to a great extent by internal tensions set up by the Superego. The ancestral cult was largely the result of the outward projection of the memories of the dead father and mother, and the sacrificial offering was in this respect the result of the individual's desire to please his parents and to make amends for any guilt feelings the individual might possess. The receiving of the medal coin was equivalent to receiving the esteem of the parental figures. The desire to acquire money was thus motivated by the wish to be loved by the father and mother. (This is, of course, commonplace in the observations of psychoanalysts. Abraham [1], incidentally, suggested that the spending of money in certain cases is a substitute for the libidinal cathexis of the parents.)

The expression of unconscious early sibling rivalries in competition to acquire money is also well known to psychoanalysts. The offerings of votive objects and the receiving of the medal coin in the ancient ancestral cult were to a great extent expressions of this competition; and the patterns of jealousy and envy, which are so disruptive of harmonious social organization, no doubt also stemmed from the emotional fixation of ancient men upon the parental love. (The Bible, by the way, tells us that the first murder occurred as a result of Cain's hurt feelings when Abel's offering was accorded preferential blessing.) The quest for grace—the desire to become one of the "elect"—which enters so strongly into the desire to obtain money was to a great extent motivated by the desire on the part of the quarreling siblings to be the most favored by the father and mother, and enthusiasm, in its infantile aspect, was the feeling by an individual that he had obtained this special blessing upon receiving the medal coin.

Oedipal Symbolism of Early Monetary Forms

Following along the lines of Freud's *Totem and Taboo* theory, we may also suggest that early money represented repressed incestuous desires for the mother, as well as hatred, fear, and guilt toward the father image. In addition, following Freud, it may be suggested that the ancient monetary forms were compulsively sought symbols at the center of a mass obsessional neurosis stemming from ancient man's inability to accept emotionally the instinctual renunciations necessary for civilized living.

In order to apply Freud's *Totem and Taboo* theory,

it should be proved that totemic survivals existed in the ancient bull sacrifice and in the early forms of money. Scholarship, however, is divided on the question of the survival of totemism in ancient Greece. In his recent authoritative work on Greek religion, Martin P. Nilsson (25) states that all attempts to prove this hypothesis have been fruitless.

Many other scholars, however, have supported this theory, two of the earliest being Andrew Lang and McLennan. Farnell (7) regarded certain ancient Greek rituals as containing traces of an earlier totemic period. A. B. Cook (3) regarded as totemic survivals the various types of animal cults in which the participants dressed themselves as animal gods in order to symbolize their identification with them. George Thomson (27) states that totemism survived in ancient Greek religion, and regards the Roman *gens* as having originated in totemic clans. In her last work on Greek religion, the distinguished Jane Harrison (15) based much of her analysis of primitive ritual on Freud's theory of totemism and exogamy.

Initiation ceremonies in early Greece show striking similarities to the totemic rites of primitive societies. This has been commented upon by such writers as Hutton Webster (29), Andrew Lang (19), and van Gennep (28). Jane Harrison (7) also devoted much attention to these anthropological parallels. Numerous scholars, such as Francis Macdonald Cornford (4), have traced the origin of higher aspects of ancient Greek culture to magic rituals and religious practices similar to those found in primitive cultures.

Jane Harrison (16) regarded the bull sacrifice as totemic in nature, and the possibility of a totemic origin of the animal images on Greek coins was already advanced by McLennan (24); a similar point of view was expressed by Cook (3). D. P. Costello (5) states that early Athenian institutions present striking affinities with the totemic system, and that the coats-of-arms of some of the cities (which often appeared on their coins) may have originated a totemic insignia.

If the sacrificial ritual and the symbols on coins in ancient times can in some sense be regarded as totemic survivals, then it may be said that there existed an oedipal symbolism in the early forms of money. We have seen that possession of the medal coins represented the desire for union with the mother, and this probably had an important incestuous component. The representation of the father image by the bull has already been mentioned, and we may regard the killing and eating of this sacrificial animal as a symbolic parricide. In so far as the bull rituals were propitiatory and atonement ceremonies, they may have expressed oedipal guilt feelings.

The food rituals from which money arose may have had a compulsive aspect, expressing irrational guilt, hatred, and anxiety. Ancient law, as such authorities as Fustel de Coulanges (11) and Sir Henry Maine (23) have shown, arose from the funeral rituals of the cult of the dead. The strictness and rigidity of the legal practices in the ancient city, in which immutable verbal adherence rather than intelligent acceptance of the law existed, indicates that ancient law was obeyed to a great extent out of anxiety and compulsion. The sacrificial meal (originally the totem feast) would represent simultaneously the breaking through of irrational hostility toward the father (repetition of the "primal crime") and the atonement for the guilty wishes. The two laws of totemism—the incest taboo and the prohibition against killing the father—are perhaps the prototype of all later legal prohibitions. Various rigidities and irrationalities in the performance of the animal sacrifice indicate the presence of compulsions in this activity.

> The nature of the victim, the color of the hair, the manner of slaying it, even the shape of the knife, and the kind of wood employed to roast the flesh—all was fixed for every god by the religion of each family, or of each city. In vain the most fervent heart offered to the gods the fattest victims: if one of the innumerable rites of the sacrifice was neglected, the sacrifice was without effect; the least failure made of the sacred act an act of impiety.

> The slightest alteration disturbed and confused the religion of a country, and changed the protecting gods into so many cruel enemies [11, p. 224].

Some of the findings of psychoanalytic writers on modern attitudes toward money would seem to add weight to the interpretations we have made above. G. Pederson-Krag (26) suggests that the modern corporation unconsciously represents the pregenital mother, and Geoffrey Gorer (14) has offered the hypothesis that the attitude of many Americans toward money is related to early feeding practices. The work of Bergler is also to be considered in these connections. Research on the etiology of ulcers and other psychosomatic disorders has indicated that the quest for money in modern man is often motivated by powerful unconscious wishes stemming from infantile relations to the parents (13). Our hypothesis that the first coins were medals suggests that the need to acquire money is closely associated with the body image. Lauterbach (20) has discussed some of the theories offered by psychoanalysts to explain modern attitudes toward money, and has correctly pointed out the necessity for considering changing sociological, economic, and political conditions in attempting to apply such hypotheses.

Sublime Aspects of Early Money

In its higher symbolism, and apart from its magical and infantile significance, early money represented the vital powers of nature with which each person identified in the sacrificial meal. As a symbol of the heroic dead, the coin medal embodied the tradition of cultural progress springing from the creative forces of nature expressed in human society. Money was the core of the individual's emotional life, for participation in the divine communion served to inspire each person with an enhanced feeling of noble commitment.

Early money, which symbolized the common meal, thus revivified the spirit of creative cooperation which is the higher aspect of the division of labor, and reintensified the bonds of loyalty and love among the members of the group. This symbol of the sharing of the flesh of the sacrificial bull established a loving union, or contract, among the participants, each individual committing himself to the renunciations and efforts involved in the mutual aid (right and correlative duties) which are at the basis of all law and social organization.

The medal symbolized the continuity of the tradition which gave meaning to each individual's existence. The fullness of life was experienced in the dedication of each communicant to the welfare of the community, and each member of the congregation could feel secure that he had not lived in vain, for his descendants would continue to appreciate his work and honor his memory in the rituals of the dead. Thus, despite the irrationality, ignorance, superstition, and intellectual rigidity of the ancestral cult, it preserved the strength of character of the heroic predecessors, symbolized by the medal, and inspired each later generation with the creative spirit which leads men to the development of high civilizations.

Notes and References

Notes

1. The writer has made a Freudian study of the relation of the ancestor cult to ancient social organization in his articles, "Psychoanalysis and Legal Origins" (*Int. J. Psychoanal.*, *34*, 1953), and "Compulsive Aspects to Ancient Law" (*Am. Imago*, *11*, 1954).

2. It is generally accepted that coinage originated among the Lydians in the seventh century. This paper will not deal with the origin of coinage in China and India or with the moneys found among primitive cultures.

3. This topic has been discussed more fully in the writer's article, "The Bull-Fight as a Religious Ritual," *Am. Imago*, 9, 1952.

4. Bernhard Laum, a well-known philologist, is now Professor Emeritus at the University of Marburg in Germany. Our discussion of his work is based mainly on his two books, *Heiliges Geld* (Tübingen,

Verlag von J. C. B. Mohr, 1924), and *Ueber das Wesen des Münzgeldes* (Halle a.d. Saale: Abteilung Verlag der Münzhandlung A. Riechmann & Co., 1929).

References

(1) Abraham, K. "The Spending of Money in Anxiety States." *Selected Papers on Psycho-Analysis*. London: Hogarth Press, 1927.

(2) Burns, A. R. *Money and Monetary Policy in Early Times*. London: Kegan Paul, 1927.

(3) Cook, A. B. "Animal Worship in the Mycenaean Age." *J. Hellen. Stud.*, *14*, 1894.

(4) Cornford, F. M. *From Religion to Philosophy*. Cambridge: University Press, 1952.

(5) Costello, D. P. "Notes on the Athenian TNH." *J. Hellen. Stud.*, *58*, 1938.

(6) Curtius, E. "On the Religious Character of Greek Coins." *Numismatic Chronicle*, *10*, 1870.

(7) Farnell, L. R. *The Cults of the Greek States*, Vol. II. Oxford: Clarendon Press, 1896.

(8) Farnell, L. R. "Sacrificial Communion in Greek Religion." *The Hibbert Journal*, *2*:309, 1903-04.

(9) Frazer, J. G. *Spirits of the Corn and of the Wild*, Vol. I. London: Macmillan, 1925.

(10) Freud, S. *Group Psychology and the Analysis of the Ego*. London: Hogarth Press, 1948.

(11) Fustel de Coulanges: *The Ancient City*. Boston: Lee & Shepard, 1874.

(12) Gardner, P. *The Types of Greek Coins*. Cambridge: University Press, 1883.

(13) Garma, A. "On the Pathogenesis of Peptic Ulcer." *Int. J. Psychoanal.*, *31*, 1950.

(14) Gorer, G. *The American People*. New York: Norton, 1948.

(15) Harrison, J. E. *Epilegomena to the Study of Greek Religion*. Cambridge: University Press, 1921.

(16) Harrison, J. E. *Prolegomena to the Study of Greek Religion*. Cambridge: University Press, 1908, p. 545.

(17) Harrison, J. E. *Themis*. Cambridge: University Press, 1927.

(18) Head, B. V. *Historia Numorum*. Oxford: Clarendon Press, 1911, p. lvi.

(19) Lang, A. *Myth, Ritual and Religion*, Vol. II. London: Longmans, Green, 1906, p. 294.

(20) Lauterbach, A. *Man, Motives, and Money*. Cornell University Press, 1954, pp. 138-44.

(21) Lewin, B. D. *The Psychoanalysis of Elation*. New York: Norton, 1950.

(22) Macdonald, G. *Coin Types: Their Origin and Development*. Glasgow: James Maclehose & Sons, 1905.

(23) Maine, H. S. *Ancient Law*. New York: Henry Holt & Co., 1864.

(24) McLennan, J. F. "The Worship of Animals and Plants." *Studies in Ancient History*. London: Macmillan, 1896, p. 569.

(25) Nilsson, M. P. "*Geschichte der Griechischen Religion*," *Handbuch der Altertumswissenschaft*, Abt. 5, Teil 2, Bd.I, p. 37.

(26) Pederson-Krag, G. "A Psychoanalytic Approach to Mass Production." *Psychoanal. Quart.*, *20*, 1951.

(27) Thomson, G. *Studies in Ancient Greek Society*. London: Lawrence & Wishart, 1949, p. 114.

(28) van Gennep, A. *Les Rites de Passage*. Paris: Libraire Critique, 1909, p. 114.

(29) Webster, H. *Primitive Secret Societies*. New York: Macmillan, 1908, p. 189.

Contribution 9

Primal Forms and the Origin of Property

Géza Róheim

When we make the attempt to select from the vast amount of data only what is indispensable to the task we have set ourselves, we find that the first question we have to answer is this: to what extent does "production" on the level preceding hoe culture, the collecting and gathering of what nature provides, proceed collectively and to what degree individually. No matter what primitive society we examine, we always obtain the same result. The food gathering of men may be classified under two clearly defined headings: 1. The individual will ambush and track the game by himself, and pursue it until he kills the worn-out animal. 2. The second form is the battue, undertaken collectively by a large number of men and usually aided by a brush fire. Grey writes that natives will sometimes pursue a fleeing kangaroo for days across the endless scrub of Western Australia, go to sleep on the trail, and resume their pursuit the following morning. During this time, they eat only very small quantities of plant foods.[1] It would therefore seem that the killed animal provides the body with only little more energy than is expended in hunting.

The information about New South Wales also seems to indicate individual effort. When someone is about go to on a hunt, he uses the magical bones of the lower thigh of a dead person to make a spear of them. When he sees a kangaroo or an emu, he need only raise this weapon and the animal stops as if spellbound. If the hunter knows magic, he can even cast a spell on the tracks of the animal and thereby insure success.[2] Among the Eskimos on Point Barrow, the hunter leaves his hut on the lake shore by himself and proceeds inland. If he sees a deer on the open field, he simply runs in its direction. If the deer also begins to run, he speeds up, hoping that the animal will be so curious about its pursuer that it will begin running in a circle and thus come within range.[3] The technique used by the Narrinyeri in Southern Australia and described by Angas is very curious. Someone lies down on his back on a rock, holding a piece of fish in his hand. The birds of prey swoop down on the fish and the hunter simply seizes them by their feet.[4] For the following procedure, two men are necessary: one creeps up on the nest and injures the bird by throwing a spear at it. The other clubs the bird as it tries to fly away.[5] We do not come across one primitive people where hunting is done exclusively by either the single individual or the group. About the Karaia in Brazil, Krause writes: "hunting is done by both individuals and in groups. Wild boars especially are always hunted by a group."[6] In Southern Australia, the bandicoot is hunted by burning the grass of the steppe; everywhere, the animals emerge from their holes in the ground and run straight toward the boomerangs of the hunters. On Lake Eyre, the Dieri surround a stretch of land and the entire tribe participates in the drive on the emus.[7] Among the extremely primitive Seri Indians, hunting pelicans is the communally executed, well-organized enterprise of the entire tribe. The shaman sets the precise time, and the whole tribe proceeds to the swampy region to "harvest pelicans."[8] The Greenlanders kill reindeer by having the tribe encircle an area and start a battue.[9] Among the Kai, the beaters drive the game into nets where it is killed by others with spears. Over a large grassy area, partially enclosed by nets and surrounded by the men, fires are lighted on all sides. The flames spread rapidly, particularly when there is a strong wind. Soon the fires become a single, closed circle burning toward the center and progressively narrowing the area. During such a hunt, some pigs, many rats and mice, numbers of kangaroos, and perhaps a giant snake are also bagged.[10]

Two fundamental types emerge as one looks at these two ways of obtaining food:[11] the pursuit is either individual or collective. But in a third variety, neither the principle of mutual aid nor the individual element predominates. If a Bororo goes hunting, the woman uses a pointed stick to dig roots and tubers out of the earth.[12] Among the Euahlayi, it is the woman's task to dig the roots out of the ground with a stick.[13] In the swampy regions of New South Wales, the women pull the roots out of the ground.[14] They collect resin from the trees, and various kinds of berries. They do the gathering even where animal products are involved. They collect eggs, berries, larvae, and honey although the men also frequently join in gathering the latter.[15] This form of food gathering may proceed both individually and collectively. Where a fairly large group lives together, it is probably the women who leave jointly, separate in various directions in the forest, and then bring to their respective huts what each has collected. When we consider that this simple gathering is undoubtedly the most primitive and, among contemporary aborigines, the most important human economic activity, we will see immediately the decisive role the *praeconcepta opinio* usually hidden in definitions plays in the formation of synthetic judgments concerning the most fundamental questions, and how little one may trust such carelessly formulated views as, for example: at the beginning of development, we find economic communism or, conversely, individualism.[16] For this gathering may be viewed either as unorganized and collective or as undifferentiated and individualistic activity. What we can say is that the complex prohibitions and commands governing the distribution of game which are claimed to be vestiges of a primal food-gathering community have not so far been demonstrated to obtain when what has been gathered is distributed. This accords with what is normally observed, i.e., that the person embodying the principle of the horde community is not the woman (who gathers) but the man who is the hunter.

Before dealing with the problem of the distribution of food and in connection with what has been said so far, the much-disputed question of the primal economic unit must be discussed. It is Moszkowski's view that the men originally made up an economic unit and occasionally joined together for purposes of hunting. And basing himself on his experiences in New Guinea, he says that the women gather plant food and that then an exchange between the sexes takes place. "But this is not to be taken to mean that within a closed economy the man provided the animal and the women the plant food. Generally speaking, the men, including the married ones, live and procure food together, and this also applies to the women." He imagines economic development in this way: the original food communism of the sexes is infringed by the custom of "ephemeral love economies." The enamored man elopes with the woman and spends a honeymoon of a few weeks' duration in the dark of the forest after which the partners return to their respective communities. When these ephemeral associations stabilize at a later time, the family develops as an economic unit.[17] This is undoubtedly an ingenious hypothesis and open to no objections. The only trouble is that it does not accord with the facts. Particularly as regards New Guinea, our sources permit us to infer that marriage is not a temporary but a permanent companionship. It is also evident that Moszkowski very much exaggerates the importance of the economic units consisting of persons of the same sex. Hagen writes: "As may be expected in what are predominantly marriages of inclination, love is strongly developed among the partners. In Bogadijm, there is an old couple where the man and the wife still show each other the same tenderness and attention that is customary among newlyweds. I know of a younger couple where the man picks up his wife on the field, the woman her husband when he has finished fishing."[18] Moszkowski is refuted even more decisively by Seligman. "Among the Koita, each house contains only members of a single family, and typically consists of parents and children with perhaps a surviving grandparent or great aunt or uncle."[19] Moszkowski would undoubtedly object that this may be correct as regards present conditions but that the "ephemeral love economies" represent survivals of a more primitive phase of development. If that is correct, that primal state or at least a general approach to this hypothetical state must be shown to exist on the directly preceding, more primitive cultural level which predates Papua culture, and that would be in Australia.[20]

But as we cast a glance at conditions there, we discover the precise opposite of what we would have to expect on the basis of Moszkowski's statements. In Port Stephens, the individual families wander about in the forest and form a tribe only for important celebrations.[21] On Moreton Bay, eight or ten men with their wives and children form one group.[22] Among the tribes of central Australia, a group living together consists of one or two families.[23] The Kabi and the Wakka live in groups of a few families.[24] On King George Sound, the inhabitants of six or eight huts constitute a local group.[25] Although some of our Australian sources mention larger hordes which come together at the time of year when hunting is best,[26] most indications suggest quite clearly that as we move back from the higher cultural level of the Papua to the next lower one of the Australians, the importance of the family increases to the same degree as that of the tribe diminishes.[27] *In all this, we merely see a phylogenetic confirmation of the ontogenetic findings of psychoanalysis, according to which all possible attitudes, both social and antisocial, are rooted in the family constellation.*

In all its acts, humanity is guided by two fundamental principles, hunger and love, the reality principle and libido. At first glance, it might appear that the concept of property belongs predominantly into the area of the reality principle. But the simple fact that the distribution of food occurs within the limits of the family, i.e., within that social unit which is based on conscious and unconscious erotic instincts, cautions us against underestimating the importance of libidinal factors: in the social unit that is the family, the conscious erotism between man and wife, and the unconscious erotism between parents and children is the "spiritual bond." In addition to these predominantly heteroerotic ties (homoerotism is represented in the ties to the parent of the same sex),[28] we have the association of males whose unconscious libidinal structure is based on a result of repression, i.e., the homoerotic sublimation of the family complex. It is precisely to Moszkowski that we owe the demonstration of the homosexual significance of the wood carvings and data on homosexual orgies.[29] Yet there can be no doubt that our interpretation which has the inner life as its starting point contains only one part of the truth and only casts light on one side of the coin. For it is perfectly obvious that it is the less favorable conditions for the gathering of food that are the reason for the smaller size of the units in Australia. The food found on a relatively large terrain suffices only for a single family. Conditions in New Guinea are considerably more favorable. We find cultivation of the soil, villages, and a denser population. The unconscious and the tendencies of the libido then adapt to the possibilities of the environment. This digression may not have been superfluous, for it turns out that it is *the family which is the primal social and economic unit. Within it, we find both the gathering of food and its distribution. With equal justification, we may therefore call this level one of loose, indeterminate communism or one of as yet undifferentiated individualism.* I believe that an investigation of the pattern of food distribution will serve to confirm the results obtained so far. It is hardly necessary to affirm that the hunter will himself eat the game he has killed, for this constitutes the natural conclusion of a series of acts. But it is worthwhile to examine somewhat more closely those cases where this does not occur, where the sequence of acts appears inhibited and shows the first traces of renunciation. "The Australian native cannot be accused of a lack of generosity: what he has he distributes freely to those whom tribal custom tells him that he ought to, and it may be added that he obeys to the letter the injunction of taking no heed for the morrow."[30] When we look at the persons to whom the hunter owes this kind of tribute, we shall have the key for an understanding of these contributions. A man may eat no part of an animal that has been touched by his father-in-law, his sister's son (to be understood in the classificatory sense), his mother-in-law, or his maternal grandmother. If he wants to eat what he has hunted, he first has to offer it to his father-in-law. The Arunta does not like going hunting with his father-in-law, for he runs the risk that the latter will keep the entire kill for himself.[31] Among the Warramunga, the custom survives only in the convention that the son-in-law gives his father-in-law meat as a present.[32] If a Kurnai kills five opossum, two of them go to his wife's father, two to his brothers, and the remaining one is his. Howitt writes: "As I investigated this matter further I discovered that both the game hunted and killed by the men and the vegetables[33] gathered by the women are distributed among the tribe according to certain rules. . . . Thus there is a certain community of food and there was an acknowledged obligation to supply certain persons with it."[34] If three go hunting together, and one of them bags a kangaroo at a certain distance from the camp, the other two who help him in cutting up and cooking the animal are given a foot and the tail. The rest he takes back to camp. Head and back belong to the wife, who gives them to her relatives; the rest goes to the parents of the hunter. If the latter is very hungry, he may retain a small piece for himself, but if there is something else for him to eat, he is obliged to distribute all of it. On the other hand, he will be given fish if his mother or his wife's female relatives bring some home, and the small children are always well taken care of by their grandparents. The next day, after he has supplied his wife's relatives with food, they are obliged to give him some. This is based on the juridical fiction that he is hungry now and must be well fed so that he may once again go hunting.[35] The share the hunter turns over to his relatives is called "Neborak," and Howitt reports that it is always the larger and better part of the bag which falls into this category.[36] If the hunter kills a number of swans, he retains a piece for himself and his entire family while the larger share of the remainder belongs to the relatives, particularly the parents of his wife, and the smaller to the parents and relatives of the man.[37] An eel always goes to the father-in-law.[38] In New South Wales, these same customs are called "djimber," and the pattern of distribution is approximately the same. Neither the young man nor his sister may eat of the game he has killed. It is the father and sometimes the mother who eat it. If two brothers have killed an animal, they exchange it for what another young man has hunted. The fisherman retains one-fourth of his catch; the rest is distributed.[39] Among the Ngarigo, the head of the wombat goes to the hunter, the ribs on the right side to the father, those on the left to the mother. She also receives the spine but gives it to her parents. The right shoulder goes to the elder brother, the left to the younger, his elder sister receives the right rear leg, the younger sister the left, while the rump and the liver go to the young who share their food.[40] Among the Manero, the entire kangaroo belongs to the father, who gives the hunter only a small piece if he happens to be hungry.[41]

To "explain" this orderly distribution of food, we have to proceed from two different perspectives. First, we must look at these customs from the functional and Darwinist-teleological point of view. We read the following about the Kulin: "According to their view, everything in the forest is common property. Only the tools everyone keeps in his bag are private property, and the right of the community to the gifts of nature even extends to the daily kill. At dusk, those who hunted successfully during the day share with those who returned empty-handed so that no one may suffer while someone else enjoys his abundance. The gift is not seen as a present but a rightful share. The person giving it throws it down at the feet of the other."[42] From the sociological point of view, this primitive food communism functions as a mutual life insurance. Without such safeguards, these primitive peoples could not survive the struggle for existence. On a certain level of cultural development, a selection must take place which will favor the peoples that practice such customs. Among the Lengua Indians, every tribe is obliged to feed those who could not participate in the harvest or were unable to obtain food for some reason.[43] The members of a Malayan Suku, i.e., gens, deal with each other as if they were the parts of a single body. Those who live in a great house share foliage and roots, debts and claims. All of them share disgrace and honor equally.[44] "We find striking proof of solidarity in our sources. In the Dalebura tribe, a woman who had been a cripple from her birth was carried about by the tribes-people in turn, and this was done until her death, when she was over sixty years of age."[45] But this biological explanation does not enlighten us concerning the specific forms of this custom. It does not tell us how these acquired characteristics (in the Lamarckian sense) came about. It does not make clear the psychic aims which express themselves in this custom.

We thus need an additional explanation which should be genetic and psychological. The question has to be formulated differently: who gives, and who receives in these customs? It is primarily the son-in-law who gives and renounces. The person who receives is the father-in-law. So the matter seems quite simple: these regular tributes are a further development of the bride-price.[46] But things aren't that simple, for, to begin with, it isn't just the father-in-law but the entire class of fathers-in-law which is involved. And it is not only the father-in-law but also preeminently one's own father and, more generally, one's ancestors. If we do not go beyond this simple finding for the time being, we will note that both this aspect of the distribution of food and also the special significance of the father-in-law can be explained by analogous phenomena. For there is a number of customs of distribution and renunciation to which primitives ascribe magico-mystical significance. Just as we can most easily obtain an insight into the darkest regions of psychic functions among civilized peoples by looking at neuroses, it is also the apparently nonadaptive acts among the primitives where the workings of unconscious mechanisms can most easily be studied.

In Australia, young men are not allowed to eat certain foods prior to their initiation and especially during the period of their novitiate.[47] Among the Kakadu, the listing of prohibited foods would cover half a printed page and includes various species of yams, snakes, lizards, turkey, cassowary, opossum, tortoise, etc.[48] In New South Wales, the newly initiated are not allowed to eat the meat of the Australian bear, opossum, kangaroo, bandicoot, emu, pelican, and duck.[49] From childhood on, the male is accustomed to eat only female animals. Male animals have to be brought into camp by him and given to the elders. With every successive step of initiation, one of the prohibitions is lifted. By the time he may eat everything, he has become an old man.[50] On the Pennefather River, the eggs of the wild hen, the snake, the emu, and the tortoise are forbidden foods. On the Tully River, it is salmon. Those who eat it will become prematurely gray.[51] Among the Koita and Motu, the young must take care not to eat certain fish. In cases of transgression, they are punished by hardening of the skin and the loss of favor of the females.[52] In the Bartle Bay region, the young men may not eat meat or fish during the initiation ceremonies.[53] Among the Kaitish, the young man who eats forbidden foods soon becomes gray and his body swells.[54] The Warramunga lift the prohibitions one by one, and usually the native is already past his prime before he is allowed also to eat the larger animals.[55] In Australia, the entire system prescribes that the more nourishing or rarer foods are withheld from the young and set aside for the older population.

From the sociological point of view, these customs seem to be natural and necessary expressions of social solidarity since they withhold food from that part of the population which has greater physical vigor and nimbleness and can therefore survive in the struggle for existence without it. At the same time, these measures benefit the weaker who would probably be doomed to an early death without them. The dominant fiction rests on a *reversal of physiological facts*, for these people proceed from the assumption that certain foods which a frail old person can eat without harm may endanger a robust youth. The society thus appears as a *system of balances* which overcompensates the decline of physical vigor by a corresponding increase of fictitious social energies.[56] If we ask what the origin of these customs may be, we will not be able to endorse the views of those ethnographers who see in them a product of selfishness and cleverness on the part of the old. This is similar to the views of a prescientific era in the study of comparative religions according to which religion was allegedly "invented" by the priests for their own benefit, etc.[57] We are firmly anchored in a deterministic science. If the old forbid something, if the young renounce a certain food, there can be no question that they act under the influence of *unconscious, surviving infantile memory traces*. Among the Yualaroi, the old have a large influence in determining what food the young may eat, and the reasons for this taboo are striking. The Wotjobaluk, for example, say: if a man under forty eats emu meat, he turns gray on the spot.[58] An inner inhibition resists the eating of the animal, and the root of these inhibitions is the feeling of a difference vis-à-vis the older generation, the fathers, for if a young man eats of the forbidden animal, he moves up into the older generation with undesirable speed: he turns gray. *In the infantile memory traces, we actually discover the prototype of this inhibition, for the child does in fact receive all of its food from older people, i.e., its parents,*[59] and these memory traces established in the unconscious tend toward repetition.[60] The adult must also receive his food for some authority, and this authority is the surrogate parents, the older members of the tribe. The internal inhibitions which resist the eating of the food are the survival of the inhibition of the child which is rooted in external conditions. Just as the child can realize its desires only through the mediation of its parents, the adult looks for a repetition of this situation, i.e., he does not directly proceed to an implementation of his desires, he needs his surrogate parents to give him their permission.[61] The older one becomes, the more one rids oneself of these inhibitions. The psychic situation gradually shifts and the attitude characteristic of a son is replaced by that of the father. Of course, the small child can eat only a small portion of the wild animal, and thus the hunter distributes everything except a small piece. And for the young man, everything is taboo except the smaller and less highly regarded animals. But every child also desires to become an adult, to reverse the situation and to be the father's provider. With frequent shifts this desire is realized, though not vis-à-vis the father but rather vis-à-vis the father-in-law. In this process, the unconscious identifies the spoils of the hunt with those possessions of the father-in-law which were taken from him by his son-in-law, i.e., the daughter. Just as before he owned his daughter who now belongs to the husband, so the latter first has to offer his catch to him before he may eat it himself.[62]

Another widespread category of renunciation among the primitives concerns the fact that no one may eat his own totemic animal, and Freud has convincingly demonstrated that the relationship between the primitive and the totemic animal corresponds to that between father and child, that the totem is a father symbol.[63] Here, we are not so much interested in the symbolic repetition of the primal prohibition not to kill the father but rather in those rites in central Australia where the old men of the totem clan, i.e., the fathers, first taste a piece of their totemic animal and thereby grant permission to the other members of the tribe, i.e., the children, to eat it.[64] It is for the benefit of the gods that one foregoes a certain portion of the food during sacrifice in order to be able to eat the rest without anxiety. Functionally interpreted, the gods are a projection of the socially conditioned inhibitions, and ontogenetically they are the projections of the father imago. But the power which man acquires over the gods as a result of the ritual of sacrifice can also be partially explained by this relationship, for the gods depend on the tribute of their followers in precisely the same way the father-in-law depends on the game his son-in-law brings home. Our premise *that the patterns of the distribution of food among the primitives are rooted in the family constellation* thus turns out to have been correct. But we can also fully endorse the views of Bastian concerning this matter: "at an early time or, rather, from the very beginning, the concept of property, of possessions, will turn out to be the necessary enlargement the sphere of the personality must undergo in society. When someone plucks a fruit and is about to eat it, he is governed by a decision of his will whose motives are hunger, the expected sensation of taste and the flavor, all of which can activate much more complex muscular movements rapidly and easily."[65] "Just as involuntary muscle combinations come into play to avoid being struck by a falling tree, living with one's neighbors also has created a certain causal nexus between giving and receiving, where every such act, being a clear symbol, immediately called forth its implementation without first having been analyzed into all its individual components. In the neighbor's threatening facial expression, his commanding tone, this sign language is mirrored as a strong motive for passing over the desired object. When the strength of the adversary was known to be far greater, this motive could also compensate and overcome a strong desire for food."[66] The primal form of property as an extension of the personality is thus that part of the external world which is directly incorporated by the self, food, while the origin of its social distribution must be looked for in an unconscious readiness to avoid those conflicts, in the establishment of a pattern of evasion. From the ontogenetic point of view, we merely add that these inhibitions in the life of the individual must be seen as originating with the father.

We now move on to the delimitations of private and communal property which may in fact be shown to exist among primitives. How far does the absolute right to dispose over things extend, and what are the objects in which he has a share only as a member of the community? Darwin made the observation that apes carefully hide the rocks they use in opening nuts after they are through with them.[67] Concerning the Eskimos, Rink writes that the houses in which they live together are also common property, whereas weapons and tools belong exclusively to the person using them.[68] On the Nicobar Islands, private property comprises all those objects a person has made himself;[69] and since the Karaya Indians, for example, also make all their own utensils,[70] there is an a priori probability that, next to food, these things constitute the second level of private property among primitives. Among the aborigines of Brazil, Zartius writes that huts and tools are private property, but that they are also familiar with the idea of communal property, for use is frequently by all. Only weapons, ornaments, pipes and hammocks are private property in a narrower sense.[71] K. von den Steinen writes about the Bakairi: the plantations were common property, but inside the house everyone has his own property, even women do, and we often saw them object to our being given some of their property. The property is passed on to children, daughters and sons.[72] All our sources agree that in Australia everyone can freely dispose over his ornaments, blankets, weapons, and tools. The hut belongs to the family, the hunting grounds to the tribe.[73] The same was probably true for the even more primitive Tasmanians. La Billiardère tells how he gave his pants to a girl in exchange for a kangaroo hide.[74] The borders of the hunting ground of the individual tribes are strictly observed: crossing them is a declaration of war. Land is never private property.[75] The Comanches know the difference between mine and thine only as regards objects most intimately connected with the individual. The land they roam and the game they kill belong to the entire tribe.[76] Among the Sioux, land is the common property of the tribe or group while there is a combination of individual and communist ownership of movables which accords with practical requirements. Everything perishable such as foods or firewood, for example, is common property and distributed according to carefully elaborated rules. Objects of lasting value, however, such as tents, clothing, dogs, and weapons are individually owned.[77] Among the Moannus, the concept of property is completely conscious. It lays claim to cooking utensils and hogs and, more generally, to everything made by the individual himself.[78] Concerning the Solomon Islands, Thurnwald writes: "The land is the property of the district. All its residents claim the right to use the forest, to go hunting couscous, to catch wild pigs, to cut Sago palms, etc." "The forest of the district forms the large larder where all kinds of fruit and raw materials for tools can be obtained." "Property is primarily the product of labor. For that reason, it is mainly plants and their yield which are claimed as property and also animals that have been caught."[79] As regards the primitive food gatherers, Hobhouse is unquestionably correct when he says that private property consists of weapons and tools—and we add ornaments and amulets—which are considered direct extensions of the body, while the land which serves as the group's livelihood is considered communal property. "Now the recognition of individual property in personal belongings and of communal property in land and its produce may both be explained as resting on one and the same principle, the principle of occupation and use."[80]

We thus find here the representatives of both views: is production and work, or occupation, the taking possession of, the act from which the concept of property may be derived?[81] Before we give our opinion concerning this question, another form of property should be mentioned which is usually neglected when matters of this sort come up, perhaps because no one thinks that a cultural institution of this sort exists among primitives. I am referring to intellectual property.

There are primitive peoples who are familiar with the notion of copyright and they also effectively protect it. If among the Baining someone becomes the lucky inventor of a new dance and a melody and text to go with it, he gathers his friends and works on a performance of the new creation.[82] In Australia, the singer or narrator claims that he owes the story or corroboree to an inspiration that came to him in a dream. While the dream is still vividly remembered, he goes to the chief and tells him the story. If the latter should find the matter sufficiently noteworthy, the content of the dream is made known and actors are brought together.[83] In Western Australia, songs are called after their composers, and guests bring new ones.[84] Among the Arunta, every totemic rite belongs to a specific individual, while among the Warramunga, it belongs to the totemic group as whose representative the chief acts.[85] For the North Americans, the possession of certain cults, rites, and songs constitutes a particular form of property which is legally defined in the same way material property is. Thus the right to tattoo belongs to certain members of the tribe. The recitation of a myth or a song is the prerogative of a specific individual[86] and may be purchased from the owner. Although a member of the audience may remember the entire performance, he yet would not dare stage his own as long as he has not paid the fees for this privilege.

The cult objects of secret societies were entrusted to the care of one of their members, and certain forms of the cult constitute an inalienable possession of the secret society.[87] In such cases, one can speak neither of acquisition nor of work in the material sense of the word. Here, property has to be considered as the *projection of a psychic process*. Generally speaking, the following observation might be made from the psychological point of view. Among the primitives, *part of the external world becomes the property of some individual or group when certain experiences or acts come to be attached to the object*. On the one hand, we are thus dealing with *a form of adaptation to the external world, and an introjection of part of the external world into the Ego*.[88] On the other hand, from the point of view of those who are not owners, this is *the formation of a permanent associative nexus between a person or a human group and part of the external world*. In short, property is an act before it becomes a concept, and as a concept it is first merely preconscious, something that we would tend to call a sense of union rather than of property. This also explains the privileges in the process of production and the origin of the law of inheritance.

In the region of a tribe in New South Wales, there occurs a kind of rock which readily lends itself for making stone axes. Tribes came from considerable distances to pick up the material for such axes. Gradually, the tribe in question, and especially its chief, began to claim certain special rights over this rock.[89] In the interior of New Guinea, there is a considerable shortage of salt. In earlier times, the Kai went to the sea, drank their fill, collected as much as they could carry in bamboo tubes and on slices of pumpkin and also picked up large numbers of pieces of wood soaked in sea water. This wood was carefully burnt at home and the ash used as table salt. But then the coastal inhabitants used this opportunity to parade as the masters and owners of the sea and to demand appropriate payment of the tribes living in the interior. The unauthorized scooping of water was considered theft.[90] Such a conscious exploitation of the resources of the external world develops only gradually and cannot simply be explained on a purely intellectual-rationalist basis, for it presupposes the emotional solidarity of tribe and external world. Among the Bakairi, the various animals were the "lords" or "owners" of cultural products and it is from them that the culture hero took them. The lord of medicinal tobacco and cotton was the kinkajou, of ordinary tobacco the electric eel, of the cassava the Bagadu fish, of sleep and the hammock the lizard, of water containers the river snake, of the sun the king vulture. It is only natural that the lizard which sleeps for several months should be thought of as the "owner" of sleep and the hammock which goes with it. The sun can only "belong to" the high-flying king vulture, and similarly the water containers to an animal living in that element. Medicinal tobacco comes from the North where the kinkajou lives, and similarly fire and the silver fox whose eyes shine in the dark belong together.[91] If we reduce the concept of property to an associative unity, we can also understand the absence and the genesis of the law of inheritance. On the most primitive level, there is nothing to inherit, for all things—and this means movables exclusively—are buried or burnt with the dead or destroyed in some other way. For the primitive, the associative unity between man and his possessions is indissoluble and not affected by death. The Kakadu break or burn the tools of the woman and the weapons of the man when death occurs.[92] The Karkurrera place drinking utensils, digging implements, and the small objects she owned on the woman's grave.[93] The Kukata bury weapons and drinking utensils with the dead.[94] We must postulate the interference of another psychic chain if we wish to explain the development of inheritable property. In line with biological facts, the primitive also sees the child as a continuation of the personality of the parents, but since this knowledge is unconscious, it takes on magico-symbolic forms.[95] The son is the small father, the Baikiri say.[96] Among the Euahlayi, the grindstones used to make a kind of flour from various seeds are passed on from one generation to the next. A spirit inhabits these stones, they move automatically, they can even speak.[97]

Both psychic complexes, the unity of the generations and the unity that exists between property and owner, are found in the unconscious. But it is that complex which better corresponds to the reality principle which becomes reality. The principle of the unity of generations will appear more important than the nexus between the individual and his property where more valuable, i.e., less easily made objects are involved. At the beginning of development, only valuable objects are passed on,[98] and in European folk belief, inherited objects still have a special magical value.[99] The reversal of the relationships between cause and effect happens to be a pervasive quality of the magico-mythical.[100]

Another important question still has to be settled. What are the primal forms of the ownership of land?: first, among gatherers and hunters; second, on the level of the most primitive form of hoe culture. Among the most primitive peoples, the land is the communal hunting ground, it is the property of the entire tribe, and when we consider that the fleeing animals are pursued over considerable distances, we realize that only common and far-flung borders are possible in this type of economy. If the entire region were split up among individuals or families, constant border violations would be unavoidable. The previously mentioned battues also naturally lead to the recognition of an integrated hunting ground. Fletcher writes: "Among the North American Indians, the land was not considered property initially. Like the air, it was an indispensable condition for the life of the race. For that reason, neither an individual nor a small group had exclusive claim to it."[101] Among the Kurnai, land belongs to the tribe and everyone has an equal share in the rights arising from this fact.[102] In view of the perfect homogeneity of the material, it is unnecessary to provide additional data. We will, however, examine the question regarding the ownership of land by smaller units such as the family or the individual on this level.

Concerning the tribes along the lower Murray, Eyre

writes that every adult male owns a piece of land whose borders he can define with precision.[103] In Western Australia, every family has a piece of land but uses it together with others if their relations are friendly.[104] Along the Swan River also, individual ownership of land is known, but in a sense this land also belongs to the tribe. The owner must be present when fire is put to the grass on his tract for a communal battue. About Queensland, there is the complementary and additional information that the owner of the land decides the time of the hunt, that he must be present when the grass is set on fire, and he also directs the ceremonies which take place on this land.[105] The so-called owner thus has a formal, ceremonial rather than a practical relation to his property. Information about the Yaraikana that live at the northern end of Australia shows us a concept of property even more remote from ours. During initiation, every man has a tooth knocked out. But this is not done by a single but repeated blows of the stone hammer. As each blow is struck, the name of some region is given, and that region which happens to be mentioned as the tooth falls out belongs to the boy.[106] It is evident that property in this form is neither exclusive nor of practical significance. When his tooth is knocked out, the Yaraikana youth receives something else: a personal tutelary spirit.[107] For the old examine the blood which drips on the ground as the tooth is knocked out. The similarity they discover between that pattern and some animal leads them to specify the personal totem of the boy. It thus seems that among the Yaraikana, *the connection between an individual and a region has no practical but a magico-mystical significance. There seems to be some sort of nexus between this magical meaning and the totem, and the visible sign, the symbol of the nexus between the self and the external world, is a severed part of the body.*

Among the Vedda, landed property is transferred by having the former owner give the new one a quartz crystal or one of his teeth that has fallen out, and perhaps a lock of hair.[108] We know that there are Australian tribes where the teeth knocked out during initiation ceremonies mediate a transfer of a different sort between the self and the external world: the knocked-out tooth is hidden under the bark of a tree, and now this tree becomes the tree of that person. Its flowering means happiness for the young man, its withering, death.[109] Just as among the Yaraikana the tooth serves to establish a magical connection with a plot of ground, the knocked-out tooth is used to find the future wife on Princess Charlotte Bay. As the tooth is being knocked out during initiation, girls' names are recited, and the one that is mentioned as the tooth flies out of the mouth is the right one.[110]

When we see that the concept of property, i.e., the introjection of part of the external world into the self, comes about 1. through the mediation of a severed part of the body, 2. is tantamount to an erotic tie (cf., above the appearance of the wife at the same point during the ceremony where the landed property is named), it is perhaps not too bold to infer that in *those parts of the body that can be severed and are autoerotically cathected, we have the physiological prototype of property*. The fear which attaches to these parts of the body is a certain sign of strong libidinal cathexis.[111] In the Theddora tribe, the girl is promised to a man at the time of her birth. To assure him of this, his living property, the man is given a lock of hair as a pledge. If the girl refuses to become his wife, he only has to place her hair into water, and just as that hair rots the recalcitrant girl will also die.[112] The Cherokee bury the sputum of their enemies under a tree that has been struck by lightning; the enemy will then die within six days.[113] These rites which ordinarily are classed as sympathetic magic are actually determined by the autoerotic phase of the psychosexual development of the libido. They contain a piece of the pre- and primal history of property which is suggested by the role of food,[114] for example, to which we pointed above as the primal form of property. It is that part of the external world which is the first to be introjected both physiologically and psychically and is therefore strongly cathected by fear. As the food disappears, the person who ate it dies. As confirmation of the erotic origin of the magic significance of severed parts of the body and as a parallel to the previously mentioned customs where the nexus with the external world is established by such a severed part, the following custom might be mentioned. In Northwest Australia, the detached foreskin of the young man who has just been initiated is either hidden in the bark of a tree or eaten by the young man.[115] Among the Unmatjera, the youth hides the foreskin in a tall tree, and the place is a carefully guarded secret, particularly from the women.[116] Frazer, who perspicaciously connected these customs with the idea of rebirth, calls attention to the fact that according to Unmatjera tradition, the Alcheringa ancestors stored their foreskins in their Nanja trees, and it is this Nanja tree which serves as the seat of the soul and the starting point of reincarnation, according to central Australian conceptions.[117]

There is much that tends to corroborate Frazer's view. From our perspective, we have to say that if we see the phylogenetic prototype of property in the severed parts of the body, *decisive importance from the point of view of ontogenesis must be attached to that moment where the close community is terminated and detachment from the mother occurs, the body being given over to the external world*. The rest will be explained by the curious connections between birth and property,[118] between landed property and the mother's body.

Along the Pennefather River, the soul is called *choi*. Every human being has a choi, beginning at the very minute when Anjea (a so-called spirit of nature) places the already existing creature into the mother's body. But at birth, part of the choi remains attached to the placenta and is buried with it in the ground. From the placenta, or rather from the choi in it, Anjea then keeps forming the children who are being incarnated. When the umbilical cord is cut, the names of various regions are called out. The region mentioned during the moment the umbilical cord breaks is the future home of the boy; it is his land where he may roam and hunt. It is characteristic that this region with which he becomes so intimately associated by what is really a magic act often lies a number of miles away from his real place of birth. The mystical connection with the fictitious birthplace also finds expression in the name, for children are called "come from a tree," "sprung from a rock," or "sprung from fresh water."[119] The inadequate material available to us justifies the guess that such customs were widespread in Australia. Usually, children are named after a bird that happens to fly by as they are born, some other animal that may be noticed, or their place of birth. Since the belief in a magical nexus between man and these animals has been demonstrated in some cases, we may assume that it is general and perhaps also the reason for place names being used as personal names.[120]

It seems that we are dealing here with a preliminary stage of landed property which is not wholly clear. Most plausibly, it might be called *a sense of a closer nexus with part of the external world*. This spiritual and physical bond is also somehow connected with totemism. We know more about conditions in central Australia than elsewhere, and it is here that we are most likely to obtain an insight into these connections. All these tribes are made up of local groups which own certain clearly defined sections of the tribal territory. No individual may own a piece of land, the smallest unit always being the local totemic group.[121] The members of a totemic group roam the common region in small groups, gather berries, hunt or fish, but always remain within the area of the group.[122] From the point of view of the reality principle, such would be the connection between totemic group and land; these are the acts through which the connection is established. This external reality, however, is based on a fiction which appears in the unconscious as the opposite of this reality.

The tribal region is divided into various oknanikillia, i.e., totemic centers. Usually, such a center is a point in the landscape which is remarkable for some reason. It may be isolated rock formations, trees, etc., where, according to legend, some totemic ancestor died and entered the earth after hiding his churinga and leaving behind a number of child-seeds which there await reincarnation. When a woman passes by the totemic center and senses the first signs of pregnancy, they believe that a child-seed of the totem in question is being born anew in her. In such cases, the child is a member of the local totemic group. If signs of pregnancy are felt near the center of the emu group, for example, the child will belong to the emu totem and be given a personal name such as "small emu," "emu feather," or something of the sort.[123] Today, the concepts "local group" and "totemic group" no longer wholly coincide for the simple reason that these women sometimes leave the area of their own totemic region as they roam about and experience their malaise also in the vicinity of a different totemic center. It may be assumed, however, that on a still more primitive level, the population was less dense and that the various small groups hardly ever came into contact with each other. But today, the local totem predominates among members of a local group, i.e., women notice the signs of pregnancy usually near their own totemic center.[124]

Totemism as such can hardly be explained without the presupposition that it is a magico-mystical projection of the actually existing nexus between man and the biosphere, particularly between man and those animal species with which he shares his territory. This means that the totem of a group is originally some animal species in his environment which is conspicuous by its size or importance.[125] Strehlow writes, for example, that in ponds with a great many fish the rapata of a fish totem await the time of their birth.[126] When the Warramunga advance as the reason for the bipartition of their tribe that the ancestors of every phratry roamed those regions in very early times which the same phratries still occupy today, their explanation is perfectly valid,[127] except that it should be phrased a little differently. *The magico-mystical nexus between a human group and the zoögeographic and territorial milieu is merely the "psychic" extension of the locally established acts of several generations*. The characteristic element in this totemistic complex is a far-reaching identification between man and the animals living in his environment, for the existence of the human group depends on the incarnation of the kangaroo, emu, etc., rapatas, and in the same way the increase in the animal species is merely a result of the Intichiuma rites held by the human members of the tribe.[128] On this level, we thus have a situation where man and the world in which he lives "own" each other reciprocally,[129] if such a term may be used here. That is to say, *the active and passive elements of the attitude taken toward the external world are still indifferently contained in the same complex.*[130] *In the course of development, these opposing attitudes become increasingly differentiated. The passive attitude, the sense of dependence on the environment manifests itself in the various local taboos, cults, and local demons, while the fact of active intervention in the world around them crystallizes in the concept of property.*[131]

In Florida, the sacred places are called vunuha. Here, the Tindalo is sacrificed to and everything that grows on the sacred spot is taboo, i.e., the property of a spirit. One may only come to such a spot in order to sacrifice to it. Those who accompany the person bringing the sacrifice walk in his tracks. The individual performing it may not glance back, otherwise his soul will be caught in the vunuha.[132] The belief of the Koita in certain beings whose sphere of power extends over specific regions is probably connected with this taboo, or prohibition. It is through the presence of the spirit that they become sacred, i.e., taboo. Usually, they are headlands, swamps, mountains, which are considered the property of the taboo spirits and which either may not be visited by human beings at all, or only if certain expiatory sacrifices are performed.[133]

The fact that there are areas which are considered sacred and as belonging to the spirits is to be understood as the psychic symptom of an as yet imperfect mastery over nature. The Indonesian peoples really do not know the concept of landed property. The tribe, the horde, or the village merely enjoy the usufruct of certain regions. Since all have this right, it is also the right of the community to define the extent of the individual's usufruct. The unrestricted property right of the individual extends only to objects he himself has made, and this is also true for the community. "But the right to the ownership of all those things which have not become the property of persons through labor is not man's but the spirits'." They live everywhere in the ground, in the water, on fields, in mountains and bushes; the earth is theirs. Everything that comes into being independently of human labor is their property, and man must purchase the right to use the earth through sacrifice.[134] Those magico-mystical notions which have to be understood as psychic reflections of action patterns tied to specific localities thus have to be viewed as the precursors of the practical juridical concept of landed property. This primal complex becomes differentiated into an active and practical component which develops into the concept of landed property, and a passive and ideological one which gives rise to the various local prohibitions and cult sites. Landed property in the real sense of that term exists only on a much higher level of cultural development, but even among the most primitive peoples we see the first outlines of this idea which becomes a reality only much later. Particularly as regards the landed property of the individual and the family, it seems that we are dealing with certain inhibitions of the other members of the society vis-à-vis certain regions which are somehow connected with important phases in the development of the individual who is tied to these regions and manifests this fact ceremonially. We know, for example, that every Watchandie has to visit the place of his birth three times yearly,[135] and on Cape Bedford the place of birth of a person is taboo for everyone except his parents.[136] In these mystical connections, it is particularly the place of birth that is significant. In central Australia, the individual belongs to the totem in whose region as incarnation of the embryo soul occurred. In the West and on Cape Bedford, there is a mystical nexus between the individual and his place of birth; in Queensland the region where his placenta was buried belongs to him. Following Bastian, we established earlier that food is the first property; now, we merely add that from the ontogenetic point of view, the mother's milk is of course the first property of the neonate, his first extrauterine property being the mother's breast. *All this suggests that it is in the feeling of a more intimate connection with the environment from the point of view of ontogenesis that we have to see the unconscious survival of memory traces from the embryonic period*. Just as the embryo is the exclusive owner of the space taken up by it within the mother's body, *the individual also experiences a more intimate nexus with that part of his environment which is closest to the intrauterine, and that is his place of birth*. Already in Australia, there are many indications that both the idea of a mystical nexus with the external world and the concept of individual property consisting of immovable objects attaches primarily to trees,[137] and the fruit-bearing tree is one of the most frequent symbols of the mother.[138] Among the Yaraikana, landed property is determined when the tooth is knocked out in precisely the same way as the future wife is on Princess Charlotte Bay.[139] Among peoples that till the soil, the connection between the earth and woman, particularly the first woman, the mother, becomes perfectly conscious by virtue of the return of the repressed. The North Americans, for example, call the earth mother since it provides food for her children like a good mother.[140]

Of course, landed property in a practical sense only exists on the level of the most primitive hoe culture. Conditions here are perfectly homogeneous among all primitive peoples, and the causal nexus is also completely transparent. Among the Baining in New Pommerania, the plantations constitute the most significant property. "Individual property in land has not developed because the most important presupposition, sedentary life, is missing." Land is the common property of the inhabitants, and everyone has the right to cut down trees in the unoccupied parts of the forest, to plant trees in clearings, and to harvest on his plantation. The usufruct, the crop, is the exclusive property of the person who started the plantation, and if someone plants coconut palms on a neglected one, for example, the nuts belong to him alone. If the original owner again plants in the clearing, the entire harvest reverts to him.[141] Among the Kai, every field is used only once. Already at harvest time, weeds grow in such abundance that the papua have to desist and go on to another piece of land. On the harvested field, dense bushes and bamboo then begin growing. After six or eight years, a new crop can be planted on the old field. Every year, a piece of land is designated as a new field and every villager claims his share in advance.[142] Parkinsons also writes about the Baining: "The Baining are wandering farmers. Where they start a taro field, they immediately settle. When the field begins to yield less, they choose a new area which is sometimes quite some distance away from the former one, and build their huts there." "The land also does not belong to individuals. The place where they plant seems to be considered property for a time but they know no such thing as a permanent claim, nor are they familiar with the transfer of property through inheritance, purchase, gift or exchange."[143] On Milne Bay, the region adjacent to settlements of the tribe is its common property. The gardens of the village and the surrounding land, however, belong to the totemic clan which lives in the village. Unused forest land is common property. If someone clears part of it, that part temporarily becomes his, but later the permanent property of his clan. If a stranger wishes to join the tribe, a plot of ground is assigned to him, but under the condition that he accepts one of the tribal totems.[144]

This is the same sort of nexus we demonstrated between territorial distribution and totemism on the level preceding hoe culture.

In Florida, we also have the so-called "matanga" property, the boundaries of the village which never belongs to an individual but always to the maternal clan, the "Kema."[145] Among the Mafulu, the house and the ground on which it stands belong to the individual, but when the pillars rot and the house collapses, the land reverts to the community. Houses of this type stand for only a few years. Clearings are individual property only in a restricted sense, for the right to hunt and fish belongs to the community.[146] In Bogadjim also, new plantations are started yearly, for the inhabitants are well aware of the advantages of virgin soil. They clear the ground jointly and then assign to each family a plot for cultivation. Here, conditions are no longer so simple, for the land is owned by individual families. But since plantations are often started far from the family's landed property, it follows that they cultivate land that isn't theirs. Let us assume a village with three family groups, A, B, and C. In a given year, the plantation owned jointly is started on the land belonging to family A, the next year on the land belonging to family B, but the so-called owner derives no particular rights from this fact, for the crop belongs to the person who did the planting. This means it belongs to the individual families of group A, B, or C, the only restriction being that the head of the family is obliged to turn over part of the yield when feasts are held by a group of families.[147] This is probably the nonpractical, preagricultural form of the concept of property, or, more accurately, its survival in the property of the family groups which were in all likelihood totemic clans originally. The practice of moving on from one agricultural site to the next also explains Romilly's remark that the natives are unfamiliar with the idea that land can be sold. Gifts are accepted by the natives but they are profoundly astonished when one tells them that they, the original inhabitants, no longer have any business on their land.[148] Berkusky writes similarly about the most primitive Indonesian tribes that the land is common property. The individual who clears land or starts a plantation is entitled only to the harvest. This is hardly surprising, for land exists in such abundance that only the labor spent on it has value; the land itself has none. The individual who cultivated a particular piece of land the year before is already working elsewhere the following year and would not know what to do with the tract of land he tilled a year ago.[149]

Among the North Americans, land originally belonged to the tribe. With the coming of agriculture, family property developed, but this never reached the point where the Indians felt that the land could be sold.[150] For the Bakairi, the plantation is communal property.[151] Among the Lengua, land belongs to the entire tribe and no one is entitled to a greater share than his neighbor. What the forest produces belongs to all, the herds graze on the communal pasture, and the land belongs to the individual only as long as he cultivates it.[152] Generally speaking, the concept of property is no more than the expression of the continuity of a series of acts, and that is the reason that large bags of game or fish belong to the village, the crop from the plantation to the family, weapons and tools to the man, the hut and the boat to the woman, toys to the child.[153] In the same way, conditions characteristic of a kind of nomadism obtain among the Awemba in Rhodesia. The land belongs to all, the crop to the person that cleared the forest. The land is so sparsely settled that no one is obliged to cultivate the same area twice in succession. Everyone owns what he has harvested, but not the land which is without value in any event.[154] Berkusky demonstrates convincingly that permanent possession of land developed as the population density increased. As soon as the agriculture of wandering tribes is superseded by the sedentary forms of hoe culture, we see property emerge as the psychic product of what are now established sequences of actions.[155] And this also means that we have reached the upper limit of conditions that can be called primitive. We will therefore simply cast a final glance at further lines of development. In Florida, the sacred spot, the vunuha, is often also the cemetery, and the "genius loci" is the soul of a dead person.[156] As living space contracts and nomadism comes to an end, we observe that man and earth come to form a more intimate unity in Indonesia. The spirits to whom the earth belongs now are no longer alien demons but ancestors. The cult connects the generation now living with its predecessors, and it is from this that everyone derives his actual claim to a share of landed property. That is the reason why on the Watebela islands, in Flores and Sumba, they say that it is due to consideration for the ancestors that land may not be sold, and that in Halmahera selling the land is viewed as an act violating the commands of the ancestors.[157] When the primitive considers his fatherland sacred because it belongs to the ancestors, this means that the psychic background of the tie to the surface of the earth is given in the infantile attitude toward the long sequence of fathers. *Mother earth belongs to the ancestors, i.e., the mother belongs to the father*. This is what we find projected in the magic tie to the earth during the totemistic phase, and it is by virtue of this psychic attitude that social and economic equality gradually disappears, for the chief as the actual embodiment of the father imago becomes increasingly prominent. The only thing that distinguishes the chief of a totemic group in central Australia from the other members is his closer relationship to the cult of the Alcheringa ancestors. He thus becomes the focal point of the father images surviving in the infantile unconscious, the visible object of the infantile tendency to obey. The members of the tribe have the same attitude toward him as they do toward the demon and the totem: *it is the attitude of inhibited aggressiveness, of partial renunciation*. The chief reserves the right to the first-fruits and a part of the land which originally belonged to the tribe.[158] And in these symbolic prerogatives which reflect the right of the father to the mother, we have the beginning of the development of capital and of social classes.

Notes and References

1. G. Grey, *Journals of two Expeditions of Discovery in North West and Western Australia*, (1841) I, 259-299. N. W. Thomas, *Natives of Australia*, (1906) 103, 104. For the uncertain results and the disproportionate effort required in this kind of hunting, see A. Oldfield, *On the Aborigines of Australia. Transactions of the Ethnological Society*, (1861) I, 294. Kurt von den Steinen, *Unter den Naturvölkern Zentral-Brasiliens*, (1894) 233. Koch-Grünberg, *Zwei Jahre unter den Indianern*, (1910) II, 50 ("The great fishtraps . . . and all the fish caught in them belong to the entire community.") E. Nordenskiöld, (1912) 184, 185.

2. R. H. Mathews, *Ethnological Notes on the Aboriginal Tribes of New South Wales and Victoria*, (1905) 52, 53.

3. J. Murdoch, *Ethnological Results of the Point Barrow Expedition, IX. Annual Report of the Bureau of Ethnology*, (1887/1888) 264.

4. G. F. Angas, *Savage Life and Scenes in Australia and New Zealand*, (1847) II, 231. One may perhaps be inclined to see a survival of this primitive method of hunting in a mythical motif. Cf., K. von den Steinen, *Unter den Naturvölkern Zentral-Brasiliens*, (1894) 324. Stucken, *Astralmythen*, (1907) 1.

5. N. W. Thomas, *Natives of Australia*, (1906) 97. Western Australia. See also A. F. Calvert, *The Aborigines of Western Australia*, (1894) 26.

6. F. Krause, *In den Wildnissen Brasiliens*, (1911) 247.

7. E. Eylmann, *Die Eingeborenen der Kolonie Südaustralien*, (1908) 273, 274. Cf., also "Sometimes they join in company for the chase. . . . These public battues are governed by certain rules. . . . The animals are surrounded and each man has his position assigned; then the circle gradually closes in on the terrified creatures, but few of them escape." A. F. Calvert, *The Aborigines of Western Australia*, (1894) 25. "In the Boulia district when a mob of emus happens to come within the neighbourhood of a camp all the men and women may assist in surrounding and mustering them like cattle, subsequently driving them down to the nearest waterhole." W. E. Roth, *Food, its Search, Capture and Preparation*, (*North Queensland Ethnography*. Bulletin No. 3, 1901) 26. J. F. Bennet, *Historical and Descriptive Account of South Australia*, (1843) 361, 362. A. Oldfield, *The Aborigines of Australia*, (*Transactions of the Ethn. Soc*. III) 272. All of the members of the tribe and sometimes even two neighboring ones take part in the battue. H. Ling-Roth, *The Aboriginals of Tasmania*, (1899) 97, 98.

8. W. J. McGee, *The Seri*, (Indian Bureau of American Ethnology, XVII, 1895/96) 190, 191. Perhaps these jointly held battues are the first expression of the communal life of the horde. They are probably more primitive than war which may well have developed from them. The similarity to the hunting techniques of wolves when they attack in packs is conspicuous.

9. J. Murdoch, *Ethnological Results of the Point Barrow Expedition*, (*IX. Report of the Bureau of Ethnology*, 1887/88) 265.

10. Ch. Kaysser, *Aus dem Leben der Kaileute*. R. Neuhauss: *Deutsch Neu Guinea*, (1911) III, 19.

11. Cf. Alfred Knabenhans, *Arbeitsteilung und Kommunismus im australischen Nahrungserwerb*, (*Festschrift für Eduard Hahn. LX. Geburtstag. Studien und Forschungen zur Menschen-und Völkerkunde*. XIV, 1917) 79, 80. In fishing, we can also distinguish individual and collective procedures. The method of the Euahlayi, for example, is individual. The women lie down completely naked in the ponds and wait there until the prawns bite them. Then they can catch them. K. L. Parker, *The Euahlayi Tribe*, (1905) 110. In shallow water, they simply step on the fish. N. W. Thomas, *Natives of Australia*, (1906) 89. Or they hit them with arrows or spears. See op. cit. and A. W. Howitt, *Native Tribes of South Australia*, (1904) 461. K. von den Steinen, *Unter den Naturvölkern Zentral-Brasiliens*, (1897) 223. C. G. Seligman, *The Veddas*, (1911) 333. The most rudimentary form of cooperation is encountered where the fish are driven from one end of the pond to the other by the use of twigs and branches. Eylmann, *Die Eingeborenen der Kolonie Südaustralien*, (1908) 276-277. Spencer and Gillen, *The Northern Tribes of Central Australia*, (1904) 677. A. Oldfield, *The Aborigines of Australia*, (*Trans. Ethn. Soc*. III) 274. Weirs and fishgarths belong in this context. N. W. Thomas, *Natives of Australia*, (1906) 92. K. L. Parker, *The Euahlayi Tribe*, (1906) 109, 110. (Every tribe has its own fishgarths. If a stranger takes fish, this is considered theft. Along the Upper Nile, lakes and ponds are respected as the same sort of valuable property as farmland and vineyards are in Europe. Ratzel, *Völkerkunde*, [1894] I, 118.) W. E. Roth, *Food, its Search, Capture and Preparation*, (*North Queensland Bulletin* No. 3, 1901) 23. (Details about the various kinds of fishing in that work.) Morgan, *Houses and House Life of the American Aborigines*, (*Contr. to North American Ethnology*, IV) 77. Discusses "communism in husbands as well as wives" in connection with "communism in food." An incisive critique of both one-sided views in F. Somlo, *Der Güterverkehr in der Urgesellschaft*, (*Institut Solvay*, 1909) 166, 175. See also Knabenhans, *Arbeitsteilung und Kommunismus im australischen Nahrungserwerb*. (*Eduard Hahn Festschrift*, 1917) 74. And Fr. Ratzel, *Völkerkunde*, (1894) I, 117.

12. K. von den Steinen, *Unterden Naturvölkern Zentral-Brasiliens*, (1894) 206.

13. K. L. Parker, *The Euahlayi Tribe*, (1905) 115.

14. R. H. Mathews, *Ethnological Notes on the Aboriginal Tribes of New South Wales and Victoria*, (1905) 91. J. Fraser, *The Aborigines of New South Wales*, (1892) 51.

15. C. Lumholtz, *Au Pays des Cannibales*, (1890) 145, 189. Cf., Ed. Hahn, *Die Entstehung der Pflugkultur*, (1909) 6. O. T. Mason, *Woman's Share in Primitive Culture*, (1895) 14.

16. Cf., K. Bücher, *Die Entstehung der Volkswirtschaft*, (1911) 27. "Level of individual search for food." Moszkowski, however, writes in *Vom Wirtschaftsleben der primitiven Völker*, (1900) 227: "Within these economic units, there is at first absolute communism." H. Schurtz, *Urgeschichte der Kultur*, (1900) 227. "Communism, which some see as the highest and most desirable flower of cultural development seems on the contrary to have long since been transcended by the more progressive groups of mankind, while there are others which still adhere to it."

17. M. Moszkowski, *Vom Wirtschaftsleben der primitiven Völker*, (1911) 10.

18. B. Hagen, *Unter den Papuas*, (1899) 243.

19. C. G. Seligman, *The Melanesians of British New Guinea*, (1910) 66.

20. A discussion of the differently oriented type of research done by adherents of the theory of culture complexes (see Schmidt and Koppers, *Völker und Kulturen*, III, [1924]) will be presented elsewhere.

21. R. Dawson, *The Present State of Australia*, (1831) 326.

22. M. Hodgskinson, *Australia from Port Macquarie to Moreton Bay*, (1845) 222.

23. Spencer and Gillen, *The Native Tribes of Central Australia*, (1899) 16.

24. J. Matthew, *Two representative tribes of Queensland*, (1910) 128.

25. Browne, *Die Eingeborenen Australiens. Petermanns Mitteilungen*, (1856).

26. See the material in B. Malinowski, *The Family among the Australian Aborigines*, (1913) 146-148, who also quotes the sources mentioned above.

27. The even more primitive Tasmanians, on the other hand, are said to have roamed about in larger groups. H. Ling Roth, *The Aborigines*

of Tasmania, (1899) 105. In the primal state, individual families of the Veddas roamed the forest individually. Seligman, *The Veddas*, (1911) 81. Among the pygmies of central Africa, we seem to be dealing with larger tribes. A. B. Lloyd, *In Dwarf Land and Cannibal Country*, (1907) 268.

28. Cf., S. Freud, *Totem and Taboo*. Th. Reik, *Probleme der Religionspsychologie*, (1919) 119, and Blüher, *Die Rolle der Erotik in der männlichen Gesellschaft*, (1917) I, II, but Blüher does not recognize repression, the secondary element in the homoerotism of male associations.

29. Moszkowski, *Vom Wirtschaftsleben der Naturvölker*, (1911) 24. Cf., Schurtz, *Altersklassen und Männerbünde*, (1902) 20, 22, 52.

30. Spencer and Gillen, *The Native Tribes of Central Australia*, (1899) 469.

31. Spencer and Gillen, ibid. On the tribute payments to the father-in-law, see also B. Spencer, *Native Tribes in Northern Australia*, (1914) 36.

32. Spencer and Gillen, *The Northern Tribes of Central Australia*, (1904) 610.

33. We maintained above that rules of distribution do not apply to what has been foraged. Here, we find an exception. Yet I nowhere find precise information on the rules governing distribution similar to those covering game. Cf., Knabenhans, *Arbeitsteilung*, (*Hahn-Festschrift*, 1917) 162, "that on this level, the man is still much more caught up in all sorts of sociological ties than the woman."

34. A. W. Howitt, *The Native Tribes of South East Australia*, (1904) 756.

35. Howitt, *Native Tribes*, 756, 757.

36. Cf., "The hunter only eats the lesser parts; he distributes the rest." This custom is practiced by appealing to an etiological myth where "Selfish" suffers death for his lack of altruism. J. Dawson, *Australian Aborigines*, (1881) 22, 23. Cf., further material in Knabenhans, loc. cit. 95-97.

37. Howitt, loc. cit. 758.

38. Howitt, loc. cit. ibid. In the case of Polynesian or other material, this suggests the meaning of the eel in sexual symbolism. But here it is probably only the eel as food which is relevant.

39. R. H. Mathews, *Ethnological Notes on the Aboriginal Tribes of New South Wales and Victoria*, (1905) 56, 57.

40. Howitt, loc. cit. 759.

41. Howitt, loc. cit. 760.

42. Howitt, loc. cit. 767. This act of throwing something at another's feet must not be considered a humiliation of the person receiving the thing, as it would be in Europe. Howitt explains that this is intended to avoid the possibility of a spell which might come about if food is passed directly from one person to another. Psychologically speaking, the fear of a spell corresponds to the suppressed selfish impulses of the giver (the repressive authority being, of course, society). Therefore there is general fear of the evil eye while eating, for example. E. Crawly, *The Mystic Rose*, (1902) 151, 161. On the magic dangers of accepting gifts, see E. Westermarck, *The Origin and the Development of the Moral Ideas*, (1906) I, 593. Concerning the hospitality of the Lengua Indians, Grubb writes "but this apparent hospitality is given grudgingly, though ostensibly with good grace. They are compelled to share by native law." W. B. Grubb, *An Unknown People in an Unknown Land*, (1911) 189. The Erinys, the avenging spirits who turn on those that violate the sacred laws of hospitality, the *dei hospitalis*, are the projected feelings of the offended guest. Cf., Westermarck, loc. cit. 585.

43. W. B. Grubb, *An Unknown People in an Unknown Land*, (1911) 189.

44. G. A. Wilken, *De Verspreide Geschriften*, (1917) I, 314. (*Over de verwantschap en het huwelijeksen erfrecht bij de volken van het Maleische ras*.)

45. A. W. Howitt, *The Native Tribes of South East Australia*, (1854) 766. Cf., also "whether their bag is large or small, everyone receives his share. The young and the weak, the old and the helpless are treated no differently from the strongest." W. Campier, *Early Voyages to Australia by B. H. Major*, (Haklyut Society, 1959) 103. "The fortunate hunter distributes the meat with a liberal hand to his comrades, reserving but a comparatively small portion to himself." A. Oldfield, *The Aborigines of Australia*, (*Transactions of the E. S.* III) 271. Everyone who passes at the time of the evening meal simply sits down without waiting for an invitation and receives his share. "So great was the hospitality of the people to equals and superiors that food could almost have been termed common property." G. Mc. Theall, *The Yellow and Dark Skinned People of Africa South of the Zambesi*, (1910) 229. Customs similar to those of the "Neborak" of the Australians are also encountered in Africa where they have developed into what can only be called a system of taxation. It seems likely that we are dealing here with one of the primal forms of taxation generally. (Primitial sacrifice and various taboos may also be involved.) The spoils of the hunt belong to the person who is the first to mortally wound the animal with his spear. "Various relatives, head-men, or

chiefs have rights over certain parts of an animal killed by a relative or a member of the town. A child takes a leg or a shoulder of the animal slain by his father, a mother receives the belly piece or neck from her successful son. These bespoke portions that belong to the family are called *bilelo*. The head-man receives the head or neck and his portion is called *motamdo*." Frequently, hardly anything remains for the hunter. John H. Weeks, *Among Congo Cannibals*, (1913) 231, 232. The kidneys of the killed antelope belong to the chief, one rear leg to the men of the town who share it with their wives, one shoulder goes to those who helped during the hunt, the heart is the father's, the rest goes to the hunter. J. H. Weeks, *Among the Primitive Bakongo*, (1914) 185. The head belongs to the hunter's coevals. If it is a small bush animal, his oldest brother on the father's side receives the head and shares it with his younger brothers. The jaw bone of the animal, one hind leg and the kidneys go to the older uncle on the father's side. When a hunter dies, this uncle has to request from whatever creditors he may have had that his debts be reduced, i.e., "he must strain his jawbone." The neck of the animal goes to his sisters on the mother's side because they lend their neck and carry the burden when the dead hunter leaves debts behind. The hunter's mother receives the breast. For both in joy and in grief, she beats her breast with her hands (the real symbolism, of course, is more profound). The loins go to the hunter's wife because her loins become tired as she works for her husband. As the body rests on the loins, so the entire house does on the woman. The grandfather is the root of the entire family whose members are merely his branches and twigs. He receives the tailhead, that part where the strongest muscles and nerves come together, etc. J. Spieth, *Die Ewe-Stämme*, (1906) 384-388. (A similar symbolism probably underlies the Australian rules governing distribution, though it is unconscious.) When large game is hunted, the "lord of the earth" receives the head, and this is also true of the tail of buffalo and elephant, and of the tusk of the latter which touches the ground, or both tusks if the elephant was kneeling and supporting itself on them while dying, etc. Pechuel Loesche, *Die Loango-Expedition*, (1907) II, 2. Teil, 218.

46. This is Malinowski's view, *The Family among the Australian Aborigines*, (1913) 290.

47. See also Th. Reik, *Probleme der Religionspsychologie*, (1919) 7. G. Róheim, *Australian Totemism*, (1925) 276-280.

48. B. Spencer, *The Native Tribes of Northern Australia*, (1914) 323.

49. R. H. Mathews, *Ethnological Notes on the Aboriginal Tribes of New South Wales and Victoria*, (1905) 57.

50. J. Fraser, *The Aborigines of New South Wales*, (1892) 54.

51. W. E. Roth, *Tabu and other Forms of Restriction*, (*North Queensland Ethnography Bulletin* II, 1908) 76.

52. C. G. Seligman, *The Melanesians of British New Guinea*, (1910) 139.

53. Ibid. 496.

54. Spencer and Gillen, *The Northern Tribes of Central Australia*, (1904) 611.

55. Ibid. 612. Ch. Wilhelmi, *Manners and Customs of the Australian Natives*, (*Royal Society Transactions*, 1862) 16. H. E. A. Meyer, *Manners and Customs of the Aborigines of the Encounter Bay Tribe*. J. D. Woods, *The Natives Tribes of South East Australia*, (1879) 187.

56. That this overcompensation can become one in the derogatory sense is proven by an Australian custom which certainly cannot be approved of from the point of view of eugenics (although secretly, a balance is created of course). It involves the old men's keeping all the young women for themselves so that the young find it difficult to get a wife. Conditions are not much different in certain strata of civilized European peoples: there occurs a significant socio-economic shift favoring the older, physically less effective men.

57. Cf., "The boys are also forbidden to eat thirteen different sorts of game and it is said that if they eat them they will become prematurely gray. I have no doubt that this custom was originally intended to make provision for the old people and women, for the game which is forbidden the boys is easily obtained and is nourishing food. If therefore they were allowed to partake of it, it would probably soon be exterminated for the whole tribe would feed on them to the neglect of those animals which are more difficult to obtain." G. Taplin, *The Narrinyeri*, (1878) 16.

58. A. W. Howitt, *The Native Tribes of South East Australia*, (1904) 769.

59. In New South Wales, food taboos do not as yet apply to young children. They may eat everything their parents or other relatives give them. R. H. Mathews, *Ethnological Notes on the Aboriginal Tribes of New South Wales and Victoria*, (1905) 56, 57. It is in the food provided by the parents that we must look for the root of the category of "permitted" foods. But such a category also presupposes the existence of another, forbidden one. Perhaps the child also notices that the larger share of the food goes to the adults, and this experience is then activated in the category of "sacred," "taboo," "forbidden" food.

60. On the repetition compulsion of the unconscious, see Freud, *The Uncanny*.

61. On Encounter Bay, the distribution of food proceeds by age levels. "At certain seasons of the year when a particular kind of fish is abundant, the men frequently declare it to be *rambe* (holy) after which all that are caught must be brought to the men by whom they are cooked and the women and children are not allowed even to approach and eat of what the men choose to give them after having eaten themselves." H. E. A. Meyer, *Manners and Customs of the Aborigines of the Encounter Bay Tribe*. J. D. Woods, *The Native Tribes of South Australia*, (1879) 187. At certain times of the year, fish are declared taboo. This appears to be a selfish exploitation of unconscious strivings already rooted in the preconscious. In any event, we see in the food set aside for the men the prototype of the gods receiving the sacrifice, and in this infantile attitude the root of all later "religious" or "social" renunciation rites.

62. Connections with the custom of bride purchase also should not be discounted (cf., above) and as regards the nexus between the food forbidden the young men the custom of giving the best piece of the kill to the father-in-law, we remind the reader of the custom of the Aluridja where it is precisely the father-in-law who performs the rites of initiation. H. Basedow, *Anthropological Notes made on the South Australian Government North West Prospecting Expedition*, (*Transactions of the Royal Society of New South Wales*, XXVIII, 1904) 22. The father-in-law takes the father's place, just as the wife takes the mother's. See Reik, *Pubertätsriten der Wilden. Probleme*, (1919). On the connection between wild animals hunted and killed, and women, see Róheim, *Die wilde Jagd. Imago*, XII. *Australian Totemism*, (1925) 101. Dr. H. Goja, *Das Zersingen der Volkslieder*, *Imago*, VI.

63. See S. Freud, *Totem and Taboo*, (1914).

64. See also the material provided in Róheim's *Psychoanalysis es ethnologia. Ethnographia*, (1918), and, for more detail, *Australian Totemism*, (1925) 245.

65. A. Bastian, *Der Mensch in der Geschichte*, (1860) III, 216. (In spite of derogatory criticism in the *Année Sociologique*, X, 446), see also the profoundly reasoned comments by Petrucci, *Les Origines Naturelles de la Propriété*. (*Institut Solvay*, III, 1905) 14, concerning the "*réserves nutritives*" of plants and animals as primal forms of property.

66. Bastian, loc. cit. III, 218.

67. Ch. Darwin, *The Descent of Man*, (1898) I, 125.

68. H. Spencer, *The Principles of Sociology*, II, 540.

69. E. Westermarck, *The Origin and Development of the Moral Ideas*, (1908) II, 42 (ex. Kloss, *In den Andamans and Nicobars*, [1903] 240).

70. F. Krause, *In den Wildnissen Brasiliens*, (1911) 280. Among the Assiniboin, everything one has made oneself is one's property. J. D. Dorsdy, *Siouan Sociology*, (*Bureau of Ethnology, XV. Report*, 1897) 225.

71. Royal Geographical Society, II, 195, 196.

72. K. von den Steinen, *Unter den Naturvölkern Zentral-Brasiliens*, (1897) 285. "At an earlier time during the nomadic state, no property existed except personal equipment." B. Hagen, *Die Orang Kubu auf Sumatra*. (Veröff. Städt. Völker Museum II, 1908) 156. Kohler, *Zeitschrift für vergleichende Rechtswissenschaft*, VIII, 86. P. E. Goddard, *Life and Culture of the Hupa*, (*Univ. Cal. Rebl*. 1903/04) 59.

73. See W. E. Roth, *Notes on Government, Morals and Crime*, (*N. Q. E. Bull*. VIII, 1906) 9. (Footprints as mark of property, few personal possessions.) J. Fraser, *The Aborigines of New South Wales*, (1892) 67. (Markets, weapons, tools, marks of property). Spencer and Gillen, *Northern Tribes of Central Australia*, (1904) 632. (Trade in stone weapons.) A. W. Howitt, *The Native Tribes of South East Australia*, (1904) 718, 719. (exchange value of weapons and tools, prices in trade.) R. Andree, *Ethnographische Parallelen und Vergleiche*, (1889) II, 82, 83. W. E. Roth, *Transport and Trade*, (*North Queensland Ethnography*. Bull. 14, 1910) 17. W. E. Roth, *Huts and shelters*, (Bull., 16, 1910) 60. (On landed property of the tribe, see below.) Kohler, *Zeitschrift für vergleichende Rechtswissenschaft*, VII, 359.

74. H. Ling Roth, *The Aborigines of Tasmania*, (1899) 27.

75. Ling-Roth, loc. cit. 59.

76. Schoolcraft, *Information respecting the Indian Tribes of the United States*, (1853/56) I, 232.

77. W. McGee, *The Siouan Indians*, (*Bureau of Ethnology, XV. Report*, 1897) 177, 178.

78. R. Parkinson, *Dreissig Jahre in der Südsee*, (1907) 398.

79. R. Thurnwald, *Forschungen auf den Saomo-Inseln und dem Bismarck Archipel*, (1912) III, 34.

80. L. T. Hobhouse, *Morals in Evolution*, (1908) I, 332.

81. See also A. H. Post, *Grundriss der ethnologischen Jurisprudenz*, (1895) II, 602-614. Post, *Die Anfänge des Staats und Rechtslebens*, (1878) 276-298. W. Wundt, *Völkerpsychologie*, (1917). *Die Gesellschaft*, II, 86-87. See also 93 on magic ornaments and property. L. Dargun, *Ursprung und Entwicklungsgeschichte des Eigentums*, (*Zeitschrift für vergl. Rechtsw.*, V, 1884). I. Wilutzky, *Vorgeschichte des Rechts*, (1903) II, 63. Avebury, *The Origin of Civilization*, (1902) 478, 479.

82. R. Parkinson, *Dreissig Jahre in der Südsee*, (1907) 154.

83. E. V. Palmer, *The Australian Corroboree*. (*Nineteenth Century*, 1906) 317.

84. G. Grey, *Journals of two Expeditions to North West and Western Australia*, (1841) II, 304.

85. Spencer and Gillen, *The Northern Tribes of Central Australia*, (1904) 193.

86. The lines dividing preference, habit, and right waver. In the Hungarian Lowlands, the peasant not only has his own song but every one of them also has his own fairy tale. While he also knows those of others, he only tells a certain fairy tale, "his fairy tale," during work they all do together. Kalmany, *Hagyomauyok*. (*Traditions*), vol. II, p. VII.

87. A. C. Fletcher, *Property and Property Rights*. F. W. Hodge, *Handbook of American Indians North of Mexico*, (*Bureau Am. Ethn. Bull. XXX*, 1910) 308. See J. R. Swanton, *Contributions to the Ethnology of the Haida Jesup*, (*North Pacific Exp*. v, P. I, 1905). "Prerogatives of Families," 105-121. "Crest Songs," 180. "Ceremonials." F. Boas, *The Social Organization and the Secret Societies of the Kwakiutl*, (*Smithsonian Report*, 1897) 336.

88. Introjection in Ferenczi's meaning of the term, *Introjektion und Ubertragung*, (1901). When we discover in the psychoanalysis of neurotics or in dreams that every object has symbolic value, i.e., has become the embodiment of certain affective and libidinous contents, we observe in that fact an ontogenetic repetition of phylogenesis: originally, the psychic apperception of an object is identical with its being cathected by pleasurable qualities.

89. A. W. Howitt, *The Native Tribes of South East Australia*, (1904) 311, 689.

90. Ch. Keysser, *Aus dem Leben der Kaileute*. Neuhauss, *Deutsch New Guinea*, (1911) III, 17.

91. K. von den Steinen, *Unter den Naturvölkern Zentral-Brasiliens*, (1894) 306-310. The entire visible world is ruled by supernatural powers or "owners," each of whom holds sway within certain limits and is called "iuna" (viz., its or his "muk," which word signifies man and also owner or inhabitant). Dr. H. Rink, *Tales and Traditions of the Eskimo*, (1875) 37. See K. Breysig, *Die Völker ewiger Urzeit*, (1907) 435.

92. Here, there also exists a specific expression for all personal possessions ("ardi"). B. Spencer, *The Natives Tribes of Northern Australia*, (1914) 342.

93. H. Basedow, *Anthropological Notes made on the South Australian Expedition*, (*Trans. Roy. Soc. South Australia*, 1904) 35.

94. A. W. Howitt, *The Native Tribes of South East Australia*, (1904) 450, 458.

95. For more detail on this, see Róheim, *Australian Totemism*, (1925) 143.

96. K. von den Steinen, *Unter den Naturvölkern Zentral-Brasiliens*, (1897) 292.

97. K. Langloh Parker, *The Euahlayi Tribe*, (1905) 117.

98. Róheim, *Adalekok a magyar nepnithez* (Contributions to Hungarian folk belief), (1920) 64, note 2.

99. See Róheim, *Psychoanalysis es ethnologia*. (*Ethnographia*, 1918) XXIX, 88. L. Kaplan, *Psychoanalytische Probleme*, (1916) 55, 69. Concerning the inversion of psychic processes.

100. Everything is buried with the dead except stone axes. J. Dawson, *Australian Aborigines*, (1881) 62. A. W. Howitt, *The Native Tribes of South East Australia*, (1904) 455. Some brother inherits the weapons. W. E. Roth, *Burial ceremonies and Disposal of the Dead*, (*North Queensland Ethnography*, Bull. No. 9, 1907) 367.

101. A. C. Fletcher, *Land Tenure*. F. W. Hodge, *Handbook of American Indians*, (1910) I, 756.

102. L. Fison, *Land tenure in Fiji*, (*Journ. Anthr. Inst.* X, 351). See B. Thompson, *The Fijians*, (1908) 355. "Every tribe possesses a certain tract of country called after the name of the tribe." W. Landor, *The Bushmen*, (1847) 212. See K. L. Parker, *The Euahlayi Tribe*, (1905) 12.

103. E. J. Eyre, *Journals of Two Expeditions of Discovery into Central Australia*, (1845) II, 297. See also G. Grey, *Journals of two Expeditions of Discovery in North West and Western Australia*, (1841) II, 232-236. E. M. Curr, *Recollections of Squatting in Victoria*, (1883) 243.

104. R. Salvado, *Memoires Historiques sur l'Australie*, (1854) 256.

105. J. D. Lang, *Queensland*, (1861) 335, 336.

106. A. C. Haddon, *Cambridge Anthropological Expedition to Torres Straits*, (1904) V, 221.

107. Ibid., 193. A. C. Haddon, *Head Hunters, Black, White and Brown*, (1901) 19.

108. C. G. Seligman, *The Veddas*, (1911) 113, 114.

109. J. G. Withnell, *The Customs and Traditions of the Aboriginal Natives of North West Australia*, (Roebourne, 1901) 9. See R. Oberländer, *Die Eingeborenen der australischen Kolonie*, (Globus) IV, 281. Spencer and Gillen, *The Native Tribes of Central Australia*, (1904) 341. Blandowski, *Trans. Phil. Soc. Victoria*, L, 72. F. Bonney, *On some customs of the aborigines of the River Darling*, (*Journal Anthr. Inst.*) XIII, 128. Ch. Wilhelmi, *Manners and Customs of the Australian Natives*, (1862) 28.

110. W. E. Roth, *Marriage Ceremonies and Infant Life*, (*North Queensland Ethnography Bull*. 10, 1908) 4.

111. On organism and property, see R. Petrucci, *Les Origines naturelles de la Propriété*, (Institut Solvay, Fasc. 3, 1905) 15, "une trasition entre la réserve nutritive, fabriquée par l'organisme, et la réserve nutritive extérieure à l'animal."

112. A. W. Howitt, *The Native Tribes of South East Australia*, (1904) 196.

113. J. Mooney, *Sacred Formulas of the Cherokees*, (VXX. Report, 1891) 392.

114. See J. G. Frazer, *Taboo and the Perils of the Soul*, (1911) 126-130.

115. E. Clement, *Ethnographical Notes on the Western Aborigines*, (*Internationales Archiv für Ethnographie*, XVI, 1904) II.

116. Spencer and Gillen, *The Northern Tribes of Central Australia*, (1904) 341.

117. J. G. Frazer, *Totemism and Exogamy*, (1910) IV, 184.

118. Traffic in goods between two tribes is handled by two individuals who anxiously avoid contact with each other (neurotic reaction to close affinity), but of whom one is in possession of the "kalduke" (umbilical cord) of the other. G. Taplin, *The Narrinyeri*, (1878) 33. Turning over the umbilical cord is a prelude to turning over property.

119. W. E. Roth, *Superstition, Magic and Medicine*. (*North Queensland Ethnography Bull*. 5, 1903) 18.

120. See J. Dawon, *Australian Aborigines*, (1881) 7, 41. D. Rudesindo Salvado, *Memorie Storiche dell' Australia*, (1851) 310. E. J. Eyre, *Journals of Expeditions into Central Australia*, (1845) II, 324-325, 326. Collins, *An Account of the English Colony in New South Wales*, (1804) 364. J. Fraser, *The Aborigines of New South Wales*, (1892) 4. R. Brough-Smyth, *The Aborigines of Victoria*, (1878) I, 55. G. F. Angas, *Savage Life and Scenes in New Zealand*, (1847) I, 92. J. D. Woods, *The Native Tribes of South Australia*, (1879) 186, 187.

Strehlow and Leonhardi, *Die Aranda und Loritjastämme in Zentral-Australien* (Veröffentl. des Völkermuseums Frankfurt a.M. I, 1907) I, 53. Daisy M. Bates, *The Marriage Laws and some Customs of West Australian Aborigines*, (*Victorian Geographical Journal*, XXIII-XXIV) 49. J. G. Fraser, *Totemism and Exogamy*, I, 564.

121. Spencer and Gillen, *The Northern Tribes of Central Australia*, (1904) 27.

122. Spencer and Gillen, *The Native Tribes of Central Australia*, (1899) 16.

123. Ibid., 124. Strehlow, *Die Aranda und Loritjastämme in Zentral Australien*, (1908) II, 53.

124. Concerning the large and small totemic centers, the primitiveness of the Arunta, and whether we should view the localization of the totem as a primary or secondary phenomenon, see P. W. Schmidt, *Die Stellung Aranda. Zeitschrift für Ethnologie*, (1908) 882. A. van Gennep, *Mythes et legendes d'Australie*, (1905) p. XXXIV. A. Lang, *The Secret of the Totem*, (1905) 75. Since it seems unlikely that the Arunta are the original inhabitants of the regions occupied by them today, the localization of the totemic centers must be secondary since the distribution of the individual groups can only have occurred after immigration. But this does not preclude a later dislocalisation in the sense discussed above. On these questions and those of totemism generally, see Róheim, *Australian Totemism*, (1925).

125. See Fr. Gräbner, *Das Problem des Totemismus*, (*Korrespondenzblatt der deutschen Gesellschaft für Anthropologie, Ethnologie und Urgeschichte*, XLI, 1910) 81. E. Reuterskjöld, *Die Entstehung der Speisesakramente*, (1912) 88. B. Ankermann, *Das Problem des Totemismus*, (*Anthropos*, X/XI) 592. A. C. Haddon, *Address to the Section of Anthropology*, (Roy. Brit. Ass. Adv. of Science, 1902) 745. Haddon believes the totem to have originally been an animal species which constituted the main food of the tribe. It is noteworthy how the lines of origin of the concepts "food-property-totem" seem to converge at one point. The above hypothesis does not of course solve the strongly overdetermined phenomenon of totemism. Cf., *Australian Totemism*, (1925). (That work was actually written in 1918.)

126. Strehlow, *Die Aranda und Loritjastämme in Zentral Australien*, (1908) II, 52. Cf.: "One origin frequently assigned by the natives to these family names is that they were derived from some vegetable or animal being very common in the district which the family inhabited and that hence the name of this animal or vegetable became applied to the family." G. Grey, *Journals of two Expeditions to North West and Western Australia*, (1844) H. 225. Grey, *Vocabulary of the Dialect of South Western Australia*, (1844) 4. R. Brown, *Description*

of the Natives of King George Sound, (*Journal of the Royal Geographical Society*) I, 42-44. In mythological times, the Upper Bridge River Country was inhabited by the Deer people who were afterwards transformed into deer. For that reason, deer are most plentiful in that country at the present day. J. Teit, *The Lillooet Indians*, (*Jesup North Pacific Exp*. V) 275.

127. Not of the two-class system, of course, but of the connection between a region and a human group. Spencer and Gillen, *The Northern Tribes of Central Australia*, (1904) 28, 29.

128. See the books by Spencer, Gillen, Strehlow, Leonhardi, A. R. Brown, Basedow, etc. More detail in *Australian Totemism*.

129. Cf., the totemistic marks of property. R. Andree, *Ethnographische Parallelen und Vergleiche*, (1889) II, 82, and on the so-called sub-totems. "The objects, which are claimed by each totem, are also called mir (totem) but no one is named after them. They only *belong* to a person because they belong to the totem to which the person belongs. Thus one of my informants was Krokitch ngaui and therefore claimed kangaroos as belonging to him. Another man of the same class and totem claimed Bunjil as belonging to him, but he is not Bunjil and does not take it for a name; he is ngaui but not Bunjil. *The true totem owns him, but* he owns the sub-totem." A. W. Howitt, *The Native Tribes of South East Australia*, (1904) 123. The verb "to belong" refers both to a property relation and also a general belonging together. But in the expression "to own" the idea of property is very clearly expressed. Accordingly, what we have is that among tribes which have sub-totems, i.e., where all of nature is incorporated in the totemistic system in the form of sub-totems (among the Wotjobaluk, for example, the main totem "sun" includes as sub-totems Alpha Crucis, the plain turkey, the opossum, the grey and red kangaroo, and a tuber) someone is the "owner" of various animal species, and even of a star (the members of the sun totem are all "owners" of the gray kangaroo and of Alpha Crucis). On this level, we are therefore not as yet dealing with property in the practical sense but merely with a feeling of belonging together which expresses itself vis-à-vis the principal totem (the representative of the father imago) in a more passive, and vis-à-vis the sub-totem in a more active form. Through these sub-totems, man fictitiously takes all of nature as his own, and this fictitious property stands in inverse relation to the actual influence he can bring to bear on his environment. Here we find the fiction of the domination over nature as an overcompensation of the opposite, the total dependence on nature. In the course of development, we note a progressive diminution of the fiction and a corresponding strengthening of the reality. The prohibition regarding the eating of the totem (in this respect, see various attitudes toward totem and sub-totem in Fison and Howitt, *Kamilaroi and Kurnai*, [1880] 169) is the neurotic

reverse side of the desire to do precisely that. The wish to take possession of the totem, especially the woman of the totemic clan, encounters an inhibition; she is negative property. Since we could also show the presence of a libidinal nexus to the outside world in the act of taking possession of things, we can appreciate Malinowski's view according to which a sort of class relationship between man and woman exists in Australia, that woman is man's first property (Malinowski, *The family among the Australian Aborigines*, [1913] 288). Here we should also point to the inner connection between the chain of hypotheses "horde-sexual promiscuity-original communism" on the one hand, and "family-monogamy-level of individual search for food" on the other (the tendency to "communize women," partly falsely imputed to communists in our time, but also partly something that does exist among them is to be understood as the real, unconscious motive of the entire movement). If therefore we find in our sources that children and especially girls are the property of their parents, women the property of their husbands (cf., the custom of bridal purchase, etc.), this characterizes not only the share of the reality principle (power relationship) in the relation between parents and children (or men and women), but also the libidinous nexus between owner and property. See H. J. Nieboer, *Slavery as an industrial system*, (1900) 8, 426.

130. This is an ambivalent attitude toward the mother's body. The Nanjaa tree of the Arunta and the Anjea spot of the Pennefather River inhabitants are both psychologically and linguistically the same (the mythical place of birth). On the Pennefather River, this is precisely the place where the boy may hunt, among the Arunta it is the place where he may not. This ambivalent attitude derives from the Oedipus complex (cf., above on hunting and coitus). Spencer and Gillen, *The Native Tribes of Central Australia*, 133. Roth, *Superstition*, 18.

131. An early mystical form of the concept of property is already noted by Malinowski but not explained by him. B. Malinowski, *The Family among Australian Aborigines*, (1913) 144, 146, 150.

132. R. H. Codrington, *The Melanesians*, (1891) 176.

133. C. G. Seligman, *The Melanesians of British New Guinea*, (1910) 183-185. The dangerous spots were considered taboo, and as belonging to the Nuliayoq. F. Boas, *Second Report on the Eskimo of Baffin Land and Hudson Bay*, (*Bulletin of the American Museum of Natural History*, 1907) 498.

134. H. Berkusky, *Das Bodenrecht der primitiven Stämme Indonesiens*, (*Zeitschrift für vergleichende Rechtswissenschaft*, 1912) 65. About ancestors as spirits of sacred mountains, see Andrian-Werburg, *Der Höhencult*, (1891) 144, 145 et passim.

135. A. Oldfield, *On the Aborigines of Australia*, (*Transactions of the Ethnological Society*, III, 1865) 252.

136. W. E. Roth, *Tabu and other forms of restriction*, (*North Queensland Ethnography Bull.* II, 1898) 77. Cf., "Should a child of another family have been born on the estate it is looked upon as one of the family and has equal rights to share in the land. Each family has exclusive rights by inheritance to a part of the tribal lands which is named after its owner and his family and every child born on it must be named after something on the property." Dawson, *Australian Aborigines*, (1881) 7.

137. "Individuals claimed special favorite trees as their own." J. Matthew, *Eaglehawk and Crow*, (1899) 90. Particularly trees in which honey is found. See K. L. Parker, *The Euahlayi Tribe*, (1905) 144. R. Brough-Smyth, *The Aborigines of Victoria*, (Melbourne, 1878) I, 145. "A married woman had selected a certain tree according to their practice when in the bush, which tree, in such case, is considered representative of the person who makes choice of it and is regarded as their inviolable property at all times to be held sacred." H. Ling-Roth, *The Aborigines of Tasmania*, (1899) 60. In Indonesia also, the first beginnings of family- and private property center on fruit-bearing trees (in contrast to tribal property). H. Berkusky, *Das Bodenrecht*, (*Zeitschrift für vergleichende Rechtswissenschaft*, 1912) 51, 54. A particular importance also attaches to the specific property rights to swans' eggs. Fison and Howitt, *Kamilaroi and Kurnai*, (1880) 226, 232.

138. C. G. Jung, *Wandlungen und Symbole der Libido* (*Transformations and Symbolisms of the Libido*), (1910) 250, 254.

139. On initiation and the knocking out of teeth as symbolic castration, see Róheim, *Spiegelzauber*, (1919) 11, 12. Reik, *Probleme der Religionspsychologie*, (1919) 59. The old men will allow the youth to receive a woman (symbolically, the earth) only after he has been symbolically castrated. This symbolic castration is the sacrifice he brings to avoid real castration. From the analysis of neurotics, we know that some react to the loss of property by fear of castration.

140. A. C. Fletcher, *Land Tenure*, (*Handbook of American Indians*, 1911) 756. "When a man has selected a site for a new garden, he marks the place, and bespeaks or as the natives say, betroths the ground." A. C. Werner, *The Natives of British Central Africa*, (1906) 179. (Additional material is being set aside for an essay dealing with this particular problem.)

141. F. Burger, *Die Küsten und Bergvölker der Gazellehalbhinsel*, (1913) 52. Yet one must be careful not to overestimate the universal validity of the pattern and must also not underestimate local differences. On Jap Island, for example, land is pure private property, and even the idea of family property is unknown among its inhabitants. "Even the most barren grassy plot has its owner, and everyone can

define the borders of his tract with precision." W. Müller, *Jap. Ergebnisse der Hamburger Südsee Expedition*, (1917) I, 249. But a propertyless class also already exists there, the "milirai" of the serfs, ibid., 250, 751. "Each man in the mountains would have a patch of oaks (trees!) . . . and no one else was allowed to go there and gather acorns." Du Bois, *The Religion of the Luiseno Indians*, (1908) 103.

142. Ch. Keysser, *Aus dem Leben der Kaileute*. Nehuauss, *Deutsch Neu-Guinea*, (1911) III, 13. "Land as land has no value. Its value arose only from its potential produce. The thing treated with most consideration among primitive peoples is human labor and the products of it." B. Thomson, *The Fijians*, (1908) 364.

143. R. Parkinson, *Dreissig Jahre in der Südsee*, (1907) 158.

144. C. G. Seligman, *The Melanesians of British New Guinea*, (1910) 467, 468.

145. R. H. Codrington, *The Melanesians*, (1891) 62, 63.

146. R. W. Williamson, *The Mafulu of British New Guinea*, (1912) 117.

147. B. Hagen, *Unter den Papuas*, (1899) 197, 198.

148. H. H. Romilly, *From my Verandah in New Guinea*, (1889) 269, 270.

149. Berkusky, *Das Bodenrecht der primitiven Stämme Indonesiens*, (*Zeitschrift für vergleichende Rechtswissenschaft*, 1912) 49, 50.

150. A. C. Fletcher, *Land Tenure*, (*Handbook*, 1911) I, 756.

151. K. von den Steinen, *Unter den Naturvölkern Zentral-Brasiliens*, (1897) 285.

152. B. Grabb, *An Unknown People in an Unknown Land*, (1911) 188.

153. F. Krause, *In den Wildnissen Brasiliens*, (1911) 323.

154. Gouldsbury-Sheane, *The Great Plateau of Northern Rhodesia*, (1911) 60.

155. Berkusky, *Bodenrecht*, (*Ztsch. für vergl. Rechtsw.*, 1912) 51.

156. Codrington, *The Melanesians*, (1891) 175.

157. Berkusky, loc. cit. 65, 66.

158. The whole of the land is owned by one or other of the chiefs and the boundary of one chief's property is the beginning of the next chief's estate. H. H. Weeks, *Among the primitive Bakongo*, (1914) 179. "Prince . . . or really owner of the earth." E. Pechuel Loesche,

Die Loango Expedition, (1903) II, 175. "La terre appartient au chef comme représentant de la sous-tribe et ne peut être vendue." E. Torday and T. A. Joyce, *Les Bushongo* (*Doc. Ethn. conc. les. Pop. du Congo Belge* II, I, 1910) 90. Property among the western Dene is private and personal such as hereditary estates or hunting grounds the limits of which were always clearly defined. The other men of the clan were supposed to hunt with and for the tenezas, receiving from them such of the spoils of the chase as they are pleased to bestow upon them or permit them to retain." C. Hill-Tout, *British North America*, (1907) 147.

Translated by Michael Shaw

Contribution 10

Yurok Shell Money and "Pains": A Freudian Interpretation

S. H. Posinsky

In the course of an intensive study of Yurok ritual (Posinsky, 1954), done primarily in terms of interaction theory, the writer was impressed by a remarkable if inverted similarity between the dentalium shells (the aboriginal money of the Yurok[1]) and the *telogetl* (the material but animate "pains" which are the primary cause or manifestation of illness among them). It was suggested that the *telogetl* or "pains"—which are finger-like in shape and covered with blood or slime when extracted and displayed by the shaman—are suspiciously similar in appearance to dentalia, except that the *telogetl* are maleficent rather than beneficent (ibid., pp. 161-165). Since Yurok values and morality are couched in financial terms, virtue and asceticism are expected to result inevitably in dentalia (wealth), whereas violations of morality and taboo produce the *telogetl* (that is, the maleficent dentalia) in the victim's body.

As the literature was insufficiently corroborative, the problem was kept in abeyance. However, a further consideration of the data confirms the original impression but necessitates a psychoanalytic level of interpretation and a somewhat different hypothesis: that the dentalia and *telogetl* are respectively the positive and negative aspects of an infantile introject, the breast and/or penis.

It has been established psychoanalytically that these parts of the body, or their psychic representations, undergo a symbolic equation—an *assimilation*, as Abraham (1924, p. 490) describes it—and that such symbolism is generally overdetermined.[2] It is also known that "other parts of the body, such as the finger, the foot, hair, faeces and buttocks, can be made to stand for those two organs" (ibid.), and that money frequently symbolizes the breast-penis equation. Thus, Onians (1951, pp. 124-125) notes that *caput* ("head"; our "capital") refers to money which produces "seeds" (interest); and he writes: "The custom of making money-boxes in the form of the female breast and other shapes of fruitfulness . . . seems to derive from the same thought" (ibid., p. 124, n.).

Unfortunately, the Yurok ethnographies are so deficient in primary data on anal functioning that the additional excremental quality of both the shell money and "pains" can be elucidated only by inference. At any rate, note has already been made of the physical resemblance of the shell money and "pains," in addition to the moral antithesis which exists between them in consciousness. After touching on several preliminary considerations, the writer will return to this problem and attempt to prove that the shell money and the material "pains" refer *unconsciously* to the breast-penis equation.

II

Yurok culture, which is patently anal, is marked by unusual legalistic tendencies and litigiousness (Kroeber, 1925, 1926); by a zealous concern with "face," honor, and prestige; and by a tendency to flare up at the slightest provocation, whether real or imagined. There appears, in fact, to be an alternation between meek passivity and almost "manic" aggressiveness. Daily life is ritualized to a marked degree; the sexes sleep apart (women and children in the "living house," post-adolescent males in the "sweat house"); there is a taboo on sexual intercourse for six months of each year, beginning with the autumn rains; and there is a great emphasis on reserve, self-control, and dignity. Nevertheless, the society is described as "tense" and "anarchistic" (Kroeber, 1925, pp. 4, 38).

In cultural terms, the anarchy rests on the simplicity of the subsistence and industrial techniques and on family self-sufficiency in a large sedentary population where little co-operation, exchange, or mutual interdependence is required. The great World Renewal rites and the Wealth Display dances, whatever their psychic determinants and consequences, involve feasts and the lending of dance regalia, and operate against familial and local self-sufficiency. And the crassness of the Wealth Display dances does not disguise the fact that these contests, like the ball games between villages and the related gambling, serve to channel intense and disruptive rivalries into socially controlled oppositions which run their course outside of subsistence areas or war.

The unresolved struggle for prestige is carried on with wealth and property but also with numerous symbolic privileges. Thus, among the coastal Yurok, certain families possess and jealously guard the right to take the flippers when a sea lion is killed, and the right to take a specific number of cuts from a stranded whale. The flipper rights are transferable, though not without anguish, and are the basis of a celebrated feud in which they were demanded, and finally ceded, as compensation for a murder (Spott and Kroeber, 1942, pp. 182-199). The division of a stranded whale is roughly proportional to status, and the rich are permitted to take double the amount available to the poor. The rich man's privilege in this matter is symbolized by the packstrap with which he drags home his portion of the whale. The rich and poor of the village take their allotted shared in prescribed order, and the remainder is left to visitors from communities which are not included in this division. Any violations of established procedure lead to brawls and killings. The prestige factors are so strong that a man who exceeds his rightful cut by a few inches may be killed for his presumptuousness.

The florescence of the World Renewal rites is certainly correlated with the absence of social or political controls outside the family. It may also be, though the data are lacking in time depth, that the more complex World Renewal rites—for example, the one at Kepel (Waterman and Kroeber, 1938)—are a response to the disruptions produced by the coming of the Americans to California.

In a deeper sense, as the writer has indicated elsewhere (Posinsky, n. d.), the inordinate Yurok passion for wealth, like the unrealistic fear of starvation, may be seen as a reaction to an infantile deprivation. Thus, pregnant women work hard, eat sparingly, and avoid prolonged sleep. Late in her pregnancy, the woman is required to rub her abdomen in the midafternoon in order to keep the fetus awake. (This is the period of greatest interaction within the family, and apparently also a period of great magical danger.) During delivery, the mother must keep her mouth closed, or the fetus will not leave her body.[3] The newborn infant is not nursed for the first five or ten days (or more), and it "is fed only a little water in which hazel or pine nuts have been rubbed, and which looks milky" (Kroeber, 1925, p. 45; cf. Erikson, 1943, p. 285). The explanation is that "if the child . . . were to take nourishment from its mother, the Yurok believe that its jaws would become affected and it would soon starve" (Kroeber, 1925, p. 45).

The infant is permitted to nurse in due time; but it does not partake of any other food until weaning, and it is not even permitted to "steal" a drink of water during its baths. Weaning is early by American Indian standards and must occur no later than the child's first birthday, though it should take place ideally at six or seven months. From birth until it is able to walk, the child is forcibly kept awake from midafternoon until sundown. Sleep during this period, the time of the main family meal, puts the child in danger of being bewitched, from which death is expected to follow.[4] Creeping, which lifts the dietary and sexual taboos imposed on new parents, is encouraged: The feet are left free in the cradle basket from the time of birth, and the infant's legs are massaged daily from the twentieth day on. Bowel training is instituted as soon as the child can walk, when it is led out of the house by an older sibling for bowel movements.[5]

III

It has been hypothesized in the foregoing that the dentalium money represents the positive aspect of an infantile introject—"good body contents," in Kleinian terms—and that the symbolism, deriving from the various levels of psychosexual development, is overdetermined. It has been noted also that, in consciousness at least, the Yurok shell money is antithetical to food and genitality. Thus, the Yurok eat moderately and conserve their genital resources in order to acquire or retain dentalia; this is a conscious formula for wealth which they practise in their daily behavior and in magic. Unconsciously, however, there is a synonymity of dentalium-breast-feces-penis, with anal retentivity the dominant theme.

Kroeber (1948, p. 618) has noted that the anal-type description fits the Yurok strikingly; and Róheim (1950) has summarized their anality in the following formula: "Hold everything inside, extend *sphincter morality* (Ferenczi) both backward to the oral and forward to the genital zone. The most stingy of all human beings—that is what I would call the Yurok" (p. 272; his italics).[6]

However, just as there is a danger of emptiness, there is a comparable danger of fullness—of holding everything inside (cf. Burlingham, 1955); and it is this dilemma which places the Yurok in a tenuous psychic balance. Róheim (1950) has pointed out certain aspects of this dilemma in his interpretation of the Yurok passion for wealth:

> The men have to become rich, i.e., mothers full of "*good body contents*" (food, feces, embryo, etc.), because they

> have been frustrated by their own mothers. Hence their oral aggression is directed against the mother's body, and what follows is the corresponding talio anxiety. They will be "scooped out," empty—i.e., poor. To be rich means to be full of *good body contents*, i.e., food stabilized into a fecal symbol. It also means to be magically and ambivalently identical, both with a *full*, i.e., gratifying, mother and with a bad, withholding mother (p. 275; his italics).

But Róheim's interpretation is incomplete because he stresses only the alimentary quality of Yurok wealth; and in connection with the dentalia he writes: "The shells themselves are probably female symbols" (ibid.). On a pre-Oedipal level the shell money is certainly equivalent to a positive introject, or "good body contents"; but it also develops a phallic component which reinforces the previous ones. (Similarly, as will be noted presently, the *telogetl* or "pains" constitute a negative introject or "bad body contents," with components that also mark the several phases of psychosexuality.)

The most powerful evidence about the phallic aspect of the dentalia comes from the stringent taboo on sexual intercourse within the "living house":

> The Yuork hold a strong conviction that dentalium money and the congress of the sexes stand in a relation of inherent antithesis. This is the reason given for the summer mating season: the shells would leave the house in which conjugal desires were satisfied, and it is too cold and rainy to sleep outdoors in winter. To preserve his money, in other words to prevent his becoming a spendthrift, a man bathes after contact with his wife, and is careful not to depart from the natural positions. Strangely enough, the Yurok have a saying that a man who can exercise his virility 10 times in one night will become extraordinarily wealthy; but there are not wanting those who consider this ideal unattainable by modern human beings (Krober, 1925, p. 41).

It may also be that intercourse away from the house is necessary in order to avoid children's witnessing a primal scene.[7] That is, the parents project their own infantile aggressiveness and sexual curiosity onto their young children, who in turn become the potential cannibals, voyeurs, and castrators. Interestingly enough, this compulsive avoidance, with its Old Testament rigor, is negated by the unrestrained license and aggressive exhibitionism which prevail during the summer—when food is most plentiful and conscious and unconscious enemies may be taunted with wealth and bountifully appeased with food. Thus, conscious rivals (and mere onlookers) are taunted and feted in the World Renewal rites; so, unconsciously, are the basic enemies, originally the parents, but also—by displacement and projection—the children.

At any rate, the basic taboo, the postulated flight of the shell money (which here refers to semen or penis), and the poverty which will result inevitably from intercourse in the living house and from a failure to bathe after coitus—these are patent rationalizations which spring from a deep-seated castration anxiety. And, as always, this castration anxiety is overdetermined. It is intensified during the Oedipal phase, but it is very important in the pre-Oedipal period and may be traced to the original oral trauma. Thus, to be poor means originally to be hungry or empty, but it also comes to mean *to be without a penis*.

There is, again, a danger in emptiness (starvation, lack of love, poverty, castration, death), *and* a fear of fullness. The danger of fullness grows not only from the projection of oral aggressions onto the mother (and father) and the consequent fear of retaliation, but also from the ambivalence involved in fullness—which means both good and bad body contents. Thus, the fear of emptiness makes the Yurok greedy and retentive, while the fear of fullness makes them moderate eaters who must keep the alimentary passage open: Death is ascribed to a *visceral constriction*, and the material but animate "pains" are both *obstructions* and *parasites*.

As indicated, ambivalence toward the body contents

(and toward the internalized parental images) is laid down during the oral-anal period and is reinforced by the negative and positive aspects of the Oedipus complex. There is thus an identification with, and an ambivalence toward, both sexes, with a marked tendency of males toward the avoidance of women; this is accompanied by a homosexual, but aim-inhibited, turning and submission to men in the exclusively masculine (and ascetic) atmosphere of the sweat house. In fact, the paucity of evidence about conflicts between fathers and sons would appear to indicate that the basic anxiety is pre-Oedipal and grows from the wish to rob the mother's body of its contents with this wish being projected onto others and being reinforced by the castration fears (and wishes) of the Oedipal phase (cf. Jacobson, 1953; Loewald, 1951; Muensterberger, 1955, pp. 14-17).

The resulting personality is remarkably *akin* to the configuration found in a compulsion neurosis. The libido has regressed, or is fixated, at the anal-sadistic stage; while excessive cleanliness, conscientiousness, and the like are reaction formations. (So is Yurok generosity with food, which results from an unconscious identification with the withholding mother.)

One can now understand the tenseness of this society; the heavy ritualization of daily life, which goes so far as to place a taboo on the use of personal names outside the immediate family; the emphasis on reserve and self-control, and the fluctuations between passivity and aggressiveness. Tempers flare up, feuds and lawsuits are instituted at the slightest pretext; but the encroachments of the white man were ignored, and the Yurok remained detached and apathetic (when they were not actively directing the white aggressor toward fellow-tribesmen and neighbors). They are given to tantrums and anal sadism when such behavior is safe, but they can be remarkably passive and submissive when force (or authority) is demonstrated. Similarly, they aspire to Herculean sexuality and achieve it, partly in fantasy, partly in the carnival atmosphere of the summer festivals; but they are fixated in the *preparatory and defensive asceticism*.

As may be expected, anality overshadows whatever genital sexuality they achieve. Thus, to "do business" refers both to a bowel movement and sexual intercourse (Erikson, 1943, p. 285). This is notably similar to the "Protestant" or "Puritan" ethos and emphasis on "doing one's duty" in life, with "duty" becoming a childish word for excrement. It is significant that a number of "Protestant" or "capitalist" traits may be delineated in Yurok culture (Goldschmidt, 1951), and that Brierley (1951, pp. 177, 214) correlates the Protestant or Puritan tradition with the *maximum denigration of the sexual instinct.* Be that as it may, sex is a dangerous and dirty business for the Yurok; but it is also aggressive and manly, both in a phallic and anal sense. Nevertheless, the anal contradictions cannot be resolved; for genital sexuality may eliminate the dangers of fullness, but it also results in emptiness (starvation, poverty, castration).

The alimentary dilemma (fullness vs. emptiness) explains many of the paradoxes of Yurok behavior: the fear of starvation in the midst of plenty; the tendency to eat moderately and to accumulate large amounts of food; the generosity with food and the miserliness with everything else; the anti-genital attitudes and the periodic license; and the accumulation, by borrowing and hoarding, of large amounts of wealth which have no realistic value in terms of adaptation and survival, and are never consumed, but which are aggressively exhibited and thus arouse great fears of envy, damage, and robbery.

The conscious antithesis between wealth, on the one hand, and food and genitality, on the other, like the unconscious need to avoid fullness and emptiness, is further revealed by the need to abstain completely from food and water when practising wealth magic, and by the general emphasis on slow and modest eating which must be accompanied by thoughts of wealth:

> The father teaches the boys and the mother the girls how to eat. They are told to take a little food with their spoon, to put it into their mouth slowly, to put the spoon back into the eating basket, and to chew slowly and thoroughly, meanwhile thinking always of becoming rich.

> Then the food is to be swallowed and the child may again reach, without haste, for the spoon. Nobody is supposed to talk during the meal, so that everybody can concentrate on thoughts of wealth. While there is still food in one's basket or in one's mouth, one does not ask for more. If a child eats too fast, the father or the mother silently takes his basket away from him and the child is supposed to rise silently and leave the house (Erikson, 1943, p. 286).

These and other restraints generate additional aggression against the mother (and/or father), as Róheim (1950, p. 273) has noted, but they also require a stronger repression of the basic infantile hatred. Since the "pains" result primarily from a violation of food taboos (but also from incestuous fantasies), the inverse relationship between dentalia and "pains" grows clearer: Slow, modest, *unaggressive* eating appeases the withholding mother and results in the acquisition of her favors (wealth, good body contents), while aggressive eating results in hunger, poverty, "pains" (bad body contents). Thus, once again, the ambivalence which is inherent in the infantile introjection and identification necessitates an avoidance both of fullness and emptiness.

The literature indicates considerable hostility between the sexes, with a powerful drive toward (and avoidance of) incest. Since the human race, according to Yurok mythology, was sired on a bitch, intercourse with a dog, here a kind of incest, is the ultimate offense and will result in the communal delegation of a villager to slay the offender. This is perhaps the only occasion when the village functions as a political unit, and no indemnities are payable for such a killing; otherwise, self-help and retaliation are in effect.

The rigid dichotomy of the sexes, and the underlying hostility and castration anxiety which it reflects, begin at birth and are not permitted to lapse even in old age, as they do in many cultures. Thus, the tattooed chin of a woman keeps her separate and apart until death: "They say that an untattooed woman looks like a man when she grows old" (Kroeber, 1925, p. 78). Similarly, in Yurok mythological projections, the unnamed *woge* or prehuman ancestors—who occupy certain of the rocks along the river—cannot abide menstruating women or corpses. The result is that if there is a menstruating woman or a corpse in a boat, the woman or corpse must be removed from the boat at these points, carried around the rocks, and returned to the boat.

The power of this castration anxiety is indicated by its persistence. After the century of intensive acculturation which followed the inundation of northwestern California by the gold-seeking "Forty-niners," most of Yurok culture has disappeared; but the menstrual taboos remain: "The understanding between the sexes in these matters goes so far (or can go so far) that one informant defined a 'nice girl' as one who always tells the boy beforehand when she is menstruating, thus saving him ritual trouble and subsequent loss of working time" (Erikson, 1943, p. 298).

Love, even for one's wife, is considered an aberration; and, like affection for a dog, it exhausts one's emotional reserves (or libidinal bank account, as is noted in certain neuroses) and results inexorably in weakness and poverty. A benevolent contempt is expressed toward women in general. Based on the infantile abandonment and colored by a fear of rejection and genital injury, this contempt is really a mixture of hostility and dependence. The genital aims are devoid of emotional commitment, even in marriage, and the rationalization is that women are little better than animals. (Was not the human race sired on a bitch? What can we expect from our women—are they not bought?) The social significance of the bride-price is thus reworked. The bride-price is not, of course, a commercial transaction but the means by which one kinship group relates itself to another and by which a man can appreciably raise his own prestige and the status of his future children. Nevertheless, the social meaning of the bride-price becomes overlaid with hostile sexual attitudes.

Thus, women are inferior (damaged, castrated), yet sexually seductive and promiscuous, like bitches. But sexuality leads to poverty, starvation, and castration, with the threats emanating both from the mother and father. The pronounced castration anxiety leads to anal-passive behavior (an identification with the mother and a self-castration), but this is as dangerous as the anal-aggressive behavior, which leads to retaliatory sadism.

Although the female psyche is inadequately explored in the literature on the Yurok, an identification with the hostile and withholding mother appears indicated by the unusual deprivations which are inflicted on the newborn infant. Significantly, the unconscious rejection of children is paralleled by a conscious wish for 20 *children* (10 boys, 10 girls). This theme enters symbolically into the female puberty ceremony (Kroeber, 1925, p. 45), with 20 sticks being laid out on the river bank. The female wish for great fecundity appears to be another demonstration of the fact that *one is not empty* (or without a penis, since the woman also identifies with her father and her sons).

Since sexual intercourse must take place out of doors, lest the dentalia take offense and run away, only the most ardorous brave the cold rains which mark the six months beginning in the mid-autumn. Chapple and Coon (1942) explain it in this way:

> Among the Yurok of northern California, where there is an elaborate development of a system of ritual gifts within the political hierarchy, sexual intercourse is forbidden during the winter, which is the time of gift making (p. 478).

Unfortunately for this interpretation, there is no political hierarchy, and the incipient political organization is insignificant. Men lend each other dance regalia and other heirlooms for the competitive dances; but outright gifts are absolutely not reciprocal and are intended to ingratiate the giver with a desired ally.

The *de facto* taboo on sexual intercourse is ascribed by the Yurok to the bad winter weather and the need to retain dentalium money. A sedentary society with high standards of craftsmanship could have resolved these difficulties technologically, but the Yurok chose not to, preferring to inculcate anti-genital attitudes which are reinforced both by physical discomfort and by strivings for wealth. The simplest solution would be for them to keep the dentalia in the sweat house rather than the living house, especially since virtuous behavior connected with the sweat house is rewarded in dentalia. However, virtue really means asceticism; and the sweat house is exclusively masculine, while the dentalia have a female (alimentary) as well as a male (phallic) symbolism. It would also be very easy to erect a lean-to or other shelter where married couples could retreat; but this is not done.

It has been emphasized that the basic castration anxiety stems from the pre-Oedipal period and is the result of hostility toward the phallic mother or the undifferentiated mother and father, with the negative and positive Oedipus complex reinforcing this repressed helplessness, hostility, and guilt. On a reality level, the wealth of the mature males inculcates the same hostility and submissiveness in the young. As youths and men are socially and sexually superior to women, so older men exact a considerable degree of deference from boys and young men. In view of the wealth and power which are lodged in the hands of the father (and the father's brothers), young men are slow in achieving social and sexual maturity. The older men may be hesitant to part with their wealth in obtaining brides for the younger men (this would be especially true where there are few if any marriageable daughters in the same family); and at the same time, the older men are themselves involved in Oedipal rivalries: the never-ending struggle for wealth and prestige, as in the Wealth Display dances.

Since kinship groupings above the extended family are absent, a young man must cling to his father and paternal uncles for protection and status, and he may easily be disinherited in favor of a younger brother, a cousin, a paternal nephew, or a lifelong friend of his father. Wealth being obtained by inheritance, not by individual effort, men of all ages are urged to practise wealth magic. Young men in particular are expected to fast, abstain from sexual relationships, work hard, and observe all the taboos in order to acquire dentalia. Since the results may be expected only in old age, these various observances serve to limit the modest relationships between the men and their orally frustrating and castrating mothers (wives) and to inculcate submission to the fathers. The pursuit of wealth thus serves as a life-long instrument of social control, in addition to rationalizing the power and prestige of the rich families and of mature men in general.

The wealth magic is obviously oral in origin and involves a hallucinatory wish-fulfillment similar to that practised by a hungry infant. Although a controlled regression is involved, the megalomanic confusion between subject and object becomes clear, as does their ultimate identification:

> The persistence with which the Yurok desire wealth is extraordinary. They are firmly convinced that persistent thinking of money will bring it. Particularly is this believed to be true while one is engaged in any sweat-house occupation. As a man climbs the hill to gather sweat-house wood—always a meritorious practise, in the sense that it tends to bring about the fulfillment of wishes—he puts his mind on dentalia. He makes himself see them along the trail, or hanging from fir trees eating the leaves. When he sees a tree that is particularly full of these visioned dentalia, he climbs it to cut its branches just below the top. In the sweat house he looks until he sees more money shells, perhaps peering in at him through the door. When he goes down to the river he stares into it, and at last may discern a shell as large as a salmon, with gills working like those of a fish. Young men were recommended to undergo these practises for 10 days at a time, meanwhile fasting and exerting themselves with the utmost vigor, and not allowing their minds to be diverted by communication with other people, particularly women. They would then become rich in old age (Kroeber, 1925, pp. 40-41).

Interestingly enough, this type of wealth magic is an important part of the training of shamans, who are predominantly women. Although the wealth magic of men aims at a hallucinatory incorporation of, and identification with, the good mother, the shamanistic data will presently indicate that the phallic component of the dentalia is equally strong. For the present, however, it may be noted that the various deprivations practised, both by men and by shamans, in their wealth magic aim at achieving a reward—dentalia, or the positive aspect of the breast and penis—in those very areas where the sacrifice and atonement are greatest (that is, by oral *and* genital asceticism). Thus, oral and genital needs are deferred so that they may be more adequately fulfilled at some future date. This childish aspiration, however, is never realized; it is a compromise dictated by the needs of a compulsive and ambivalent anality which seeks solely to resolve its own dilemmas (fullness and emptiness; sadism and masochism).

In view of the fact that the symbolism of the dentalia is reinforced at each level of psychosexuality and is consequently overdetermined, it is easy to adduce considerable supplementary evidence about the basic breast-penis equation. Thus, the shell money is anthropomorphized, like salmon and deer; and it is deified in the person of Pelintsiek ("Great Dentalium"), a culture hero who sometimes assumes certain of the broadly institutory functions which are ordinarily ascribed to the two dominant *woge*, Wohpekumeu and Pulelukwerek (Kroeber, 1925, p. 74). Sometimes the dentalia appear in a female role, when, at the transition from *woge* times to the beginning of the human world, the personalized shells enter boats, and sing and dance as they leave their upriver home and go downriver into the ocean *and away from Yurok territory*, with the larger and more valuable shells going the greatest distance (Spott and Kroeber, 1942, pp. 249-250). This myth "rates the shells in value, tells where they are to be found, and explains why the precious ones now occur only at a distance" (ibid., p. 250); but it also reveals the loss of the love object at the *beginning of the world* (at birth). The breastlike character of the dentalia, together with the nostalgic yearning for them, is also revealed when "they speak in their traditions of the shells living at the downstream and upstream ends of the world, where strange but enviable peoples live who suck the flesh of the univalves" (Kroeber, 1925, p. 23).

At the same time, oral aggression—rapid eating, gluttony, cunnilinctus—will drive away the dentalia (and also the salmon and other personified foodstuffs); while the dentalia, like the salmon and deer, also suffer from castration fears and will not enter or remain in a house where there is a menstruating woman. The phallic aspect of the dentalia, which is so strikingly revealed in the taboo on intercourse within the living house, is also clarified by the sacred narratives. Thus, there is an important culture-hero of primordial times, Wohpekumeu ("Widower across the Ocean"), who constantly pursued women, often unsuccessfully, and "according as his wooings resulted, he made or marred good fishing places" (Kroeber, 1925, p. 73). (This inverts the conscious antithesis between sex and wealth, and between sex and food.) It was he who sired the human race on a female dog, committed incest with his daughter (Spott and Kroeber, 1942, pp. 233-235), and was involved in castrations and countercastrations which are reminiscent of Zeus' behavior:

> Eager for feminine conquest, he attempted to deny or evade his son Kapuloyo, and finally, in order to marry the young man's wife, abandoned him on a high tree and blinded his grandson Kewomer. Kapuloyo escaped, gathered to himself all the dentalia in the world, and departed downstream; but near the mouth of the river, Wohpekumeu overtook him and recovered enough money to restock the supply for men (Kroeber, 1925, p. 73).

It was Wohpekumeu who instituted birth, stole acorns from the sky, and liberated the salmon for the future use of mankind. However, despite his positive achievements, his erotic strivings were so intense that he was finally abducted (castrated) by the Skate Woman. The meaning of his punishment is confirmed when we learn that "a skatefish looks like woman's inside" (Erikson, 1943, p. 272).

The converse of the instinctual Wohpekumeu is seen in another creative *woge*, Pulekukwerek ("Downstream Sharp")—"so named from the horns on which he sat" (Kroeber, 1925, p. 74). These gluteal horns appear to represent an anally displaced penis. At any rate, Pulekukwerek, who is a personified Super-Ego, is "a grave, unconquerable character, who smoked tobacco but never ate, passed women by for the sweat house, and by strength and supernatural gifts destroyed monster after monster" (Kroeber, 1925, p. 74). The monsters being his own instincts, it becomes clear why he instituted (and/or drove women from) the sweat house. Unlike the unfortunate Wohpekumeu, Pulekukwerek "retired uncompelled to the far-away land of dentalia and everlasting dances. All that the Yurok have of respectful admiration in their mythology they lavish on Pulekukwerek" (Kroeber, 1925, p. 74).

We have noted frequently that money and wealth are important because they ward off starvation, poverty, and castration, and that money, on the various psychosexual levels, represents the internalized good object, whether breast, feces, embryo, or penis. The aggression and ambivalence which are involved in this incorporation and identification result in the concurrent internalization of the bad object, the "pains." The failure to achieve genital primacy or to synthesize the component instincts results in contradictions (fullness vs. emptiness; sadomasochism); and these will become clearer in a brief consideration of the World Renewal rites (Kroeber and Gifford, 1949).

The esoteric part of this ceremony is concerned with the magical replenishment of the salmon, acorns, and wild game—in a sense, with the bracing and renewing of the entire world. The secular and climactic portion of these rites is devoted to feasting and to the display of imperishable wealth. The dance sponsors, manifesting pride and apprehension, provide large amounts of food for the numerous visitors—much in the manner of the *esa-esa* ("free giver") of the Normanby Islands (cf. Róheim, 1950, pp. 151-243, 287; 1955, pp. 55-61). The Wealth Display dances, marking an aggressive display of inherited and borrowed wealth, frequently result in brawls. These outbursts of envy and pique are at times so intense as to disrupt the sacred rites, despite their cosmological importance and the mediations of the officiating priest.

Since the aggressive display of wealth takes place in the context of feasting, it would seem that the exhibitionism is made possible only by the oral abundance and reassurance. In a sense, the exhibitors will not be eaten (or castrated) if they themselves eat modestly and stuff their guests with food. And it is only during this protracted ceremony, lasting five, ten, or more days, that the ordinarily ascetic Yurok permit themselves practical jokes, sexual license, and a brief carnival atmosphere. But even these festivities are not without their profound anxieties. Marking a victory of anal and phallic aggressiveness over genital drives, there is a great fear in the dance sponsors' minds that the dancers who are displaying their wealth will break or steal it. There is also a concern about the expenditure of food. As indicated, these various fears represent not only castration anxiety, but also the fear of being hungry and empty.

Thus, in one important ceremony which is frequently terminated by brawls, the following (and contradictory) components may be seen:

1. The generosity with food is an aspect of the infantile identification with the mother; that is, an identification with the good mother (or what the mother *should* be); but there is also an identification with the withholding, narcissistic, and bad mother, and a reaction formation against this miserliness. The generosity with food, like modest eating, wards off the dangers which emanate from the projection of oral aggressions.

2. There is a victory of anal retentivity (the accumulation of food and wealth for the dances), with anal sadism manifesting itself in the practical jokes.

3. There is an exhibitionistic and aggressive display of phallic wealth, with the sadism being especially manifested in the fights, sexual license, and so on, and in the retaliatory fears of robbery, damage, and castration.

To terminate the discussion of the shell money, there is an illuminating story from the Hupa[8] which clarifies the dangers of oral aggression and takes one back to the infantile situation:

> The grandchild of the rich man of Medilding had its mouth constantly open. A shaman finally saw and proclaimed the cause. An ancestor of the rich man had asked to kiss a dead friend or relative good-by. He descended into the grave and, bending over the corpse's face, used his lips to draw out from the nose the two dentalia that are inserted through the septum, concealing his booty in his mouth until the grave had been filled. According to the report, the rich man admitted that an ancestor of his had actually risked this deed; and the shaman declared that it was the same dentalia that now kept the child's jaws apart (Kroeber, 1925, p. 42).

The identity of wealth and mother, like the projection of oral aggression onto the newborn infant, clarifies the long delay in nursing after childbirth. Like the Hupa child who has been punished in the offending organ for his ancestor's crime, the infant which nurses immediately after birth will develop a malady of the jaw and will starve to death. Unfortunately, this traumatic withholding at the very start of life sets the psychic stage for all the events which follow. The early weaning and the premature pushing of the child to independence, to lift the sexual taboo from the parents, reinforce the original trauma and result in the fear of starvation (and later, of castration). The urgent need to keep the fetus and the infant awake reveals an unconscious death wish on the part of the mother; and it is conceivable, though not verified in the literature, that the mother refrains from nursing for the first five, ten, or more days (individual variations color the cultural pattern) because she herself feels emptied and depressed by the birth of the child—which in the unconscious would be an anal birth. It is also possible, in view of the identity of feces-baby-penis, that delivery is a castration, like the first menstrual period; and that, in identification with her own mother, it is a repetition of her own birth and the original separation from the mother (cf., Orens, 1955).

At any rate, the infantile trauma is evidenced, not only by the all-consuming interest in wealth (the desire to recover the lost object), but by the unusual degree of separation anxiety (which later flows into castration anxiety). There is, thus, an intense fixation to the place of one's birth, an aversion to travel unless this is urgently necessary, a reverence for the house and the river, and the tendency to give names to houses, trees, rocks—in fact, to cathect the entire environment with libido. The negative aspects of this separation anxiety are marked by minimal eating, a fear of starvation and poisoning, the rigid separation of the sexes, and the avoidance of cathecting people or pets with libido. The need to cling to the mother with one hand and to push her away with the other is very reminiscent of the ambivalence manifested by a spoiled child.

As indicated, a resolution of this dilemma is sought in the inherently unstable compromise represented by anality. In fact, the numerous avoidances and the heavy ritualization of daily life are akin to a compulsion neurosis (Freud, 1907)—which itself reveals the instability of the anal compromise. At any rate, we can clarify the relevant aggression and ambivalence by examining the negative introjects, the "pains."

IV

As has already been noted, the *telogetl* or "pains" are *material and animate entities* which resemble the dentalia in appearance, being finger-shaped. But they have a negative meaning: They are the internalized "bad objects." It will also be recalled that the *telogetl* are the prime causes of disease and, when sucked out of the victim's body and exhibited by the shaman, are covered with blood or slime.

Like the dentalia, the "pains" are overdetermined and derive from the various phases of psychosexuality. However, there are a few illnesses which are not caused by "pains"; and these ailments require confession or a priestly formula rather than shamanistic sucking. In every case, the initial diagnosis is made by a shaman. If the somatic and psychic indications are unpromising, the shaman will not undertake the cure; and she can easily ascribe the ailment to factors other than "pains" and recommend priestly therapy—or retaliatory action if a sorcerer is causing the disease.

The "pains," in addition to being the primary cause of illness, are also the source of the shaman's power. "Pains" enter her body, sometimes through her own efforts, and make her sick; but they also give her the homeopathic power to detect and remove the "pains" of her patients. Although her own "pains" cause her lifelong distress, she has a partial mastery over them, by being able to vomit them up; and she is thus able to turn them to some personal and social good. In return, she is handsomely rewarded with dentalia; and, as will be noted presently, the joint acquisition of "pains" and dentalia is a significant theme in the training of a shaman.

Although there is no difference between the "pains" of the patient and the shaman, the latter often solicits her ailment and is considered a deviant personality by Yurok standards. In view of the vomiting which precedes her initiation and marks her personality and her professional technique, she appears to have a large admixture of conversion hysteria. That is, she relies more on repression and displacement, than on regression to the anal level (cf., Freud, 1915, 1916; Nunberg, 1955). This is also indicated by the fact that certain of her "pains" in general (for example, those sent into a person's body by a sorcerer). At any rate, the shaman is able to suck out and exhibit the negative introjects which cause many illnesses, and she thus relieves her patients of hate, guilt, and anxiety. That certain purely somatic ailments may be involved does not alter the circumstance that every ailment is moral or supernatural in its causation and that the patient reacts to it with intense guilt. Whatever psychological insight the shaman may possess, and it appears to be considerable, she is primarily treating psychic and psychosomatic disturbances—most commonly, it would appear, the alimentary symptoms which result from hysterical displacements or from the inadequacy of the anal-sadistic compromise—and she is always free to prescribe non-shamanistic therapies for which she assumes no responsibility.

It has already been suggested that, on the pre-Oedipal level, the "pains" are visceral obstructions and parasites. Thus, the "pains" always come in pairs, with the plurality suggesting breasts *and* dentalia; and, like dentalia, they are of different sizes and are butt-ended.[9] They are "little things, not bigger than a finger and often less, and are described as of various shapes and colors, although usually longitudinal" (Spott and Kroeber, 1942, p. 156). The smaller pains are less potent, as the smaller dentalia are less valuable; and, as dentalia and other forms of wealth are envied and stolen, so the shamans are envious of each other and *steal* "pains" from someone else's patients or from a shamanistic novice (ibid., p. 165).

Seen only by shamans, the "pains" fly about in the air and lodge themselves in the bodies of human beings. The "pain" of one shaman resembles a redheaded woodpecker (an object of wealth), while another is black, but tipped with red at the larger end (ibid., pp. 219, ff.). In describing one of her "pains"—which she examined after vomiting it up—a shaman notes that "*it looked like a dentalium*" (ibid., p. 160; the present writer's italics).

Since illness always has a moral or supernatural causality, the "pains," the predominant causes (or *mani-*

festations) of sickness, have a similar etiology; they result from the violation of taboo (predominantly food and incest taboos) or from hostile sorcery. Occasionally, an illness is ascribed to a shaman: She has sent "pains" into someone because she is greedy for a fee. But this is a rare occurrence among the Yurok; and it is notable that the motive is greed rather than murderous aggression. In general, Yurok shamans are not able to cause disease and are more commonly believed to effect only partial cures (that is, leave one "pain" in the sick person) in order to claim further fees for second cures. Shamans may find themselves engaged in litigation if they refuse to diagnose ailments or if they fail to return the fees after unsuccessful treatments; but, being generally unable to cause disease, they are spared the retaliatory assaults (on their life and property) which make their profession a hazardous one among many other primitive groups. It is not clear, either in historical or distributional terms, why shamanism has become an exclusively female profession in northwestern California; and this is something of an anomaly by American Indian standards. But the shamans' general inability to cause disease appears to rest on the fact that they are withholding, like the Yurok mother, and that they are as greedy for "pains" as they are for dentalia.

Hostile sorcery, to which certain "pains" are ascribed, ranges from simple envy of a man's wealth (and the accompanying wish that he will sicken and disburse all of his dentalia to shamans) to a specialized and highly potent form of sorcery called *uma'a*. Before noting the obvious phallic component of the *uma'a* "pain," it is important to point out that black magic is generally practised by men, whereas curative magic is almost exclusively a female profession. On the other hand, men replenish the food supply (and the world) in the World Renewal ceremony, while women *create famines* and *starve the world* by means of "starvation medicine" (Kroeber, 1925, p. 4; Spott and Kroeber, 1942, pp. 202, ff.).

Uma'a is a term which describes both the sorcerer

himself and the particularly malevolent "pain" which is involved. It is a type of black magic which is remarkably similar to Central Australian "boning":

> Then there are people who have learned or bought a mysterious thing called *uma'a*, with which they destroy those whom they envy or hate. . . . Sometimes this thing is put on the end of a little arrow which is shot, at night from a distance, from a miniature bow at the house of the victim, one of whose inmates soon sickens. At times an *uma'a* can be seen at night, traveling on his nefarious errand. He may be carrying his charm concealed under his arm, but the thing is strong, breaks out, and is visible as sparks or a bluish light that shoots or rises and falls. If this enter a man, he is likely to sleep unto his death. Some shamans, however, can suck it out (Kroeber, 1925, p. 67).

As in the case of Central Australian "boning," the dreaded (and desired) homosexual assault by the *uma'a* results in a fatal sleep (regression, castration, death) (Róheim, 1945, pp. 120-134).

The Oedipal dream of a shamanistic novice reveals the phallic character of the *uma'a* sorcerer and of the flying "pains" in general:

> Thus, once while the others slept, I dreamed I saw an *uma'a* coming. One of his legs was straight, the other bent at the knee, and he walked on this knee as if it were his foot, and had only one eye. Then I shouted, dashed out, and ran down along the river. My male relatives pursued me and brought me back unconscious. Then I danced for three nights more. At this time I received my four largest pains. One of these is blue, one yellowish, another red, and the fourth white. Because I received these in dreaming about the *uma'a* they are the ones with which I cure sickness caused by the *uma'a* (Kroeber, 1925, p. 65).

Concerning the *uma'a* "pains," another shaman reports:

> When a doctor sucks out an *uma'a* pain she holds it between her hands, closes her eyes, chants . . . and then

> begins to sing. Then the pain flies upward, spirals in the air, and suddenly flies in a beeline to where it came from, leaving a trail of fire, by which the doctor can tell by whom it was sent. Usually she does not tell, for fear the *uma'a* will be sent back into herself (Spott and Kroeber, 1942, pp. 165-166).

The asymmetry of the *uma'a* is characteristic of phallic demons (cf. Money-Kyrle, 1939, p. 88). It is noteworthy, however, that the shaman herself is a socially recognized *phallic mother*.

As the phallic *uma'a* "pains" are stronger and more specialized than ordinary "pains," so one special class of shamans achieves the logical culmination in therapeutic specialization and is competent to treat psychoses: "There were shamans who in their initial dream ate a snake, carried it in their bodies, visible to other shamans, and sucked snakes from their patients; but the disease of which they cured was lunacy, not a bite" (Kroeber, 1925, p. 68). The shamans whose powers are derived from the internalization of a snake in a dream may be suspected of being not only more potent magically but also less pregenital than the other shamans; but the data are not adequate for a further exploration of this problem.

Interestingly enough, the peak of deviation is achieved by two male shamans (transvestites); they are not only unusually deviant, but they also clarify the basic breast-penis equation by repeatedly acting out and returning to the original infantile situation:

> There was a shaman at Murekw famous for his ability to handle hot stones and eat living rattlesnakes, and after his death one of his kinsmen continued the practise. Such arduous feats, however, are not characteristic of Yurok shamanism, in which jugglery is unimportant; and it is significant that both these individuals were men (Kroeber, 1925, p. 68).

Such acting out is not characteristic of Yurok shamans; but they do suck out and incorporate their patients' "pains" during treatment, and they incorporate "pains" or snakes in a dream—all of which are identical in motivation. Quite apart from his own infantile and homosexual needs, which are akin to the bisexual aspirations of the female shamans, it may perhaps be that the male shaman must also exaggerate and dramatize his therapeutic powers in order to compete more favorably with women in a consciously female profession. At any rate, the incestuous and infantile strivings which result in "pains," whether in the patient or the shaman, are becoming progressively clearer.

The dreams and fantasies about the *uma'a* demon reveal the maternal and paternal aspects of the "pains" in general and of the attacker, whether father, phallic mother, or the undifferentiated parents—for the *uma'a* sorcerer is both a phallic demon and a phallic mother. Sickness, then, like shamanistic potency, results from an incestuous assault by a phallic demon or from the cannibalistic incorporation of a parental figure (that is, a violation of the food taboos, which will be discussed presently). The shamans act out their infantile drives in a sucking therapy, while non-shamans attempt to negate all drives except anal retentivity.

The situation is, again, reminiscent of Central Australian sorcery, where a snake, a pointing bone, or a quartz crystal (the magic *nankara* stone, which is sometimes described as the excrement of a sky deity) is kept within the sorcerer's body but can be projected into someone else in order to kill or cure (cf., Róheim, 1934, p. 65). Interestingly enough, the shamanistic therapy of the Yurok, which is marked essentially by mouthing or sucking—that is, an assault[10] on the mother's breast or body (cf., Glauber, 1953: Róheim, 1955)—is also characterized by a phallic penetration and receptivity. Before attempting treatment, and shaman sings and dances, working herself into a trance-like clairvoyance which may even culminate in temporary unconsciousness; the the sucking therapy begins:

> The larger *telogetl* pains rest in the doctor's body enveloped in a "blanket" (*uka'a*) of something like slime (*sleyitl*). When the doctor's power comes on her, one of her pains rises in her gorge, and its *sleyitl* helps her to find the *telogetl* in the patient, as she moves her mouth over his body. She facilitates the egress of her pain by *putting three or four fingers into her throat* to retch it up. *It then passes from her mouth,* as she is "sucking" the patient, *into the latter's body,* and travels in this until it meets the pain which is causing the disease. The two slimy envelopes mingle and the doctor's pain *returns to the doctor,* drawing the other after it. Once the latter is safe in her body, she brings it up in the same manner as her own, and causes it to fly away to where it came from (Spott and Kroeber, 1942, p. 156; the present writer's italics).

This process, which is Oedipal in its positive and negative aspects, even if displaced to the oral zone, is akin to a conversion hysteria; and the shamans do appear to be hysterics. They express their genital (and incestuous) strivings primitively, whereas the more numerous compulsives in the society surrender their genital drives for a lower stage of sexual life (anal sadism).

Just as the shaman in the *uma'a* dream fled to the river (the source of salmon and life; the good mother) on awakening from her nightmare, in an attempt to protect herself against the aggressive father (or phallic mother) whom she nevertheless incorporated—so she incorporates the father and the mother in her sucking therapy and becomes a kind of phallic mother or socially accepted hermaphrodite. Her identification with the father in the dream and her ambivalent flight to the mother (the river) reveal the hostile and phallic aspect of her negative Oedipal strivings and the related homosexuality: the wish to penetrate the mother's body, in addition to submitting to the aggressive father. And she achieves both goals in her professional life, for she not only sucks out the "pains" but sends her own into the patient's body.

In reality terms, her cures bring her great wealth and power; and she is able to enjoy many masculine privileges which are strictly denied to ordinary women: She dances at certain rituals; she may enter the sweat house, but not when she is menstruating; she wears feathers in her hair rather than the basketry cap which is required of women; she exercises authority over her male kinsmen and co-residents; and she is permitted to use tobacco. The pipe, in fact, is the very symbol of her profession. It will also be seen presently that her initiation into shamanism is centered around the sweat house, that she sleeps and dances there, practises the wealth magic of the men, and so on.

Infantile cannibalism and the related food taboos further clarify the meaning of the "pains." Thus, the violation of a food taboo, in fact or in fantasy, will bring on a "pain." This circumstance makes it convenient for those young women who wish to become shamans, and they solicit "pains" by such a transgression. Other people receive the "pains" involuntarily and resist them. In either case, however, the "pains" result in illness; and the voluntary candidate for shamanism must undergo prolonged training before she is able to master her "pains."

The standardized "initiation dream" of the shaman-to-be begins with *the crying while gathering firewood* (an element of male ritual, the wealth magic) and reveals an *oral tension* and nostalgia for the *lost object* of infancy:

> This is a native summary of a shaman's inception:
>
> A woman on her way for firewood perhaps begins to think of the dead who formerly lived in her town, notes how grass-grown and dim the path is, clears it of brush and weeps in recollection. Not long after she dreams. A person says to her: "I pity you as you always cry when you gather wood. You should become a shaman. Eat this!" The woman, not knowing what it is, eats what is offered. She wakes and realizes that what she thought reality was a dream. The base of her sternum hurts, it is a pain growing in her (Kroeber, 1925, p. 64).

A more individualized "initiation dream" has been recorded:

> I began with a dream. At that time I was already married at Sregon. In the dream I was on Bald Hills. There I met a Chilula man who fed me deer meat which was black with blood. I did not know the man, but he was a shortnosed person. I had this dream in autumn, after we had gathered acorns. In the morning I was ill. A doctor was called in to treat me and diagnosed my case. Then I went to the sweat house to dance for ten nights (ibid.,65.)

The "short-nosed person" is reminiscent of the phallic demon; and, being of the despised Chilula tribe, he is an "enemy." The climbing of the mountain, significantly called Bald Hills, makes this an incestuous dream; but there are also echoes of an oral situation, in which the phallic mother is offering bad meat to a trusting child.

The ten-day dance, called the *remohpo* or "doctor dance," requires a ten-day fast (atonement). During this period, the shaman-to-be repeatedly vomits up the "pain," displays it on a flat basket, and (in the native parlance) "drinks it again." This is followed by the *ukwerhkwer teilogitl*, the "pain-cooking dance." The culinary symbolism, like the fasting and nausea, reveals that an aggressively won and basically indigestible food is involved.

Not only does the candidate fast in atonement for her oral aggression against the breast-penis, with complementary impregnation and nausea, but she must also abstain from water (a mother symbol) for variable periods. Significantly, although the trainee is generally a woman, her increasing mastery of the "pain," by self-induced vomiting, is greatly weakened by the presence of a menstruating woman (cf., Spott and Kroeber, 1942, p. 161). This marks a return to the exaggerated castration anxiety of the society, which is shared by the women—not only from their own pregenital phases, but also from the onset of menstruation in adolescence, the time when the shamanistic call is most customary. The bloody or slimy "pains" ejected from the mouth are thus overdetermined; they have their pre-Oedipal roots, in addition to being a hysterical displacement of genital libido to the oral zone.

The previously mentioned incorporation of a snake in a dream, and in reality by the male (transvestite) shamans, requires no further discussion, except that it represents a dramatic and synoptic achievement of prohibited desires.

Since "pains" also result from a violation of the food taboos, this fact affords a further clarification of the nature of Yurok illness and of shamanistic vomiting. The basic taboo, despite its numerous ramifications, is simple: Salmon and venison cannot be eaten together and must not come into contact at any time. Supplementary but related taboos prohibit the washing of hands in running water after a meal of venison; to do so would drown the soul of the deer and prevent its return to the snares of the deserving hunter. Instead, and with Hebraic legalism, the hands are washed in a basket or a wooden bowl. Persons who are most cautious may even abstain from washing their hands after eating land game and merely wipe them dry. Similarly, the wooden platters on which venison is served are washed in a basket and never in a stream.

The mysterious or bad foods which are eaten unintentionally in dreams and result in "pains" are either foods which drip with blood or slime—or worse, as the dreamer realizes later, they are a mixture of land game and fish. The foods which drip with blood or slime represent the breast, which is being consumed aggressively; they also refer to oral impregnation (cf., the need to keep the mouth closed during childbirth, and the writer's theory that an anal birth is involved). The foods that must be kept apart refer again to oral sadism (cf., the Hebraic taboo against boiling the calf in the milk of its mother), to the incorporation of both parents by the child, and to the dreaded incorporation (by projection) of the child by the parents. The compulsive separation of the maternal foods of the water and the paternal foods of the land also indicates an early sexual rivalry with the parents, an identification with both, and a powerful desire to prevent parental intercourse.

Quite apart from the food taboos, it is again clear that the emphasis on slow and modest eating, with the mind directed to thoughts of wealth, refers to eating without aggression. Thus, unaggressive eating placates the mother (and/or father) and results in good body contents (dentalia). At the same time, the suppression of oral desires also indicates an unconscious repression of Oedipal desires.[11] On the other hand, aggressive eating or the violation of food taboos, like incestuous fantasies or dreams, will result inevitably in bad body contents ("pains").

The ambivalence involved in incorporation, identification, and Oedipal rivalry is further clarified by the food taboos. Significantly, the would-be shaman who received blood-blackened venison from the short-nosed "enemy" on the Bald Hills alternated from venison to salmon in the same narrative:

> On the tenth day, while I was dancing, I obtained control of my first "pain." It came out of my mouth looking like a salmon liver, and as I held it in my hands blood dripped from it to the ground. This is what I had seen in my dream on Bald Hills. I then thought that it was merely venison. It was when I ate the venison that the pain entered my body (Kroeber, 1925, p. 65).

Another describes her great resistance to the shamanistic call, as well as her family's pressure on her:

> My mother says, "You be doctor." I say, "No." She say, "You much money, beautiful clothes; if not doctor, will have nothing." I again say, "No." She scold, she scold too rough; I go away from home, stay out at night, sleep with Nancy over in other village (Erikson, 1943, p. 262).

Although resistance is indicated, she has a dream shortly thereafter in which an old woman offers her some "bloody and nasty" substance in a basket:

> . . . she throw basket on me, it hit me on mouth; I swallow stuff, I no sense any more; I wake up with noise, Nancy wake me up. "You crazy," she says. I never tell I dreaming that night; not sleep again (ibid.).

Even though she does not communicate the dream to anyone and practises a defensive insomnia, violent nausea sets in, and she finally accepts the shamanistic call. Interestingly, this shaman, one of the most famous in the area, is disturbed in later life by "nasty dreams, dreams of snakes, which make her feel sick all over again" (ibid., p. 267); and she has to repeat her novitiate:

> I run around. Oh! *snake* all over; I hit them; all over my arm, I bite them; I like crazy; I go to sweat house, I dance, everybody sing (ibid., p. 267).

There is no question that hysteria is involved, and that the second novitiate indicates a failure of repression.

The uncontrolled, and also the self-induced, vomiting of shamans is of further interest; it indicates the special skill of the shaman, with a professional technique derived from a hysterical symptom. But it is also significant because uncontrolled vomiting is abhorrent to the Yurok. Erikson (1943), on the basis of an ingenious hypothesis which minimizes Yurok anality, assumes that the aversion to vomiting is based on the "tube" configuration of the Yurok: that they have assimilated the geography of the area into their anatomical and physiological concepts, and that uncontrolled vomiting is dreaded because it reverses the normal vectors of the river and the salmon.

Such geographical determinism is simply too convenient. It ignores the infantile situation and ascribes an unwarranted causality to the physical environment. Insofar as there is an assimilation of geography to physiology, it is the result of a previous projection, with the river symbolizing the mother. The "tube" configuration, then, represents merely another type of animism, with the environment understood and described in visceral (that is, internal physiological and psychological) terms. In other words, there is a projection of internal experiences and affects onto the geographical environment.

The literature is not sufficiently corroborative, but it may be suspected that diarrhea, which does *not* reverse the vectors of the river and of food, is as dreaded as vomiting, with both representing the fear of emptiness—as is constipation, which represents the fear of fullness. (Cf., Erikson, 1943, p. 286, for the folktale in which the hungry bear overeats and then suffers alternately from constipation and diarrhea. It may also be noted parenthetically that diarrhea, like childbirth, may constitute a symbolic castration.)

Further, an environmental explanation of the Yurok psyche is too particularistic. How, on the basis of Erikson's *ad hoc* hypothesis, can one explain similar attitudes toward vomiting and the like in different, *non-riverine* environments: Conversely, how can one explain the general absence of Yurok attitudes (and a completely different character structure) in an environment which is comparable to that of the Yurok, and even more intensively riverine, as among the peoples of the Northwest Coast (the Nootka, Kwakiutl, Haida, Tlingit, and so on—of whom the Yurok are only a culturally impoverished periphery)?

It would seem, rather, that uncontrolled vomiting, which is the predominant symptom in the candidates for shamanism, refers to a variety of stimuli and is overdetermined. It derives generically from an incorporative hostility toward the mother, and it results in the rejection via the mouth of bad body contents. It may also be reinforced, of course, by fantasies of oral castration and/or impregnation, or by fellatio and its negative (repulsion). This hysterical symptom is especially dreaded, it would seem, because of the delicate and unsuccessful compromise which the Yurok collectively achieve in their regression to anal sadism (compulsion neurosis), with its marked tendency toward self-control and self-deprivation, retentivity, and ritualization. Thus, among non-shamans, vomiting, "pains," or any other gastro-intestinal ailments represent a victory for ambivalence and the failure of the anal compromise. *Regression* having failed, the supplementary repressive powers of the shaman are introduced; whereas the shaman herself, who is primarily a hysteric, relies most heavily on the *repression* and *displacement* of her own genital strivings and regresses only briefly to orality during the time of therapy. The self-induced or controlled vomiting of the shaman places this dreaded hysterical process in the safe area of ritual, where it is used to exorcise the ambivalence and guilt of the patient.

In view of the synonymity of breast-feces-embryo-penis, it is possible that a supplementary coprophagous fantasy underlies the vomiting, whether in the sick person or in the shaman; but this is impossible to document because of the inadequacy of the literature. At any rate, the breast-penis meaning of the dentalia and the "pains" is further clarified in the training of the shamanistic novice. After partaking of a forbidden food or a forbidden mixture of foods in a dream, the young woman finds that a material and animate "pain" is growing within her. Whether solicited or not, the taboo-violating dream is productive of illness and requires therapy. In some cases, the young woman resists the shamanistic call and has the offending "pain" sucked out. Such a choice apparently is related to the personality of the young woman, and to the circumstances which obtain in her family. For example, there are some families in which the profession of shaman descends matrilineally, but not by inheritance. In addition to family pressures, certain deviant traits begin to differentiate the candidate: These ego deviations and weaknesses, together with inadequate, object-relatedness, are summed up by excessive sleepiness, vomiting, and a variable degree of homosexuality. Further, since the arduous novitiate takes upward of two years, the call generally comes to adolescent girls, though they may marry later. If already married, a woman must be childless (itself a dreaded condition) at the time of the call.

At any rate, the preliminary rites test the candidate's qualifications, after which the prolonged novitiate is begun. The novice abstains from food and water for ten-day periods, she sleeps and dances in the sweat house, she undergoes training in self-induced vomiting, and she demonstrates her powers at various ceremonies.[12] Not only is she acquiring mastery over her "pains," but she is also acquiring more of them.

As indicated, the shamanistic pursuit of "pains" is similar to the wealth magic of the men; both are accompanied by abstentions from food and sexual intercourse, by crying aloud when gathering wood for the sweat house, and the like. In fact, the special affinity of "pains" and dentalia—that is, their unconscious similarity—is especially clarified by the wealth magic of the shamanistic trainee. Thus, one shaman reports of her novitiate:

> All that winter I went daily high up on the ridge to gather sweat-house wood and each night I spent in the sweat house. All this time I drank no water. Sometimes I walked along the river, put pebbles into my mouth and spat them out. Then I said to myself: "When I am a doctor I shall suck and the pains will come into my mouth as cool as these stones. I shall be paid for that." When day broke I would face the door of the sweat house and say: "A long dentalium is looking in at me." When I went up to gather wood, I kept saying: "The dentalium has gone before me; I see its tracks." When I had filled my basket with the wood, I said: "That large dentalium, the one I am carrying, is very heavy." When I swept the platform before the sweat house clean with a branch, I said: "I see dentalia. I see dentalia. I am sweeping them to both sides of me." So whatever I did I spoke of money constantly (Kroeber, 1925, p. 65).

Simultaneously, she is acquiring additional "pains" (cf., ibid., pp. 65-66).

As in the wealth magic of the men, one sees an oral tension and a crying for the breast. There is, again, a hallucinatory wish-fulfillment, with a confusion of subject and object, which also has its origins in the anal phase. In the wealth magic of the men, the result is limited to the putative acquisition of dentalia in old age; but the shamanistic novice is simultaneously seeking "pains" *and* dentalia. The twin themes of "pains" and dentalia are conspicuous in the novitiate, and the shaman invariably receives both of them, both in fantasy and in reality. In fact, every invitation to cure (to extract "pains") is preceded by a period of bargaining in which the payment, a string or two of dentalia, is exhibited to the reluctant shaman by the prospective patient's kinsmen.

The wealth magic of men and shamans is oral and incorporative. Like most Yurok magic, it "is of the most crudely direct kind, such as performing a simple action or saying the desired thing over and over again. The thousand and one occasions on which magic of this rather bare volitional type is employed reveal a tensity that usually seems brought on consciously. This emotional tautness, which contrasts glaringly with the slack passivity and apathetic sluggishness of the average California Indian, is manifest in other matters. Thus, restraint and self-control in manner and in relations with other men are constantly advocated and practised by the Yurok" (Kroeber, 1925, p. 4). Kroeber's descriptive summary, it may be noted, marks the transition from hunger and wish-fulfillment to anal sadism and tense ambivalence. Though self-induced and ritualized—that is, it is a controlled regression—the wealth magic constitutes a replaying of the infantile role, with oral cravings dominant but in the service of anal retentivity and phallic potency.

The flight to the mother (the river), the stimulation of the mouth and lips by the pebbles (cf., the eating of live snakes and the juggling of hot stones by the male shamans), the crying and the hallucination of dentalia—all these reveal the oral aspect of the dentalia; whereas the association of the dentalia with the masculine sweat house indicates the phallic quality of the shell money. Nevertheless, the hallucinated oral gratification fails, both in infancy and in the wealth magic of the men; and it is only painfully realized in the wealth magic of shamans, for dentalia and "pains" are introjected at the same time. The result is that the painful stimulus, originally hunger, is projected onto the mother, who becomes hungry and orally aggressive in turn. This is probably the ontogenetic precursor of the widespread Yurok fears of persecution (cf., Nunberg, 1955). Thus, there is a deep-seated fear of poisoning—by a type of black magic called *ohpok*, in which harmless but despised items (the flesh of dogs, snakes, frogs, and so on) are secreted in a person's food (Kroeber, 1925, p. 67); by drinking river water or water from strange places; and by the incorporation of the parasitic "pains," which are charged with the projected aggressions of the nursing infant. The "starvation medicine" practised exclusively by women reveals the same fears, even if it is closer to historical reality than the paranoid projections which reinforce it.

The unusual florescence of wealth magic may be understood also in the light of the realistic fact that the staple foods, salmon and acorns, and secondarily deer, deliver themselves to the very feet of the consumer. This occurs only if a person lives correctly and observes all taboos and rituals, with failures of the food supply being ascribed to moral or supernatural transgressions. Reality, therefore, reinforces the volitional magic which derives from infancy, and it also strengthens the already hypertrophied Super-Ego.

It may also be noted that the persecutory mother appears to be indicated by the persistent "looking in" of the dentalia, again with a confusion between subject and object which is typical of hallucinations. The "looking in" of the dentalia suggests not only a hallucinated breast but also a primal scene; and, as in a dream, sexual curiosity is displaced from the subject to the object—in this case, to the dentalia. (Cf., the postulated flight of the dentalia if coitus takes place in the living house.) This displacement again suggests that the dentalia, like the "pains," are a part of the subject and are also a projection of the subject.

A supplementary insight may be obtained by noting that certain shamanistic novices gash themselves in their magic. This is completely voluntary and quite unusual, since the Yurok have a general abhorrence of mutilation. It is absent from the wealth magic of the men, and is paralleled only in one type of masculine behavior. Thus, if a man has had intercourse with a menstruating woman, which is one of the most dangerous ritual offenses, he is required to gash himself during the purification ceremony (Erikson, 1943, p. 267). There is probably a similarity in the two types of behavior. The man wards off castration by sacrifice and atonement, that is, by means of a symbolic or displaced castration.[13] The shaman, on the other hand, sacrifices and atones in order to obtain (rather than retain) the male genitalia. In both cases, a defensive masochism wards off a retaliatory attack by those who have been sadistically used.

Further, in view of the intense asceticism which is characteristic of the wealth magic (the abstention from food and water), a pre-Oedipal situation is also revealed; and the aggression which was originally turned against the object, the depriving mother, is now masochistically inflicted on the subject. At the same time, the psychic and social bisexuality of the shaman, who is the phallic mother *par excellence*, clarifies the meaning of the overdetermined "pains" and dentalia. She obtains dentalia and "pains" by aggressive orality and by displacing her genital libido; while ordinary people regress to the anal stage and must give up "pains" and dentalia, oral and genital needs, fullness and emptiness, if they wish to be "healthy."

Being dysfunctionally worked out, the Oedipus complex of the Yurok results in an unusually prohibitive Super-Ego which threatens the ego constantly with starvation, poverty, or castration; hence the need to pile up good body contents, but at a price which only the deviant hysteric can pay (lifelong "pains" or bad body contents).[14]

V

In conclusion, the data appear to support the hypothesis that the shell money and "pains" are respectively the positive and negative aspects of an infantile introject, the breast and/or penis. Being reinforced at the different stages of psychosexual development, the symbolism is overdetermined in each case. The general impression is that of a tense and heavily ritualized society marked by a collective "compulsion neurosis," with a variable admixture of "conversion hysteria" which is most pronounced among the shamans.[15]

Notes and References

Notes

1. A coastal and inland tribe of Indians of northwestern California.

2. Cf., Money Kyrle, 1939, pp. 86-91.

3. The psychic identity of mouth and vagina is here revealed—and perhaps infantile fantasies about oral impregnation. At any rate, one possible exit (entrance?) is closed off to avoid a dilemma for the fetus.

4. The correlation of mealtime (eating) and witchcraft indicates deep-seated oral aggressions and talion anxiety, and will become progressively clearer during the discussion which follows.

5. Other details about toilet training are lacking.

6. Erikson (1943), though he describes the Yurok as miserly, compulsive, suspicious, and so on, does not accept the concept of Yurok anality. A detailed consideration of his objections would lead too far afield. The writer has dealt with this problem in another paper (Posinsky, n. d.).

7. Similarly, children are not permitted to talk about sex while their parents are alive. To do so is a double offense involving "swearing" and ridicule (cf., Erikson, 1943, pp. 270, 288).

8. Neighbors of the Yurok.

9. The sexuality of the paired "pains" is further clarified when they are described as husband and wife or mates.

10. A patient reports: "As she sucks, it is as if her chin were going through to your spine, but it doesn't hurt" (Erikson, 1943, p. 261).

11. Although the developmental progression from orality to genitality is basic to the understanding of the relationship between oral and genital denial, the process is not exclusively unidirectional; rather, a circular casuality or feedback is also occurring, even if secondarily and retroactively. Thus, oral and anal problems are obviously carried into

the phallic or Oedipal phase; but the phallic organization also influences the previous phases correctively.

12. Certain optional, but expensive, "post-graduate" ceremonies result in an enhanced reputation and larger fees.

13. He, too, "menstruates."

14. In view of the multiple criteria of normality, it is interesting that the shamans are deviant in terms of *social adaptation*, though their deviations are socially patterned; but they appear to be more *genital* (even if it is a displaced, hysterical genitality) than the more numerous anal-compulsives who are better adapted socially.

15. The quotation marks are used because we are dealing with analogies, not homologies. Even if the psychic mechanisms are similar, their *functions* differ. The Yurok compulsive or hysteric is acting socially, even at the cost of genital primacy. In our culture such behavior is dysfunctional and anti-social.

References

Abraham, K.: (1924) "A short study of the development of the libido, viewed in the light of mental disorders." In: *Selected Papers of Karl Abraham.* Hogarth. London. 1948.

Brierley, M.: (1951) *Trends in Psycho-Analysis.* Hogarth, London.

Burlingham, D., et al.: (1955) "Simultaneous analysis of mother and child." In: *The Psychoanalytic Study of the Child*, X. International Universities Press. New York.

Chapple, E. D., and Coon, C. S.: (1942) *Principles of Anthropology.* Holt. New York.

Erikson, E. H.: (1943) "Observations on the Yurok: Childhood and World Image." *University of California Publications in American Archaeology and Ethnology*, 35. Berkeley, Calif.

———: (1945) "Childhood and traditions in two American Indian tribes." In: *The Psychoanalytic Study of the Child*, I. International Universities Press. New York.

———: (1950) *Childhood and Society.* Norton. New York.

Freud, S.: (1907) "Obsessive acts and religious practices." In: *Collected Papers*, 2. Hogarth. London. 1924.

———: (1915) "Repression." In: *Collected Papers*, 4. Hogarth. London. 1925.

———: (1916) "On the transformation of instincts with special reference to anal erotism." In: *Collected Papers*, 2. Hogarth. London. 1924.

Glauber, I. P.: (1953) "A deterrent in the study and practice of medicine." *Psychoan. Quart.* 22: 381-412.

Goldschmidt, W. R.: (1951) "Ethics and the structure of society: an ethnological contribution to the sociology of knowledge." *Am. Anthropologist*, 53: 506-524.

Jacobson, E.: (1953) "Contribution to the metapsychology of depression." In: *Affective Disorders* (P. Greenacre, editor). International Universities Press. New York.

Klein, M.: (1932) *The Psycho-Analysis of Children.* Hogarth. London.

———: (1948) *Contributions to Psycho-Analysis*, 1921-1945. Hogarth. London.

Kroeber, A. L.: (1925) *Handbook of the Indians of California.* Bulletin 78, Bureau of American Ethnology. Smithsonian Institution. Washington, D. C.

———: (1926) "Law of the Yurok Indians." *Atti del XXII Congresso Internazionale degli Americanisti*, Vol. II. Rome.

———: (1948) *Anthropology.* Harcourt, Brace. New York.

Kroeber, A. L., and Gifford E. W.: (1949) "World Renewal, A Cult System of Native Northwest California." *Anthropological Records*, No. 13. University of California Press. Berkeley, Calif.

Loewald, H. W.: (1951) "Ego and Reality." *Int. J. Psychoan.* 32: 10-18.

Money-Kyrle, R.: (1939) *Superstition and Society.* Hogarth, London.

Muensterberger, W.: (1955) "On the biopsychological determinants of social life." In: *Psychoanalysis and the Social Sciences*, 4. International Universities Press. New York.

Nunberg, H.: (1955) *Principles of Psychoanalysis.* International Universities Press. New York.

Onians, R. B.: (1951) *The Origins of European Thought.* Cambridge University Press. Cambridge, England.

Orens, M. H.: (1955) "Setting a termination date—an impetus to analysis." *J. Am. Psychoan. Asso.*, 63: 651-665.

Posinsky, S. H.: (1954) *Yurok Ritual.* Ph.D. Dissertation, Department of Anthropology, Columbia University, New York. University Microfilms. Ann Arbor.

———: n. d. "The problem of Yurok anality." *Am. Imago.*

Róheim, G.: (1934) *The Riddle of the Sphinx.* Hogarth. London.

———: (1945) *War, Crime and the Covenant.* Medical Journal Press. Monticello, N. Y.

———: (1950) *Psychoanalysis and Anthropology.* International Universities Press. New York.

———: (1955a) "Some aspects of Semitic monotheism." In: *Psychoanalysis and the Social Sciences*, 4. International Universities Press. New York.

———: (1955b) *Magic and Schizophrenia.* International Universities Press. New York.

Spott, R. and Kroeber, A. L.: (1942) "Yurok Narratives." *University of California Publications in American Archaeology and Ethnology*, 35. Berkeley, Calif.

Waterman, T. T.: (1920) "YUROK Geography." *University of California Publications in American Archaeology and Ethnology*, 16. Berkeley, Calif.

Waterman, T. T., and Kroeber, A. L.: (1934) "Yurok Marriages." *University of California Publications in American Archaeology and Ethnology*, 35. Berkeley, Calif.

———: (1938) "The Kepel Fish Dam." *University of California Publications in American Archaeology and Ethnology*, 35. Berkeley, Calif.

Part III

Psychoanalytic Studies of Money Outside the Realm of the Anal Theory

Contribution 11

Some Emotional Uses of Money

William Kaufman

Although money is an important stimulus for many different patterns of normal and abnormal behavior, little systematic attention has been given to this subject by most psychologists and psychiatrists. This despite the fact that most people, rich and poor, are more or less continuously concerned—consciously or unconsciously—with the solution of their private money problems.

In my study of over a thousand patients from three to eighty-four years of age whom I have seen in the course of my private practice of internal medicine during the past twelve years, it has been possible to trace how concepts of money and money transactions are integrated into our lives, unconsciously or consciously influencing our conduct, our aspirations, and emotional reactions to ourselves, our families, and other people.

The symbolic meaning of money to the individual and the manner in which he uses it are determined by his culture, religion, by the attitudes of parents and teachers, by his life experiences (including the impact of the media of mass communication), by example of the people he knows, and by his personal short- and long-term goals.

Money can be translated into many of the things and services we really want. Much of what we call emotional security is soundly backed by the proper uses of money. Even part of what we call love and affection in parents stems from their ability to spend wisely for the benefit of their children.

The emotionally well-balanced use of money requires that the individual plan realistically for his present and future. His work effort must be translated into an income which will do more than support a mere subsistence level of living. If he has no emotional blocks to earning an ample income, then each expenditure he makes in a sense further tests his reality function, measures his attitudes toward himself and others, and indicates fluctuations in mood and affect.

The proper use of money creates within the individual a sense of well-being and emotional security. The inappropriate use of money becomes a serious emotional threat when the person is faced with the conflict between his desires and his conscience and with the consequences of his aberrant money-behavior. Deep unconscious motivations may prevent him from spontaneously using his money in constructive ways. Such people, regardless of income or economic reserves, often develop one of the most common psychosomatic illnesses of our time: *money-sickness*.

To delineate the complexity of the emotional aspects of money transactions in adults of our culture, I will review briefly the growing child's adjustments to money and money concepts.

A child's notions about money are usually vague until he reaches his fifth year. His first knowledge of money may come accidentally as he secretly explores his mother's pocketbook and finds a small hoard of coins and paper money. He looks at the money, clinks the coins, feels the bills. Then he may stuff some money into his mouth and quickly decide that he doesn't like its taste. Thereupon, he spits it out and throws the rest away. If strangers scramble for it, it amuses him. His emotional satisfaction comes from literally throwing money away.

From the age of three to five by passing coins to

salespeople under the direction of a parent, the child gradually learns that by giving money to the right person at the right time and in the right environment, he can get some things more desirable than money. It is at this stage that a child believes that money has magical properties, since his parents, merely by putting their hands into the right pocket, can draw on what seems to be an inexhaustible store of money and buy with it anything they want.

From the age of five to nine, the youngster learns to manipulate the pennies, nickels, and dimes at his disposal, and begins to develop some of his most important emotional reactions to the symbolic meaning and money transactions. He learns to his pleasure that he can buy certain reward foods such as ice cream, candy, and cookies. Later he realizes that money can obtain for him toys, comic books, special clothes—and admission to the movies or circus.

Because money becomes associated with pleasures in the child's mind, parents can now use it as a reward to reenforce habit development of various desirable forms of behavior. It is at this time that a child first makes the connection between love and money.

A child's income in the form of allowance or gifts is fixed by his parents. Often, when a parent refuses to give him additional money, a youngster may blurt out: "You don't love me any more!" At this point, the child still believes that his parents have unlimited supplies of money, but that for their own reasons they are withholding it from him. Depending on the way the parent handles this situation, the child may make either a good or bad adjustment to the initial situation of not having as much money as he wants.

When a child learns that he has monetary limitations, he has to solve one of the basic dilemmas in the emotional uses of money: What to do with it? One little boy, aged six, told me: "Money is nice to have—but it's nice to spend, too!" Each child must find his own solution to this ambivalent situation—to save or to spend—

and this will determine some of his adult patterns of money-use.

At about this time, he may learn that he can increase his income by running errands or doing simple jobs. He may wheedle money from his parents by nagging them till they give in—or by making such a nuisance of himself that he is paid to behave.

As the child's social life develops, he learns disquieting things. Some kids have more money than he has—and he is envious. He may have to accept as a reality the fact that he cannot have as much money as others—or he may fight it. However, he has some emotional balm when he discovers that other children may have even less money at their disposal than he has—and this gives him a sense of superiority. His already formed feelings about money will determine whether he prefers playing with children who have more money than he, or less—and this sets the stage for future relations with people whom he may always react to in terms of their economic status.

Gradually, a child's ideas of "mine and thine" become more sharply differentiated. He may share his money with others only on a this-for-that basis. But even at this early age, a child may try to buy love and friendship by giving his money to others in his play group.

As he becomes increasingly aware of the desirability of material possessions, he may wonder aloud why his parents can't have as many wonderful things as the parents of his friends. Then he learns what is a fundamental, traumatic, and almost catastrophic truth: his parents are not omnipotent. There is a limit to their buying power. This realization often creates in the growing child strong feelings of anxiety and anger.

Since his father is usually the chief wage-earner, the child's anger lashes out chiefly against him. He may kick, bite, or punch his father. Or he may try to run away from home. Parents usually do not recognize the cause of the child's anger, anxiety, mild depression, rage, temper tantrums, deep insecurity feelings, and other psychosomatic illnesses.

What this agitated child needs most is reassurance, love, and the gradually taught understanding that there is enough money to take care of all his basic needs, and even for some luxuries; and that there is no real cause for worry, since he will be well taken care of by his loving parents.

But what happens most frequently is that a parent is enraged because his child has made an unfavorable economic comparison between him and a neighbor, friend, or stranger. The father retaliates by becoming harsh and punitive toward his child. He may so criticize every money use of his child that the youngster becomes an anxious and frightened user of money. It is during this time that the parents' unconscious anxieties about money and economic security are transferred to children. From this point onward, children may develop abnormal attitudes toward the uses of money which adversely affect them the rest of their lives.

The emotionally insecure child of five to nine may try to solve his conflict about money by withdrawal from wealthier children, by subservience to them in expectation of monetary favors, by aggressive behavior intended to wrest what he wants from the richer child or to punish him for his wealth. He may limit his friendships to those having equal or lesser amounts of money than he has at his disposal. Or he may try to save or earn as much as he can to be more independent than if he had only the parental allowance available. He may feign indifference to money, emphasizing as one boy did: "What do I want money for? . . . If you don't have it, you can't lose it." A few day-dreamy children escape from realistic solution of their basic money problems by fantasying the great wealth of imaginary relatives, and savoring the pleasure of unlimited make-believe buying power.

However, a child may be tempted to solve his money problems by committing minor money crimes when he finds money that belongs to his parents or siblings, and diverts it to his own uses. To some extent these children are within their rights when they do this. Since they use so many things in common with other members of the household, they can easily assume that money too is common property within the family. To some extent, many of these children who steal money unconsciously feel rejected by their parents and substitute the things they can buy with money for the love which they believe parents have withheld from them. Formerly, most of these children could be taught over a period of time to develop a sense of honesty which precluded stealing other people's money or possessions.

However, today there is an alarming tendency in youngsters under the age of nine who, influenced by radio, television, movies, and comic books, have solved their basic money conflicts by entering into criminal activity of both amateur and professional caliber. The amateurs rob other children, short-change people they run errands for, or do minor shoplifting in stores. But some have planned and successfully executed complex and daring robberies, even opening safes, to get the money they feel they need, which their parents are unwilling or unable to give them.

The way in which a child's first money crimes are handled by his parents, teachers, or correction officers will have a marked bearing on the individual's ability to make for himself ultimately a socially acceptable life.

As the youngster grows into adolescence, he becomes increasingly aware of economic class distinctions. His increased need for money is part of his sex-awakening. The adolescent eventually spends much of the money available to him to increase his attractiveness to the opposite sex. Since he is dependent on parents, and yet desires to assert his growing independence, there is a reactivation of his earlier anger against his parents for not being able to give him all the money he thinks he needs.

The various solutions which the adolescent has at his disposal are mostly variants of those already described for younger children. The one who has developed constructive solutions of his money-problems earlier in childhood faces his contemporary adolescent money-problems with good reality function and formulates workable plans for his future education and employment. The adolescent with faulty emotional solutions to his money-problems will almost surely have a troubled adult life.

My discussion of the emotional uses of money in adults which follows assumes that the individual has at his disposal more than a minimum subsistence level of income. The major classifications indicate the predominant money behavior of the individual at the time of observation. Such behavior may be fixed for one's lifetime, or altered either spontaneously or through psychotherapy.

SOME EMOTIONAL USES OF MONEY

A. *Emotionally Well-Balanced Uses of Money*
B. *Compulsive Nonspending*
    1. conservative
    2. economical
    3. dollar-stretcher
    4. stingy
    5. tight-wad
    6. miser
C. *Compulsive Spending*
    1. infantile
    2. childish
        a. passive-dependent
        b. hostile-aggressive
        c. security-buying
    3. dreamy
    4. narcissistic
        a. self-adornment
        b. show-off spending
        c. socially competitive
        d. affection-buying
    5. expense-account
    6. self-pitying, self-rewarding
    7. gambling
    8. bargain-hunting
    9. scrimping to splurge
D. *Indecisive or Frightened Uses of Money*

E. *Denial of Economic Status*

1. pretended wealth
2. pretended poverty

F. *Use of Money as Reward*

1. constructively, to encourage socially useful activity
2. destructively, to encourage unethical, illegal activity

G. *Punitive Uses*

H. *Charitable Uses*

I. *Guilty Uses*

J. *Fetish Uses*

K. *Money Uses in the Transference Relationship*

L. *Money Uses by older People*

M.

	Mood	*Psychosis*	
1.	Euphoric	Manic	Excessive spending
2.	Sad	Depressed	Decreased spending
3.	Suspicious	Paranoic	Decreased spending
4.	Dreamy	Schizoid	Spotty, unpredictable spending

N. *Renunciation of Money*

Emotionally Well-Balanced Uses of Money

This individual may be in the low, medium, or high income bracket. He budgets his income for short- and long-term goals in a manner which shows good reality function. There is food-money, clothing-money, rent-money, money to be saved—and as an emotional safety valve, extra money set aside to be spent without guilt for trifles that seem desirable at the moment.

This person maintains as high a standard of living as possible, while allowing for reasonable savings and insurance. Fluctuations in his income are met by realistic adjustments in his spending, borrowing, and saving. His credit is good but he does not abuse it. Although he is willing to take reasonable business risks, he doesn't speculate. He is not stampeded into miserly or spendthrift uses of money. He shares his monetary resources equitably with other members of his family. Should it be necessary to do so, he can make economic sacrifices for the benefit of others.

Usually he has had a good relationship in childhood with his parents and siblings, and is free from crippling anxieties and tensions. His parents taught him reasonable ways of solving money problems, and in adulthood he has formulated his own flexible but reachable economic goals and is willing to compete fairly with others to attain these. He accepts without jealousy that there are many who have more money than he has, and often helps deserving people who are economically less fortunate than he.

Compulsive Nonspending

This individual makes enough money to maintain a decent standard of living within his low, medium, or large income bracket. But he has such a great inner fear of economic insecurity that his spending is inhibited. He tries to combat his unconscious fear by finding some minimal level of spending, and maximal rate of saving, which satisfy him. This he continues even though as time goes by both his income and monetary reserves may become so large that there is no longer any realistic basis for his inner fear of economic insecurity.

This emotionally rigid mode of inhibited spending leads to such descriptive terms as: conservative, economical, dollar-stretcher, stingy, tight-wad and miser.

The *conservative spender* is interested in getting his money's worth and no more, but limits his buying to necessities and few luxuries. The *economical* one is bargain-minded, spending much time and effort in finding goods and services he wants at the lowest prices. He is willing to sacrifice quality for price. The *dollar-stretcher* buys nothing that he can possibly make, and is constantly working during his free time to avoid spending either for finished products or services of others. The *stingy* person is self-punitive by depriving himself of things he needs or would enjoy, and which he certainly could afford. The *tight-wad* satisfies his physical needs by spending only when he must, regretting each dollar that he takes out of his purse as if it were a dear, departed friend whose loss he would never cease to mourn. The *miser* cares more for money than he does for the satisfaction of his physical needs—and gets immense satisfaction from actual contact with his money, deposit slips, bank books, and other symbols of wealth which he tries to conceal from other people.

The compulsive nonspender forms poor relationships with other people, since he unconsciously fears that they will deprive him of his money. The descending scale of warmth, scope, and frequency of human contacts starts with the conservative and ends with the miser, who often is content to lead a hermit-like existence.

These unconsciously love-hungry, money-hungry men and women set up their interpersonal relationships in a manner which causes their ultimate rejection. Their unconsciously determined notion that it is more blessed to *receive* than to *give* identifies them socially as "chiselers" or "spongers." Rejection reaffirms their belief that no one really cares for them—which is true—and this in turn makes their emotional isolation from other humans more complete than ever.

Most of these people were deprived in their early lives of love and affection, and experienced poverty, punishment, and regimentation. Symbolically, money represents the love, affection, and security which they never had and for which they have an insatiable craving.

Often anything which forcibly dislocates a compulsive nonspending pattern may cause severe anxiety, panic, depression, and many different kinds of psychosomatic illness, as well as a total breakdown in the person's capacity to adapt realistically to even minor economic reverses.

Compulsive nonspenders are especially vulnerable to confidence-men who promise them the only form of love they can understand—a sudden, large increase in monetary reserves at small expense to themselves. When the swindle is consummated, the victims turn with increasing bitterness to an even lower level of disbursement than previously.

(A few persons who originally had emotionally well-balanced uses of money became compulsive nonspenders after having lost their economic resources during the economic depression of 1929.)

Compulsive Spending

Emotionally the compulsive spender is comfortable only when he is able immediately to satisfy his slightest desire for spending. Often there is no realistic need for buying either the things or services which he purchases. Some spend their money merely for the sake of spending, and others spend compulsively for specific self-gratifying items, such as antiques, jewelry, clothing, or unusual food. If a compulsive spender is forced to save some of his money, he may become uneasy or even sick until he can resume spending at will.

These people have small, medium, or large incomes. Their main trouble in life is that they can never obtain all the spending money they need. Some work hard to earn huge salaries, and spend everything they make. Others go into debt. Still others have to resort to unethical, immoral, and illegal activities to get the money they require.

There are many emotional reasons for compulsive spending, and many kinds of compulsive spenders. Often a spendthrift gets rid of his money to obtain transient sensual gratification from the power of his money and from what is to him—unconsciously—much more important: to return to a passive-dependent status as a result of self-inflicted poverty. Many such compulsive spenders maintain a reliable economic relationship with a member of the family or a friend, who comes to his financial rescue whenever this help is needed.

The history of many of these compulsive spenders

indicates that they were overprotected in their early childhood by an overindulgent parent who guiltily substituted liberal money gifts for love and affection. Usually one parent was strict, but the other one overcompensated for his severity. The child's allowance was constantly augmented by secretly given additional sums from his indulgent parent. The child learned to spend all he had, since this was sure to bring him more money to spend. And at the same time he could punish his parents for not loving him by creating parental anxiety about his rate of spending. The constant replenishment of spending money prevented him from learning to tolerate the frustration of having to make a choice between two purchases. He never learned that money could be saved for future use.

Other compulsive spenders had neither money nor love in childhood. Their selfish spending in adulthood is an unconsciously overdetermined means of giving themselves something akin to love and at the same time creating debts which their relatives have to repay. This spending behavior is a frequent source of domestic trouble when a husband spends money needed for household expenses to gratify his own needs and to punish his wife and children.

Many compulsive spenders like charge accounts and time-payment buying even better than money itself, since this equates to temporarily unlimited spending power. The pleasurable excitement from spending exceeds the pleasure obtained from their purchases.

Many compulsive spenders have such pleasing personalities and glib tongues that it is easy for them to ingratiate themselves with others. If they need money for spending, they borrow without intention of repaying—and frequently victimize the same person over and over again. When this fails, they may have to fall back on their sex-attractiveness to get the money they need for spending. This may necessitate prostitution or marrying a bank-account.

There is the honest type of compulsive spender who suffers as he undergoes voluntary periods of great scrimping and saving until he has available the sum he needs.

Periodically he goes on a spending binge, enjoying the intense sensual pleasure of being able to buy anything he wants—until his money runs out.

Not all compulsive spenders are willing to work. Some are aggressive, hostile individuals who ultimately acquire their spending money by force. These people are rarely seen in private practice, but often in court. This is the type: He is an immature, sadistic individual, who has little patience for earning a living. He can never earn as much as he thinks he needs. He likes to live as if he were rich. Rather than face the discomfort of holding down a steady job, he flits from one job to another, hoping to find an employer who will give him a high salary. Eventually he gets his money from all sorts of unethical, immoral, and illegal ventures.

He enjoys flashy cars, flashy clothes. But what he likes most is the intense pleasurable excitement of taking money away from those who have. In the process of robbing people, he enjoys beating his victims up—sometimes even murdering them in his assaultive rage. Stealing, armed robbery, procuring, prostitution, gambling, blackmail, dope-peddling, extortion are his kind of crime.

As long as he is successful in his asocial ventures and eludes the law, he has the money and excitement he craves. He has emotional gratification of his unconscious needs, since he has symbolically attacked the parent-surrogate from whom he forcibly wrested the money he wanted.

If caught, tried, and jailed, he is actually supported and protected by the society he has harmed—and these individuals have ambivalent feelings toward incarceration. In a way it gives them a sense of security and belonging. But finally jailing acts as a further stimulus for increased antisocial activity, so that when he has served his sentence he embarks on even more vicious crimes, often culminating in murder. These individuals are sometimes described as having character disorders, as being psychopathic personalities, and some are actually psychotic.

Their history often shows rejecting parents, poverty, upbringing in a slum environment—but not always. Some come from families of high income levels in which strictness was substituted for love.

Some emotionally immature individuals are willing to work hard, but they compulsively spend all their money by giving it on payday to a parent or parent-surrogate, expecting in return to get taken care of in a manner which is symbolically equivalent to that of the passive-dependent child. An unmarried man—or woman—earning an excellent salary may be content to receive for personal use only a token sum of spending money. His parents may buy his clothes, feed him, pay his doctor's bills—and require that he spend most of his time at home keeping them company. If he marries, which he usually does after his parents die, he tries to establish the same type of relationship with his spouse. In essence, these people are willing to spend all their money as soon as they get it to buy a facsimile of the childhood type of emotional security, and when this is attained, they are satisfied.

A number of dreamy individuals who have a rich fantasy life, try to deny their poverty by compulsive spending. They have a certain hauteur which fools unwary creditors. These persons in their youth were often deprived of money and love, and were rejected and punished excessively by their parents. They are recurrently in trouble with the law because they cannot pay for what they buy. Finally, to obtain spending money, they may pass worthless checks, commit petty crimes, gamble, or give themselves sexually for money. As they deteriorate, alcoholism and increasingly prominent schizophrenic reaction patterns appear in their behavior. Many become chronic offenders who fill our city jails. Some finally are institutionalized and treated in mental hospitals. A few even commit crazy murders.

The *narcissistic* compulsive spender may disburse his money for clothes, jewelry, beauty treatments, or plastic surgery. All he is interested in is enhancing his appearance and attracting the admiration of others. The *show-off* spender must have a large audience, since what he enjoys most is astonishing people by the lavishness or unusualness of his spending. He likes to give money to institutions or organizations which will give him the publicity he craves. The *competitive* spender disburses his money to retain social prestige by outspending others in his social group. The *affection-buying* compulsive spender tries to buy love wherever he can bolster up his own feelings of inferiority. His efforts are self-defeating because he often befriends immature individuals who, instead of giving him the affection he craves, are ever-insistent for larger handouts. This compulsive spender often lapses into periodic alcoholism, during which time he throws money away to watch people scramble for it.

Some salesmen and executives who have emotionally well-balanced uses of the money they earn, obtain special gratification from compulsive spending of their company's accounts. They enjoy the feeling of being lavish hosts—at someone else's expense.

The self-pitying individual spends compulsively only when he is mildly depressed—sometimes for good reason. At such times, he may feel that no one loves him. He may shower gifts on himself till his spirits improve. I know of several patients who during hospitalization for surgical procedures secretly sent themselves flowers, fruits, and other gifts, with self-directed, self-written, effusive get-well wishes.

Sometimes a woman who has had a quarrel with her husband feels so low that she has to reward herself by buying several expensive hats which she doesn't need, and may never wear. When she makes her purchases, her anger at her husband disappears, as does her depression.

Gamblers are compulsive spenders who get excitement at the prospect of losing what they already have. They basically have the desire for big income with little work. By losing money, they punish themselves for these desires. When they win, they spend money liberally, enjoying particularly the pleasures of alcohol, tobacco, food, and sex.

Bargain hunters are often compulsive spenders, in the sense that they buy things they don't need merely because they are cheap.

The *infantile* spender is a person who literally throws money away. This behavior is normal for infants and very young children. Some alcoholics, psychotics, and senile individuals get gratification from throwing their money away and watching the furore this causes.

Indecisive or Fearful Uses of Money

Sometimes an individual has the history of having been so frustrated by his early money experiences that he has developed poor problem-solving ability in relationship to spending money. Usually, no matter how he spent money as a child, he was told he was wrong; and at unpredictable intervals he was punished for making mistakes in his use of money even when he didn't think he had done anything wrong.

In adulthood, he is often a cringing, insecure individual who is afraid to spend the money at his disposal. He wants to please others by the way he spends his money—and buys mainly to please salespeople. He deprives himself of things he wants because he fears that his spending money for this purpose would cause others to ridicule him. He usually is underpaid for his work, fearful of losing his job, and willing to lend others money in an attempt to gain their approval.

All of his money behavior tends to perpetuate his habit of making mistakes in the use of money, and thus further justifies his lack of self-confidence.

Denial of Economic Status

Pretended wealth. These people are often ashamed of their origins. Sometimes they come from well-to-do families who have lost their fortunes. They spend money to make others feel that they are wealthy, hoping thereby to attract genuinely wealthy people to them in order to gain fair or unfair advantage. Matrimony is often the object of such people who want to "better" themselves. Of course, they are seriously limited by their lack of funds, and must resort to subterfuge or illegality to maintain their front.

Pretended poverty. These individuals want to be pitied and have a passive-dependent status. They want to be given handouts so that they can conserve their own money. They secretly enjoy the potential power of their hidden monetary reserves. Many have paranoid fears that mysterious enemies are threatening to deprive them of their wealth. They believe that by seeming to be poor they will be protected against robbery. They distrust banks and often hide their money on their persons or in their homes. They are self-punitive and self-denying.

Emotional Uses of Money as Rewards

The possessor of money can manipulate the behavior of other human beings for constructive or destructive purposes through the use of monetary rewards.

When used constructively, monetary rewards encourage socially desirable activities in individuals and groups. Such a reward may reenforce desirable behavior traits in a child. It keeps adults at their daily work. It can be used to improve education, raise standards of living, improve health and welfare, and encourage creative activities in the arts and sciences. The proper uses of monetary rewards can even become an effective way of helping mentally sick patients to become rehabilitated. (In an excellent study, *Dr. Peter A. Peffer* has given a concise picture of the remarkable benefits which occur when properly selected patients in a mental institution are permitted to work for money rewards.)

Unfortunately, monetary rewards can also be used destructively to encourage unethical, illegal, or immoral activity. Bribery is often used to break down an individual's resistance to antisocial acts—and as the sum involved becomes large enough, many previously upright people succumb to the temptation. This leads to the cynical idea that every man has his price. The point of breakdown in terms of dollars and cents is a measure of the sturdiness of an individual's ethical and moral training, and of the strength of his conscience in opposing his desire for illegitimate economic gain.

Emotionally Punitive Uses of Money

Some parents control their adult children by threatening to disinherit them for disobedience. Many a passive-dependent personality will allow himself to be controlled in this way.

Sometimes gifts of money are used to disrupt the normal incentives conducive to competitive work behavior.

A grandparent may attempt to wean a grandchild's affections away from his parents by plying him with money and with luxuries that money buys. This struggle for dominance favors the moneyed grandparent and permits him to punish his own children, when symbolically buying the love and affection of his grandchildren.

A girl who learned that her father had a mistress, suddenly went on spending sprees, unconsciously desiring to punish her father and at the same time to rectify symbolically the wrong done to her mother. She opened many new charge accounts and bought expensive gifts for her mother which were charged to her father.

Charitable Uses

Many give to charity because they believe it is the duty of those who have money to share it with the needy or the sick. Some do so to gain the approval of others, and to get publicity for themselves. Many give to charity to assuage their feelings of guilt.

Guilty Uses

An individual may consciously or unconsciously wish to make symbolic or actual restitution for some real or imagined antisocial act he has committed. To do so, he may give small or large sums of money to a charity, institution, or individual—or he may even pay some of his evaded back taxes. He may do this anonymously, or he may want to have his name associated with the gift or restitution even though no one suspects his motivation.

Fetish and Ritual Uses

Some particular coin or sum of paper money may be used as a good-luck piece, and the individual's self-reliance and peace of mind seem contingent on his having the monetary fetish always with him. Sometimes the individual associates a particularly auspicious event with having this money—including having found it originally. At other times a person may carry a specific, sufficiently large sum of money to ward off possible recurrence of a previously embarrassing situation which occurred when he lacked sufficient funds for some particular purpose.

Some people are impelled to count their money repeatedly in times of stress. When the crisis in their lives is solved in a manner acceptable to them, they no longer have the need to count their money.

Emotional Uses of Money in the Transference Relationship

During the positive transference relationship, a therapist has no trouble collecting fees for his services—and his grateful patient may even shower him with handsome gifts.

However, during negative transference, the patient feels intensely hostile toward the therapist, especially with regard to fees. Symbolically the doctor is fantasied as being a parent-surrogate who should be giving the patient money instead of charging him. These intense but unrealistic feelings lead the patient to attempt to have acrimonious discussions about the doctor's charges, even though he is well able to afford the fee, which is a fair one for the professional services rendered. At a later time, when the patient regains emotional perspective, he may be contrite about the intensity of his attack against his therapist.

Since it is the husband who often pays his wife's medical bills, his latent negative feelings toward his wife may become exteriorized when he claims falsely that the charge is too high. What he really means is that he doesn't feel his wife is worth this expense.

Sometimes a person in moderate or wealthy circumstances will be well-balanced in his spending, except when he refuses to pay certain specific bills for food or clothing. It is as if he felt that his creditors as parent-surrogates owed him these specific items. He punishes them by withholding money deliberately, knowing how much trouble it is to bring suit and collect. Such a person speaks ill of those who force him to pay the bills he owes.

Occasionally a mother—less often a father—having a negative transference reaction to her own son, who declared his emotional and financial independence of her, seeks the professional services of men approximately her son's age, and stubbornly withholds payment until forced by law to settle her bills.

Older People

Older people may find it increasingly difficult to manage successfully their economic resources, and often become emotionally disturbed when they have to solve even minor problems relating to the use of money.

Sometimes an older person of this sort desires to assume a passive-dependent relationship with others, who take over his care so that he will not need to concern himself with money matters. Such an individual may be willing to turn over all his economic resources to others in return for lifelong care.

Some older people become anxious, fearful, and depressed if they have to relinquish control of their funds to others. These people have always enjoyed the power money gave them, and even though others manage their affairs, they like to feel that they always make their own final decisions.

Some senile individuals develop intense fear reactions when they imagine that their families are trying to do away with them, either to save expenses or gain control of their funds. These fears may in turn inspire self-defensive behavior which is difficult to manage in the family setting.

A few older people may literally throw their money away, sign blank checks, or give gifts to strangers. They may make punitive wills disinheriting children or relatives, for real or fancied slights.

Some older people who are well-off financially feel so insecure that they are impelled to hoard their resources to the point of miserliness. Others suddenly increase their scale of spending in order to enjoy in their declining years many of the pleasures and luxuries they formerly denied themselves.

Psychotics

The first indication of the breakdown in reality function of an adult may be his inappropriate uses of money or money transactions.

An elated or manic individual is a wild person in his spending. His interest jumps from one thing to another, with breaks in the continuity of his thinking. He tends to buy everything big, but even before a deal is consummated he is interested in carrying out some other money transaction. He cannot be induced by pleas of family or friends to be more circumspect in his spending. In fact, this angers him and may increase the rate of his disbursement of money. Sexual promiscuity, heavy eating and drinking are an important part of his spending orgies. As long as his income and spending are in equilibrium, he is not likely to have legal difficulties. Occasionally during a manic phase a man may launch a successful business project. More often he merely dissipates his resources. He may recover from his manic phase with or without treatment, and may again have better-balanced uses of money, perhaps becoming economy-minded. Or he may go into a depressive phase.

The depressed spender may spend little or nothing, and becomes more depressed with every expenditure. Sometimes, immediately before depression sets in, the patient guiltily uses some of his money to make symbolic restitution for his real or fancied anti-social acts. The depressed individual cannot continue working and earning. He feels impoverished, unworthy and unloved, and may often refuse to eat. A few seem to equate money to excreta or dirt. If the depressed individual recovers spontaneously or through therapy, he will gradually redevelop his prepsychotic uses of money.

The paranoid may spend money in a manner which indicates that he thinks someone may overcharge or rob him. He may secrete money in various pockets, in shoes, sew it into secret hiding places in his outer clothes or underwear. His spending is greatly restricted, since he fears that any display of his buying power may lead to attacks from powerful imaginary enemies. As paranoid delusions get more fixed, he is less able to get along with other people. Some emotionally sick people in this group become frankly schizophrenic paranoids.

The schizophrenic individual has erratic uses of money. He may have no recollection of what he does with his money, and may appear indifferent to the consequences of what he does with it. He may buy an expensive and wholly useful object which he adores—or may buy a piece of junk and adore it just as much. He may give money to a person whom he later assaults and kills. Or he may attack and rob a stranger. His spending behavior is unpredictable, and without recognizable reality function. Those schizophrenics in remission try to maintain a passive-dependent relationship to some person whose advice about money matters they try to follow. But even so, inexplicable expenditures occur.

Beginning with an individual's early life experiences, his use of money becomes subject to various instinctual, emotional, and intellectual reactions which ultimately lead either to socially acceptable or unacceptable money behavior. Aberrant money behavior, in turn, may create many varieties of psychosomatic illness. Moreover, mental illness may cause an individual to develop inappropriate uses of money.

Money-sickness is a clinically evident disturbance in the individual's psychosomatic health which is initiated by his excessive reaction to the stress of psycho-economic problems. It may take such forms as: headaches, anxiety states, hysterical paralysis, obsessional reaction patterns, panic reactions, depression, behavior disorders, and dysfunctions of gastrointestinal, cardio-respiratory and musculoskeletal systems.

One reason why money-sickness is not often detected is that most doctors have not been interested in studying the psycho-economic behavior of individuals. A doctor himself may have unresolved emotional problems regarding his own uses of money which unconsciously prevent him from recognizing or investigating his patient's abnormal psycho-economic behavior. He may consider it indelicate or unnecessary to ask how his patient uses money, and he certainly doesn't want to offend his patient, who may resent and misinterpret such questions as being "too personal." For these reasons, a doctor is usually content to send his bill and receive payment for his services without looking further into the psycho-economic processes of his patient. Unless the patient spontaneously talks about his financial problems during therapy sessions, this matter may never be explored. Instead, the patient may talk interminably about symptoms, troubled interpersonal relations, unhappy sex life, and dreams—all of which may be secondary to his psycho-economic problems.

In instances of money-sickness, the doctor cannot be his patient's banker or financial advisor. But he can help direct his patient's attention to the money-roots of his stressful contemporary life problems. When good rapport between patient and therapist can be established, it is surprising how rapidly progress toward recovery can be made by discussing the broad money problems of the patient at the very start of treatment. If the patient can be helped to get a new viewpoint and gain insight into the nature of his money problems and how these affect him psychosomatically, he is often able to develop good solutions leading to a cure of his basic emotional problems. This may require a change in job, a change in saving, borrowing, lending, or spending habits, a change in financial relations with members of his family, a change in his economic goals—or any other type of appropriate psycho-economic adjustment.

The psycho-economic aspects of the patient's emotional disorder must always be considered by the doctor in relation to other noxious causes which may simultaneously contribute to ill-health. The doctor should try to evaluate all the factors contributing to his patient's ill-health, so that these will appear in proper perspective and be given proper weight in the treatment of the patient as a person.

But instead of focusing all of our attention on diagnosis and treatment alone, our goal should also be prevention of the development of abnormal psycho-economic patterns of behavior in children. This can be done by helping parents to understand and resolve their own psycho-economic problems and to learn how to help their children to develop healthy patterns of money behavior.

If we could be successful in these undertakings, we might find that our world would be a much better place to live in—not only because of improvement in individual health, but also because there would be a corresponding resolution of many of the unsolved sociologic problems which plague us today.

Summary

Money is an important stimulus for many patterns of normal and abnormal human behavior. Most people, rich or poor, are more or less continuously concerned—consciously or unconsciously—with the solution of their private money problems.

In a study of over a thousand patients from three to eighty-four years of age whom the author saw in his private practice of internal medicine over a period of twelve years, it has been possible to trace how concepts of money and money transactions are integrated into our lives, consciously or unconsciously, influencing our conduct, our aspirations and emotional reactions to ourselves, our families, other people, and even to our physical environment.

The manner in which a child resolves his early conflicts about money will determine some of his basic adult personality and character traits, aspirations, and behavior patterns. The first breakdown in reality function of an adult may show itself by the inappropriate uses of money or money transactions; whereas the first signs of improvement may be the return of the ability to use money properly. Many individuals who develop emotional and psychosomatic disorders as a result of their inability to cope with their money problems—whether these be realistic or irrational—may be helped through psychotherapy.

The psycho-economic aspects of the patient's emotional or psychosomatic disorders must always be considered by the doctor in relation to other noxious causes which may simultaneously be contributing to the sickness. The doctor should try to evaluate all factors contributing to his patient's ill health so that these will appear in proper perspective, and be given the proper weight in the treatment of the patient as a person.

Contribution 12

The Hidden Faces of Money

Smiley Blanton

How sound are your money-attitudes? Is money your servant or your master? As you move into the middle years, will you manage money or will money manage you?

Silly questions? Not at all. A surprising percentage of people who come to me for counseling are in trouble because of warped money-concepts—their own or someone else's. There are, indeed few areas of living where emotional maladjustment shows itself so plainly.

Money-attitudes often become a serious problem during the middle years, not only because hidden tensions finally break through defenses, but simply because during this period the average person's involvement in money rises to a peak. To a far greater degree than in youth or old age, he earns more, spends more, borrows more, and worries more.

It's obvious to all of us that some people seem to have a gift for managing money. They make good use of whatever funds they have, be they great or small. Other people are forever being pushed around or rendered unhappy by money problems of one sort or another. Is there any basic difference between the two types? I think there is. One regards money as a medium of exchange—nothing more. The other lets money become a symbol of something else.

What this "something else" may be varies greatly with the individual. To some people, money becomes a symbol of power: they strive to amass it so that they can bend other people to their will. To some it represents virility: they hate to part with it because they fear, quite unconsciously, that their sexual or creative powers may be diminished. To some love-starved people, money becomes equated with affection; if they ask for a raise and fail to get it they are in despair because they feel nobody loves them. Some guilty souls try to throw money away because their conscience tells them that they do not deserve to have it.

As I have said repeatedly throughout this book, the ideal time to examine yourself for traces of such hidden motivation is at the beginning of the middle years, where you have at last the wisdom and self-honesty to see yourself clearly, and still retain the flexibility that makes change relatively easy. Where money-attitudes are concerned, this is doubly important, because a warped perspective has a marked effect not only on you but on those around you: your family, your dependents, and your employees.

A Check List of Money Attitudes

To make a rough check of those attitudes, let me ask you some rather personal questions, and urge you to summon up all your self-honesty before you try to answer them.

1. Do you find it difficult to buy things that you need and can well afford?
2. Are you making life drab by denying yourself or your family oridnary pleasures on the grounds of being prudent?
3. Do you justify this caution by a conviction that the country is going to the dogs?
4. Do your business ventures or financial investments have a persistent way of turning out badly?
5. Do you have a tendency to squander money, live beyond your means?

6. Does gambling mean more to you than just occasional diversion?
7. Do you fear that, unless you work constantly to maximum capacity, disaster may overtake you?
8. Are you always giving more presents than you get, especially to people whose esteem or affection you crave?
9. Do you think that if you just had more money, all your troubles would vanish?
10. Do you consider money-making ability a sound yardstick for judging people?

Admittedly, these are loaded questions. But affirmative answers to any of them may indicate a need for reappraisal and readjustment. Behind each "yes" or "maybe" lurks the possibility that money has ceased to be merely a convenient device for transferring purchasing power from one person to another and has become equated, in the deep unconscious mind, with something else.

Consider the first three questions. These are designed to detect evidence of the most common maladjustment where money is concerned: an inability to spend it sensibly—or in some cases to spend it at all.

Hardly a week goes by but some unhappy woman comes to my office in despair, not because she has emotional problems of her own, but because her husband's tight-fistedness is driving the whole family to distraction. The difficulty in such cases is almost never lack of money; usually there is more than enough for all reasonable purposes. The problem is that under the guise of "prudence" or "discipline," the person holding the purse-strings (man or woman) is acting like a miser.

The offender in such cases always has an array of arguments to justify his penny-pinching. A depression is at hand. The value of the dollar is steadily shrinking. His wife doesn't know how to manage money. His children are potential spendthrifts. If all else fails, he will fall back on the ancient and incontestable statement: "Money doesn't grow on trees, you know!"

Such justifications seem to him entirely valid. He believes them implicitly; that is why it is so hard to argue with him or change him. He cannot and will not see that his reasons are largely false reasons, carefully selected by his conscious mind to conceal and camouflage the fact that in his unconscious mind money has become the symbol of something he hates to part with, something he cannot bear to lose.

What Makes a Miser?

As everyone knows, we psychiatrists believe that adult personality traits are reflections of patterns formed in childhood. Babies and small children are completely self-centered. They resent any delay in the gratification of their desires, and they resent any outside authority. A child's first serious conflict with authority usually arises when his parents require him to control his eliminative habits. If this training is too strict or too harsh—or even if the child is praised too lavishly for cooperating—impressions are made on the receptive clay of his personality that may persist, in disguised form, throughout adult life.

Sometimes, if the child resents these attempts at regulation strongly enough, he will refuse to cooperate. He will delay, he will withhold, he will not "give." In later life, these retentive characteristics may come very much to the fore where money is concerned.

It's not always money. I know a very wealthy woman who saves string and cardboard boxes; she had two whole rooms full of them. The reason she gives, quite seriously, is that she may need them some day. Her little quirk is harmless enough, but carried to extremes it might result in one of those appalling examples of filthy, junk-crammed houses occupied by fear-ridden recluses who save everything from old newspapers to empty bottles.

The main thing to remember and ponder about such people is this: *they didn't get that way overnight*. The habit of stinginess, of closeness, of morbid prudence grew in them slowly. Had they taken time out early enough for honest self-appraisal, had they heeded the advice of their pastor, priest, or rabbi to think in terms of *giving* rather than of *getting* or *keeping*, they might have changed their thought patterns while they were still pliable enough to be changed.

Sometimes patterns formed in childhood are strongly reinforced by unconscious adult fears or resentments. A classic example of this was brought to us at the Foundation not long ago. In this case, the head of the family was a self-made man who had been forced to go to work at the age of twelve. By sheer drive and determination, he had become quite successful, and now was forging through what should have been the happiest period of his life: the middle years. But he was a very unhappy fellow indeed.

Recently, he told us, he had made a lucky investment that netted him some ten thousand dollars over and above his regular annual income. But, as so often seems to be the case, the extra money had not brought happiness. It had brought trouble.

This man had a wife whose parents were from Scotland. They had often told their daughter and their grandchildren how beautiful the old country was, had urged them to go there if they ever had the chance. Now the opportunity seemed to exist, but the husband maintained stubbornly that they could not afford such a trip. The result was great conflict in the family. The wife and children felt that the head of the house was being unkind and unreasonable. In the end, they brought the controversy to us.

"If you don't take this trip," we said to the husband, "what will you do with the extra money?"

He said that he planned to invest it. This, he added, was the prudent thing to do.

"Well," we said, "it's true that you can invest it and receive an additional income of four or five hundred dollars a year. But some of this will vanish in taxes. Besides, you don't really need the money. Is having this extra income more important to you than giving your wife and children the satisfaction of visiting a place they have always longed to see? Wouldn't their pleasure and gratitude be worth more to you than the money? Or, if not, isn't it possible that you are being dominated by some secret anxiety or resentment that you're not consciously aware of?"

Because he was an honest person, and because he did love his family, he admitted reluctantly that this might be so. A little probing then revealed the fact that he had always been jealous of his wife's pride in her Scottish ancestry. His own family had come from Eastern Europe and did not have the prestige of hers, or so he thought. His lack of formal education was also a factor in his sense of inferiority.

Basically he was refusing to pay for the trip because unconsciously he feared that his wife and children considered themselves superior to him—and Scotland was the symbol of that superiority. But his *conscious* mind saw his refusal as a wise and cautious decision based on the best interests of all concerned. It was the case of a man projecting a hidden, personal, neurotic anxiety into an outside situation—something, of course, that happens all the time.

The family did go to Scotland, and came back happier and more united than it had ever been. Why? *Because a man in his middle years sought and gained self-knowledge, gained it while there was still time to free himself from the invisible forces that were depriving him of happiness.*

That story had a happy ending. I am sorry to say that I have witnessed many that did not. All too often, if allowed to develop unchecked through the middle years, this morbid "prudence" becomes so strong that nothing can alter or arrest it. I know one multimillionaire whose compulsive drive to make more and more money is matched only by his determination to keep it. He will not give his children spending money. He makes his wife do her own housework. He pays his employees as little as he can. He wears old clothes. . . .

Such a specimen of the human race is both tragic

and terrifying. He seems indifferent to the fact that most people have come to despise him. He has no hobbies, no diversions. Like a spider at the center of a web, he watches ceaselessly for new money-making schemes and ventures. Nothing else seems to matter to him. Like Midas he goes on, day after day, loveless and surrounded by gold.

The Need to Throw Money Away

At the other end of the scale from the misers are people who seem to be determined to get rid of their money, one way or another. Again, the explanations that they offer themselves and the world in general are seldom in accord with the underlying truth.

Question 4 in our check-list, you will recall, dealt with *persistent* business failures or financial losses. Every psychiatrist encounters cases where the victims of such losses are being impelled by forces that are completely hidden from them.

One of the most common is a strong sense of guilt. Our consciences demand punishment when we have violated a moral principle, and often the self-inflicted punishment is directed at the pocketbook. I knew a woman once, an outwardly poised and handsome person in her mid-thirties, whose rather large fortune was handled for her by her father. At one point, when she questioned his judgment in some transaction, he lost his temper and told her that henceforth she could manage her own affairs. She did take over, and within a few months managed to lose almost half her holdings.

The reason was not lack of experience, or bad judgment. She felt guilty about the rift with her father and was punishing herself by getting rid of the money that had been the cause of the quarrel. When this was pointed out to her, she was sensible enough to seek a reconciliation with her father, stopped losing money, and began slowly to repair the financial damage.

Sometimes people will fling away their money or

even sabotage their own jobs in an effort to force someone else to take care of them. Not long ago an unmarried woman—also in her middle thirties—came to us at the Foundation and said that she was in trouble. She was in debt, had no job, no friends who could help her. It was really quite a pathetic story. Yet she seemed well-educated, able-bodied, intelligent.

It turned out that this woman was the only child of parents who had been divorced years before. Each parent had re-married. They had sent their daughter to good schools, and during her twenties had given her an allowance so that she could get started as a writer. But as time passed, and her writing proved unsuccessful, they urged her to get a job.

This she always avoided as long as she could. Then, when forced to go to work, she always performed badly. She would never be on time. She would fail to carry out assignments. In the end, she was always fired.

During these periods of brief employment, moreover, she would indulge in foolish extravagances. She would move to a more expensive apartment. She would buy a car, on time. Finally her exasperated father said he was through with her, that she could sink or swim. Frightened, she had come to us. She wanted us to persuade her father to change his mind.

The camouflage in this case was rather thin, although neither the woman nor her parents were able to see through it. Such willful negligence and extravagance in a potentially competent person was obviously designed to compel her parents to give her the attention and protection she felt she had been denied as a child. "Look at me," she was saying in effect. "I'm so weak, so foolish, so helpless. Come and get me out of trouble. Pay attention to me, please. Give me love—even if you give it in the form of money!"

Chronologically, this woman was thirty-seven. Emotionally, she was still a lost and bewildered child. Here she was, standing on the threshold of the middle years, facing a bleak and lonely future simply because she could not see deep enough into herself. Once she was given some insight into her basic motivation, and some hard-hitting common sense about the necessity for standing on her own feet, she began to do better. People *do* change, they *do* begin to unlock the problems that confront them once they acquire the key of self-knowledge.

This woman was mismanaging money—and indeed her whole life—because she was starved for love. I have also seen cases where people mismanaged money for revenge. A very wealthy man I once knew developed a serious heart condition in his late fifties. Through overhearing some chance remark, he became convinced that his relatives were waiting eagerly for him to die so that they could inherit his money. He had always been a successful investor in the stock market, but now he began to speculate heavily, and with disastrous results. His fortune dwindled rapidly, and might have vanished altogether if he hadn't died suddenly. Many of his associates were mystified at what seemed to be the sudden loss of his former business acumen and skill, a loss he himself had angrily attributed to bad luck. What actually took place was a reflection of his strong unconscious desire to thwart the "vulture-relatives" who, he fancied, were sitting around waiting for him to die. Without even knowing it, this man was using money as a weapon—a weapon of retaliation, of revenge.

To people who strive honestly and earnestly to earn their daily bread—and this includes most of us—the idea that some individuals are driven by a hidden need to get rid of money seems fantastic. But it is true. Chronic gamblers often belong in this category. On the surface they seem to be weak or lazy people trying to make money the easy way. Actually, they are often dominated by an unconscious desire to lose. That is why your habitual gambler almost never quits when he is ahead. It also explains some people's inability to stop gambling, even when they decide in their conscious minds that they want to.

There is nothing wrong, from the psychiatric point

of view, with winning or losing a few dollars at bridge or poker now and then, or having a friendly bet on the outcome of a golf match or a football game. But the obsessive gambler is never satisfied with such mild diversions. He is engaged in a desperate struggle to force Fate, or Lady Luck, to show him particular favor, to be especially nice to him—perhaps because as a child he felt his own mother was not so nice to him.

In his conscious mind, he is convinced that he must and will ultimately win. But in his unconscious mind he knows that he will lose, that Lady Luck will not be kind to him. And so he presses on relentlessly toward disaster, eager for the "injustice" of losing to be visited on him so that Lady Luck will be exposed as unkind and ungenerous, just as he felt the "cruel" parent was ungenerous so long ago.

If such a paradox seems incredible to the gambler—or to the average person for that matter—it is only because most of us never face up to the tremendous role that the unconscious plays in our daily lives. But where reason and logic end, the unconscious takes over. That is what happens to the compulsive gambler. He is being driven by forces beyond his conscious control.

Kleptomaniacs, too, are often motivated by strong unconscious impulses. Some steal things hoping that they will be caught and punished for real or fancied crimes that they have tried to suppress or forget. Others wish to punish their parents by bringing disgrace upon the family. The motivation need not always be so obscure; no doubt in many cases the shoplifter simply steals for profit. But when the thief doesn't need the money or the object stolen, chances are that hidden forces are at work.

It is difficult for the victim of such hidden impulses to identify them once they have seized control. But it is perfectly possible for the average intelligent person to examine himself for *tendencies* that may lead to trouble, to probe a little deeper into the underlying motives.

Take Question 7, for example. Do you work harder than is really necessary? Are you afraid *not* to work so hard? If so, ask yourself *why*. Is it normal ambition and a natural desire to get ahead? Is it an unreasonable fear of poverty, of insecurity, that may have been implanted in you in childhood? Is it a conviction that money is essential to happiness, or to standing in your community? Is it to give your children things you never had? You may not be able to give yourself conclusive answers, but at least you will be looking within yourself, groping for self-knowledge, and this in itself is a sign of maturity.

Or take Question 8. Is it possible that sometimes you attempt to use money to buy friendship? To make people like you? The answers to such questions may sometimes be disturbing, especially if they are honest answers. But you will be a broader and deeper and wiser person for having asked them.

One of the hardest things for most of us to do, as the middle years rush by, is to assign money its proper value. This, of course, varies with the circumstances, which are constantly changing. To a man with five children, for example, a dollar is more important than it is to a bachelor with the same income. The sudden outlay of a hundred dollars might mean little to a millionaire, whereas it would be a very serious matter for a day laborer, and so on.

The truth is, the more money you have, the less important it should seem to you, but this is not always the case. I am forever encountering people who, in Oscar Wilde's phrase, know the price of everything and the value of nothing.

I remember one very rich man in his mid-fifties who belonged in this category—until he was forced to change his attitude, the hard way.

This man had a daughter, his only child, who had made a very unfortunate marriage. Her husband was a fortune hunter, the worst type. He was cruel and abusive to his wife, and unkind to their two children. So obnoxious was he that the wife finally decided to sue for divorce. Thereupon the husband announced that he would contest the divorce and fight for the custody of the children—unless his father-in-law paid him fifty thousand dollars!

For fifty thousand dollars, the husband said, he would relinquish all claims to the children and never trouble his wife again. His father-in-law, naturally, was furious. He said the husband's proposal was blackmail—which indeed it was. He swore he would never submit to it.

I had been trying to help the daughter through some of her difficulties, and so was familiar with all the details of the case. It seemed to me that the father of the girl was taking a rather foolish view of the realities involved.

"What is fifty thousand dollars to you?" I asked him. "You could lose ten times that amount, and still have more money than you will ever need. You already have everything you want in terms of houses and cars and other possessions. What is fifty thousand dollars compared to your daughter's happiness and your grandchildren's welfare?"

He gave me a grim look. "You seem to think," he said, "that money grows on trees!"

"No," I said, "I don't think that. But I do think that this is a remarkable example of a case where happiness—or at least freedom from unhappiness—can be bought for a fraction of your total wealth. Imagine one of those old-fashioned balances in which people used to weigh things. On one side visualize your check for $50,000. On the other side visualize the disappearance, for good and all, of this scoundrel who is making you all miserable. Now, is there really anything to hesitate about?"

He did hesitate, for quite a while. But in the end he rethought his position. He came to the conclusion that, distasteful though it was to yield to such pressure, the value to be received far outweighed the price. He wrote the check—and redeemed his daughter's happiness.

Few of us, perhaps, ever have to choose between price and value on such a large scale. But most of us face the same choice daily, in dozens of small ways. I have a friend, for example, who thinks nothing of spending fifteen or twenty dollars on a pair of theater tickets, but will park his car five blocks away and make his wife walk in the rain rather than spend another dollar or so to put the car in a garage opposite the theater. This seems to me rather silly. I know men who persist in trying to get ten shaves out of a razor blade, although the economy thus effected is microscopic. Is their facial discomfort worth it? I shouldn't think so. But they keep on trying.

The other day when I was enjoying my favorite game, golf, someone asked me where I got the excellent sun-glasses I was wearing, and what they cost. I told him where I got them and added that they cost $45 a pair. He was absolutely horrified at the price. "How can you justify such a thing?" he asked me.

"Very simply," I said. "I have only one pair of eyes."

That same day a shower came up and we were forced to cut our game short. One of the foursome, I'm sorry to say, insisted that since we had only played nine holes, he only owed his caddie half the 18-hole fee agreed upon. The rest of us pointed out that the rain was hardly the caddie's fault, but he was adamant. In the end, the rest of us paid the balance of the caddie's fee. That man may have saved a few pennies, but he lost three friends. He thought he was managing his money, but he was wrong. His money was managing him.

The Art of Enjoying Money

Most of us, fortunately, are neither kleptomaniacs nor gamblers, misers nor wastrels; nor will we become such if periodically during the middle years we coolly and dispassionately check ourselves and our habits for tell-tale signs. But most of us, if we gave it some time and thought, could learn to be wiser about money.

One all-too-human failing that I frequently encounter is the tendency to exaggerate the importance of money where happiness is concerned. Countless patients have told me, in all seriousness, that if they just had more money, all their troubles would vanish. Nothing could be farther from the truth. It's true that at subsistence level, or below it, lack of money is a real and terrifying menace. But above what might be termed the adequate-income-level, additional funds rarely solve basic problems. In fact, sitting in my office chair, I have often had occasion to wonder if surplus money doesn't create more problems than it solves. As Richard Burton said more than three centuries ago in his *Anatomy of Melancholy*, the rich, rather than possessing their money, are possessed by it.

Money does *not* solve all problems, and if you really accept this fact your whole approach to life and to the pursuit of happiness may be subtly changed. We Americans, by and large, are good at making money, and there's nothing wrong with that; a man should be proud to be productive, and earning capacity is a reflection of productivity. Americans are also the most generous people on the face of the earth, and this too is something to be proud of. But there may well be some truth in the criticism we receive occasionally from our friends as well as our enemies in other lands: that we are likely to judge a man primarily by his dollar-value, that we tend to confuse success in life with money-making or money-making ability.

"Time is money," our captains of industry say as they hurry to work, and they say it with such conviction that most of us nod in admiring agreement. But time is not money. Time is far more precious stuff. Time is the one gift we all share with absolute impartiality: on any given day, no man has more of it than any other man. On the way we use time, not money, depends our true success in life. Coming to this realization may well be a long step toward evolving a new philosophy that will strengthen and steady us through the middle years.

Money can help us make good use of time, if we

employ it properly. But it's surprising how many people are unable to do this. All of us, I'm sure, know people of means whose money—for all the good it does them—might just as well be buried in the ground. I think it might be well for everyone in the middle years to say to himself firmly every morning for a week: "*When* I make enough money to be financially secure, or *if* I ever inherit more than I need, I am going to get some satisfaction out of it. And I'm going to see that my family and friends have pleasure from it, too!"

To convert money into usefulness or pleasure, it is almost always necessary to spend it. I say "almost always" because some people clearly get more pleasure out of saving it than spending it. I remember one gentleman, whom we treated at the Foundation, who kept a washtub full of silver coins down in his basement: quarters, half-dollars, dollars. He would plunge his arms in money up to the elbows, let it stream between his fingers, and have himself a whale of a time. He admitted a bit sheepishly that this was somewhat foolish. But since this particular activity was doing no one any harm, we didn't insist that he drop it. We merely tried to make him see that there were more productive uses for his money, and finally succeeded in doing so.

"Well," some readers may object, "a washtub full of money is hardly one of *my* problems. I don't have to worry about the conversion of surplus cash into enjoyment because there isn't any surplus cash!"

Maybe there isn't, particularly if you are at the threshold of the middle years. But you never know: there may be later. I am merely suggesting that the wise person will not let rigid habits of economy become too ingrained, that he will be sensible about money and yet retain enough flexibility to use it occasionally for some non-essential or even frivolous purpose. In my opinion, the housewife who occasionally buys spaghetti for supper instead of lamb chops, and spends the difference on a dozen gladioli, or even treats herself to a movie, is likely to be a healthier and happier person than the one who is continually denying herself small pleasures in the name of prudence or stern self-denial.

I am not, I trust, recommending a spendthrift philosophy, nor do I like to see people try to live beyond their means. But there is something both pathetic and exasperating about people who refuse to live up to anything approaching their means. They are really fugitives from living, victims of the unconscious and irrational fear that the expenditure of money will somehow make them smaller, rob them of virility, shorten their life-span.

And for what? With the whole wide world to explore, with plays to be seen, books read, concerts heard, with golf to be played, hobbies developed, people to be helped, communities to be improved, with your own personality to be enriched and broadened in a thousand different ways, why go on blindly, neurotically piling up mountains of gold which you certainly cannot take with you when you leave this troubled planet, and which may very well rob your children of initiative and self-reliance when all of it—or as much as Uncle Sam will allow—is poured into their outstretched and more-or-less undeserving hands? Surplus money just isn't that important!

Certainly religion has always known this, and has tried to teach it. The wisest man who ever lived was approached by a rich young aristocrat who was seeking true happiness. "What shall I do?" the young man said. "How can I find it?"

The Master's advice was drastic. "Give away your wealth," he said, in effect. "Get rid of the false values that it represents. Then come and concentrate on the really worthwhile things, the things of the spirit, with me."

The young man could not do it. He "went away sorrowful," and all of us know just how he felt. The conflict between the selflessness of the Christian ethic and the cutthroat competition of the marketplace is still with us, producing discords in the human spirit that go deeper than most of us realize. But we can all *try* to eliminate false values from our lives; we can *strive* for the self-knowledge that makes such improvement possible. That is the marvelous and heartening thing about human beings. We can stop at any time (what is there to prevent it?) and look steadily at ourselves, and if we do not like what we see we can resolve to change it. The change may not come overnight. But the *wish* to change is the first and by far the longest step.

No one should minimize the importance of money; it is a vital aspect of daily living. But it is an aspect that must be understood and controlled. Like all attitudes, money-concepts are formed slowly and remain plastic for some time before becoming fixed and rigid.

At some point, then, preferably early in the middle years, examine yourself for traces of extremism where money is concerned. The hoarder and the miser are extremists. So are the spendthrift and the squanderer. Remember: so long as money remains merely a medium of exchange, it is a useful servant. It's only when you let it become a symbol for something else that trouble may start.

Check your money attitudes against this yardstick. Learn to manage it. Don't let it manage you.

Contribution 13

Psychopathology of "Bargain Hunters"

Edmund Bergler

"A bargain hunter" is a person irresistibly attracted to merchandise which he does not need at the moment but which can be bought cheaply. Window shopping for a person of this type is more than simply a matter of orientation; it is an alluring situation. The difference between such an individual and the normal person, who does not want to be taken advantage of, is that for the former price is more important than usefulness, while for the latter need is of first consideration. Thus, the typical quarrel of many a marriage is: "Did you need that junk?" "Yes, I couldn't resist the price, and besides—I can use it some day."

The act of buying is for the bargain hunter not a rational situation but a battle of wits. He tries to outsmart the seller, who, on the other hand, seeks to give him, the involuntary "sucker," the narcissistic illusion of triumph. That many people buy for the sake of a bargain and not because of need is intuitively known to every merchandiser; he bases his "sales" on this fact. There are jokes as old as Methuselah making fun of this human weakness; for instance, one revived recently: A bargain hunter of antiques sees, in an antique shop, a cat lapping her milk from a saucer which the specialist recognizes as a valuable piece. He feigns interest in the cat only, and purchases it for $5. Then he asks for the saucer, too, for the cat's sake. The smart dealer feigns naiveté, too, and refuses to part with the saucer, saying: "I'm superstitious, and that saucer has brought me luck—I've sold 52 cats already this week."

Analysis of bargain hunters show that they have in common a constant need to outsmart others.[1] One bargain hunter whom I analyzed managed her business badly because of her inner self-damaging tendencies. She was constantly excited about some injustice done to her, which, however, she provoked unconsciously herself. She repeated in life, without knowing it, the situation of the mistreated child. Her whole philosophy was expressed in a little nursery rhyme which she made up and recited with gusto:

> Mother's in the pantry,
> Father's in the hall,
> I therefore put the thumbmarks
> Upon the parlor wall.
> For when the whipping's over,
> The pain will go away,
> But those thumbmarks on the parlor wall
> Will *stay* and *stay* and *stay*.

In other words, she even nursed the recollection of self-provoked humiliations, consciously regarding herself as the innocent victim reacting with righteous indignation. The objectivization ("thumbmarks on the parlor wall") of her "whipping humiliation" was in itself an alibi directed toward her Super Ego: "I am not masochistic! Mother is really cruel to me." This woman had nearly a dozen pairs of everything. Once, when she had to buy a handbag for a relative for Christmas, she increased her already large stock of handbags by a few more, on the ground that they were becoming scarce.

A second patient collected practically everything he owned via bargains. He spent his spare time visiting auctions.

A third patient believed that he could wrest a bargain, even out of analysis. He was highly indignant about the fee, and accepted it only after making the unpleasant discovery that his attempts to have it reduced resulted only in loss of expensive time, especially since he regarded the attempt to analyze his bargaining tendencies as "a waste of time." This man left analysis after ten appointments, having received one preliminary interpretation of his basic difficulty and hoping vainly that he could do the rest of the analytic work himself.

A fourth patient shifted his interests in collecting bargains. At the time I knew him, he was collecting books and tools. He soon lost interest in these, but admitted that bargaining for them had been a "strange pleasure."

A fifth patient—an habitual bargainer—once saw a microscope in a second-hand shop which he felt he must have. After much haggling, he placed a deposit on it, only to feel guilty afterward because he really couldn't afford it, especially since he had no use for it (he was a stockbroker) and was preaching economy to his wife on the ground of "bad times." Naturally, his wife took ample advantage of his purchase—as well as of other similar ones—for reproaches.

A sixth patient, a wealthy woman, was so niggardly that she never bought clothes for herself, though she indulged in constant bargaining in shops without purchasing. She allowed her mother-in-law, also a stingy person, to give her ironically "hand-me-downs." This woman happened to see in a shop an expensive dress priced a few dollars lower than an identical one in another shop. She obeyed an "irresistible impulse" and bought it.

In finding the common denominator of bargain-hunting, we must first exclude the possibility that the purchase has a symbolic meaning. Such a meaning can be found only in exceptional cases.[2] True, the tools of the passive-feminine man mentioned as Case 4 had for him the symbolic meaning of pseudo-masculinity. True, the purchaser of the microscope was in the midst of a voyeuristic conflict at the time of his purchase. But even where these considerations are of importance, they do not account for the basic bargaining "addiction." The pleasure of bargaining can go so far that its devices automatically go into play even when there is no real wish to acquire the object. The battle of wits is the thing.

We must also consider the possibility that these chronic bargainers want to get something for nothing. Could it be that they are parasites? To answer this, we must first investigate the unconscious contents of the "oral" phase of development, at which, in my opinion, all of these people are fixated. Is "I want to get" or "I want to be refused" their inner wish? In my opinion, repeatedly substantiated by clinical facts,[3] oral neurotics construct the following triad:

1. By their behavior they unconsciously provoke a disappointment, thus repeating the disappointment they allegedly experienced through the pre-Oedipal mother.
2. They are not aware consciously that they have provoked the disappointment, and believe that they may be aggressive in self-defense.
3. After being disappointed and fighting their self-constructed enemy, they indulge in masochistic self-pity.

In this triad only the feeling of "righteous indignation" and tearful self-pity are conscious. The initial provocation and the masochistic pleasure found in self-pity are repressed. We see, therefore, that their wish is not "I want to get" but "I want to be refused."

In my opinion, all of the bargain hunters whom I have observed clinically have been orally regressed neurotics. Bargaining corresponds to the second layer of this triad of the "mechanism of orality." In other words, bargain hunters behave as if bad reality (mother substitute) wants to refuse and must be outsmarted with aggression, which shows up in the tenacity of the bargaining process. It represents, so to speak, an attempt at self-cure. It fails because it is intended by the bargainer's own unconscious to fail. Part of his inner modus vivendi is that he must be the sucker in the long run, in order to enjoy his masochistic pleasure.

Men who display a predilection for bargaining usually appear on the surface to be of the passive-feminine type, with weak potency or effeminate character traits. Deeper analysis shows that they are orally regressed.

The technique of bargaining in itself indicates that the aggressive pleasure of outwitting is displayed. The bargainer first belittles[4] the object, arguing for hours about its defects, etc.

> But in the way of bargain, mark ye me,
> I'll cavil on the ninth part of a hair.
> (*King Henry IV*, p. 1, A. 3, Sc. 1).

He takes more pleasure in the negotiations than he does in making an advantageous buy. What he does not know are the following facts:

1. That unconsciously his bargaining represents pseudo-aggression toward the substitute of the bad, refusing mother.
2. That the old adage, "I am not rich enough to buy cheap, therefore poor, merchandise," is empirically correct.
3. That he is a sucker after all, if only in the sense that he invests his money in unnecessary acquisitions and spends an exorbitant amount of time on his hunt.

The attitude of these people toward the objects they have bought is strange. They are uninterested in them after a short period of reveling in them. Only the recollection of their alleged outsmarting remains pleasurable. It is, to quote a witty patient, a "sentimental journey" into the past, riding, not a "hobby horse" (*Tristam Shandy*), but a defense mechanism. Dostoevski remarked the same attitude in a "cured" gambler toward the game.

> Even now, writing it down, I love to think sometimes of the game. I have spent many hours just sitting and occupying myself in imagining the details, how I placed the stakes and how I won.[5]

In one of his letters, the same writer exclaims: "The main point is the game itself. My oath, it is not greed for money, despite the fact that I need money badly."

To summarize: The bargain hunter does not buy a bargain but pays for his pseudo-aggressive defense mechanism. He follows Jachimo's advice in *Cymbeline*, to act quickly, "lest the bargain catch cold and starve," but always finds the bargain a disappointment in the long run. Mr. Field's advice, "Never give a sucker a break," can be applied to him; indeed, he does not even give himself a break. He pays, more than he believes, but for his defense mechanism against his inner masochistic attachment.

Notes and References

1. This applies to persons who buy only when necessary, as well as to those who buy needlessly. One patient of mine started out to buy her husband a cigarette lighter which he wanted, but bought instead an umbrella, because it was a better "bargain." Of course, conscious and unconscious symbolically disguised aggression entered also into her choice.

2. In my experience, the current idea that, especially for women, purchases have a phallic significance is rarely confirmed. I would also doubt the idea that collecting gives expression to anal tendencies only, though these are always present. There are specific differences between the collector and the bargain hunter. The former even overpays for the object, because of the neurotic significance it has for him, as has been shown by Freud and, later, A. V. Winterstein. The latter shifts his interest entirely to the defense mechanism of outwitting the seller, having no specific interest in the object he buys. Bargain-hunting and collecting may be found together, but genetically they differ.

3. This mechanism is summarized in my book *Unhappy Marriage and Divorce*, Int. Universities Press, N. Y., 1946, and in "A Clinical Approach to the Psychoanalysis of Writers," *Psychoan. Rev.*, *31*, No. 1, 1944.

4. There are many forms of haggling. The impasse encountered by the small-town bargain hunter in the impersonal department store of the large city is amusing.

5. For details see "The Psychology of the Gambler," *Imago*, XX, 1936, and "The Gambler—A Misunderstood Neurotic," *J. Crim. Psychopath.*, IV, 3, 1943.

Contribution 14

A Psychoanalytic Study of Money

André Amar

In his *Introductory Lectures on Psychoanalysis*, Freud wrote: "What characterizes Psychoanalysis as a science is not the material which it handles but the technique with which it works. It can be applied to the history of civilization, to the science of religion and to mythology, no less than to the theory of the neuroses, without doing violence to its essential nature. What it aims at and achieves is nothing other than the uncovering of what is unconscious in mental life" (Freud, *Complete Works*, vol. XVI, p. 389). This statement raises two problems: can a social phenomenon be analyzed? And how does one have to go about it? We thus have to examine a question concerning legitimacy, and another concerning method.

The first has already been answered in part. Legends, myths, social and religious manifestations have been interpreted psychoanalytically. As soon as the ethnologist and the sociologist go beyond merely noting facts, as soon as they attempt the explanation of relationships, they are obliged to propose interpretations of a psychoanalytical nature. Of course, the mere existence of such interpretations does not imply their validity. Are they legitimate? Individual analysis deals with the relations of a subject to his environment. Generally speaking, a neurosis may be defined as the difficulty an individual experiences in living in his world. The conflict may take a great variety of forms. But whatever their nature, one thing is certain: the milieu is not composed of a mass of undifferentiated individuals, but of a structured social whole. Whether the relations between a subject and his environment are harmonious or disharmonious, they are social in character and are called money, profession, work, property, marriage, family, hierarchy, civil and political institutions. That the behavior of a subject is ultimately determined by love, antipathy, or anxiety does not change the fact that both illness and therapy manifest themselves in relation to individuals living in society, and that such individuals have certain functions. An analysis is considered successful not only because physiological disturbances have disappeared, but also because it has become possible for the subject to once more gain a foothold in reality. But the reality which interests us here is not physical or chemical reality, but human reality. And every individual exists only in a social constellation. Although treatment means the therapy of a certain person, it must penetrate to the network of social relationships.

On the other hand, every social or political phenomenon rests on a psychic substrate. Either/or—either a group owes its existence merely to mechanical pressure, or the social tie is of a special nature and not reducible to a physical cause. But experience itself eliminates this alternative: interpersonal relationships are of a psychic nature. Of course, economic necessities or biologic requirements cannot be underestimated, but such needs and constraints are never dealt with directly, but always through a number of social intermediaries. The individual is no Robinson Crusoe who tackles nature directly. He is always part of a collective organism, a system of production which even in a rudimentary stage includes the division of labor, functional differentiation, and economic coördination. But the cohesion of parts and social whole depends not only on the creation of institutions and mechanisms. It also needs an energy that binds, of which we are unaware during normal times but which leaps to the eye the moment phenomena of *dissociation* such as economic crises or political revolutions occur. When that happens, institutions and mechanisms do not simply disappear, but the life goes out of them; they become useless, dead objects. An invisible but real bond has been broken. New forces of attraction and repulsion change social relations, new beliefs and morals replace the old—in short, a new image of man makes its appearance.

Thus the social and the human are so closely intertwined that while the individual exists only *in* the group, the latter is traversed by psychic currents like the individual itself. It is by way of and through the individual that psychoanalytic investigation uncovers the structures of the world. Sociological investigation carried beyond superficial description grasps the group as a psychic substance. To see the individual here and the group there as one may distinguish the content from its container is to think in abstractions. Reality is neither the individual nor the group but the nature of man who both shapes and undergoes his development.

If one considers the psychoanalytic interpretation of social phenomena legitimate, there remains the question of procedure. Obviously, this does not mean that techniques by which discoveries will unfailingly be made can be prescribed; they exist in no scientific field. Whatever the methods employed, a discovery always *emerges* before the researcher. Just as there is no technique of thinking, so there is none of discovery. We can only attempt to define a way of approaching the phenomenon to be investigated.

A social phenomenon—the Russian revolution, Western capitalism, the religion of the Incas, for example—never appears in isolation. It is always part of a historical complex outside of which it has no meaning. The difficulty lies in isolating the phenomenon without removing it from its context; in taking account of all its conditions without allowing them to obscure it. The important thing is to grasp its inner unity, not its outward form. But how is this inner unity to be grasped? Unity is not a thing that one can hold in one's hands. Nor is it identity or homogeneity. A human phenomenon is always complex and differentiated. It follows that this unity must be relational, i.e., the unity of structure. This permits us to infer the fundamental rule: *a human phenomenon can only be analyzed if it is referred to a social structure*.

To make this sentence clearer, we will use a concrete example. Let us imagine that we are standing in front of the most powerful, fastest, and most modern locomotive. Whatever may be the technical perfection of this machine, the locomotive has no meaning when it is reduced to its simple appearance. Isolated from its industrial and economic framework, it is brute existence. But actually a locomotive implies tracks, and that means distance to be covered. It also implies freight cars, and that means something to be transported; a source of energy, which means a certain scientific and industrial stage. Once it has been re-integrated into its historical and social nexus, the locomotive reveals not only a specific economic civilization, but also the meaning of that civilization and its goal: the mastery over masses and speeds.

Thus it is social structures which explain individual phenomena, and not the other way around. The intellectual, social, and moral state of Europe during a specific moment of its history explains the deeper meaning of industrial inventions, the coöperation of factory and laboratory, the concentration of the means of production, economic competition. The expansion of Europe was the result of a twofold, scientific and economic, aggressiveness. The individual, physical, tangible object is only the outward expression of a psycho-social structure. If one admits that a human phenomenon must be related to the environment from which it developed, there remains the question of how the structure of this environment can be uncovered. And here we come upon the second fundamental rule: *the structure of a social environment is revealed by the works it produces*. And it is a fact that a social whole is not static, but dynamic or, more precisely, dynamogenic. Every human group has the tendency to produce itself in the external world, to express itself through visible creations. But a work is a structured creation. Political institutions, economic mechanisms, artistic or poetic achievements, temples, factories, books, roads, cathedrals—all these are works, focal points of human relationships whose structures interlock with the structures surrounding them. Mass movements, on the other hand, are not works, for they have no structure of any sort. Instead, they tend toward the abolition of all structures. A work is always of infinite depth because it refers to other works. Creative geniuses, being creators, are not travelers without baggage but individuals who carry with them the burden of an entire past, even if they only wish to express their opposition. They are inheritors, not foundlings. Even those who, like Kant or Descartes, appear to start from tabula rasa orient themselves by the lines of force of their time. They do not annul the past but illuminate or denounce it. Capitalism was denounced by Marx; psycho-social compulsions by Freud; the postulates of our cosmological world picture by Copernicus, Newton, Einstein. Every work is a link in a chain. It points to a specific state of technology, of the economy, religion, science. The work refers to social relationships, and behind these social relationships, the fundamental psychic expressions emerge: aggressiveness, guilt, anxiety. In this way, an investigation by layered zones may be made. It would move from the phenomena to the works, from the works to social relationships, from social relationships to the elemental psychic components.

But when the bottom of this analysis in depth has been reached, only part of the effort is over. What remains to be shown is the particular form these psychic components took under specific local and temporal conditions. The phenomenon has to be re-integrated in history. After the descent, the ascent has to follow. This second phase is even more important than the first, for its object is to return to reality what was temporarily removed from it. Research worthy of the name of science does not come to an end once an analysis has been completed. What has been discovered must be re-integrated in the whole of which it is a subordinate part.

In the natural sciences, this re-integration takes the form of a *law*, i.e., an atemporal constant. But in the sciences of man, there are no constants, for all phenomena are special phenomena. All attempts to generalize get nowhere; they end up as idle chatter and cliché. The only possible re-integration is temporal in nature. Every social psychoanalysis necessarily terminates in a historical re-integration. This is the only way the circle may be closed, the only manner in which a specific phenomenon removed from the historical flow for purposes of study can be put back in its place in the process of becoming.

This means that every psychoanalysis of social phenomena must be supplemented by a dialectic. Analysis digs a shaft until it gets to the ground from which the elemental psychic forces well. Then dialectics remounts to the surface, recovers the phenomenon in its particularity, and gives it its true historical meaning. This is the proper method for the investigation of social phenomena, in our opinion. We are well aware that much remains to be done in the sciences of man. It is still in its infancy. If we wish to make headway in this direction, we must constantly combine methodological inquiry and the investigation of concrete instances. In this manner, we will gradually succeed in focusing a particular mode of thought on specific problems. It is in this spirit that we attempted the analysis of a human phenomenon, the phenomenon of money.

Money

1. Psychoanalysis

We will make the assumption that we know nothing of economic and monetary theories, and of the mechanisms of credit. Having thus eliminated all a priori judgments concerning the nature of money, there remains the fact that for everyone, the man in the street, money is primarily something he worries about. Money demands constant vigilance. To become poor, one only has to let oneself go. But to enrich oneself requires greed. Our relationship to money demands a tension which is not reducible to any other. It is through money that the Other confronts us. The monetary act is always aggressive.

But to accomplish this act, aggressivity is not enough. Valid action is possible only in a world whose structure is suited to our act. That money is part and parcel of our lives not only means that it is the object of our personal experience, but also that this experience is possible only within a social universe which is structured to that end. And it is this structure in its totality and complexity that gives money its true meaning. As long as we are not hampered in our movements, we are ignorant of it. To discover it, we must sense a sudden discomfort, feel that we are being seized and swallowed by its workings. This is precisely what happened on Wall Street on a certain October day in 1929, when sudden and massive sales caused stock prices to plunge. This "Black Friday" has become famous. People who lived through those moments remember that at first no one would admit the depth and seriousness of this crisis. There was talk of a "technical adjustment," unavoidable, it was said, after an extended boom. The mechanisms had got stuck, overheated, dirty, so they said. All that was needed was a good mechanic and things would get back to normal. Experts were called in, one after the other, as physicians are called to the bedside of the dying. The fact is that an entire world became disjointed and crumbled while another arose, the world of the militant dictatorships. The economic mechanisms had nothing to do with that. The crisis occurred and spread, not because the mechanisms set in motion by capitalism did not function, but precisely because they did. Those very mechanisms which had permitted the accumulation of deposits, bullishness, speculation, and the expansion of credit, also permitted the withdrawal of deposits, the market slump, the contraction of credit. They were at work in the crisis as they had been at work during the boom, except that now it was the other way around, in the same sense in which a door may open or close, and through which one may either enter or exit, provided someone pushes or pulls it. In themselves, the mechanisms are neutral, indifferent, mere organs of transmission. They permit money to manifest itself, but they are not money. They are channels through which an *energy* flows, an energy that is called money.

Money, however, is not a physical but an economic force. Once physical force has been freed, it becomes weaker as it moves toward a position of rest. In a given system, energies tend toward a state of equilibrium. Economic force is biological; it seeks to reconstitute itself by drawing new energies from the external world. In this way, money reproduces money in an unending cycle of consuming transgression, and transforms the world through work: it destroys, dislocates, suppresses, and simultaneously creates. In the philosophical meaning of the term, every economic force is negatory, i.e., it negates what exists, not in order to destroy it, but rather in order to have it absorbed in what will come into existence. Money thus contains a negatory element. At this point, we are tempted to exclaim: "how absurd. Negatory money, what nonsense!" Doesn't experience teach us the very opposite? Don't money men always claim to be practical, realistic, positive? We seem to have come to a dead end. Suppose we look at money *as it is*: what does it consist of? Of pieces of metal? But compared to the enormous number of payments, their quantity is infinitesimal. Or is it deposits and bills? But these merely represent debts and claims. We have to conclude that money does not have the kind of existence this book here has. Money is not a thing, but a representation of debts and claims. It is something that is owed. Where it is present, it carries a minus sign. The negation it contains is revealed in the notation which expresses it. This is amply proven by double entry bookkeeping. Money that has physically been taken in is listed on the debit side of the cash account. Capital, reserves, profits, i.e., what an enterprise owns, are listed as liabilities on the balance sheet, in the rubric of debts. "He who receives, owes." Such is the fundamental rule which was worked out with painstaking precision in the fourteenth century, and still confuses apprentice accountants today.

It is true that this rule can only be acknowledged as valid if one uses a trick, which is that one makes a distinction between the function of receiving and the quality of owning something, even where only a single individual is involved. Every sum of money, including the money received by the person whose property it is, must be entered as a debit because that person owes it to someone, even if that someone is himself. The system of notation, in short, assigns a minus sign to all property and wealth. It might be said that this is merely a convention in bookkeeping, a handy device for the sake of correct arithmetic. But the fact remains that it is *this* system that was chosen centuries ago, at the very time modern economics came into being. Such tenacity, such faithfulness cannot be explained except by those profound reasons which are so firmly rooted in our economic thinking that we finally lost sight of them.

And who doesn't know that capitalism and indebtedness go together? In all stages of its development, capitalism was accompanied by an expansion of credit, i.e., a generalized indebtedness which gradually took on gigantic proportions. All crises of capitalism, whatever their causes, always manifested themselves in the malfunctioning, the jolts, the breaks in the chain of indebtedness. It is not this or that physical or moral individual that withdraws its credit. What is involved is a general process which only can be expressed by that vaguest of all pronouns: they. "They" have lost confidence, "they" demand to know what is going on, "they" want to discuss things and decide. Decision, by the way, is the etymological meaning of the word "crisis." And the moment this happens, the entire mechanism is arrested. This civilization which is based on excessive indebtedness has produced a human type heretofore unknown, the businessman. It is true that merchants have always existed, but they only dealt in supplementary products that were unessential to a social organization based on warriors, priests, and slaves. Up to today, the businessman has been the keystone of our world. Our science would have remained abstract and speculative, had it not always obeyed the call of industry, had the laboratory not been the supplier of the factory. We find the businessman at the beginnings of the transportation system, the development of sources of energy, the construction of canals, the laying of tracks. There is always an additional quantum of energy to be developed, a higher speed to be attained, more space to be conquered. This hysteria of work contributed its share to the acceleration of economic zealotry. A few generations ago, Mr. Perichon could close his shop when he had turned fifty, and enjoy life with the money he had made. The businessman of our time never stops acquiring wealth. He dies in its pursuit. The more he increases it, the greater become his debts. Without rest, without a break, as if a devilish curse lay on the monetary act, the businessman works as if he were eternally indebted and in search of an impossible salvation.

Eternal debts, impossible salvation: these words echo strangely within us. They remind us of a different drama, the drama of original sin, the punishment inflicted on mankind—the labor of man and the suffering of woman. One hardly dares admit it: capitalist history follows the pattern of the theological myth.

Capitalism could only take shape as a result of the intellectual revolution caused by rationalism. The introduction of mathematical measurements into the investigation of natural phenomena brought about a profound change in scientific thought in the seventeenth century. But this intellectual turn also left its traces in economic thought. But to translate human labor into relationships between debts and claims, to evaluate it quantitatively as was first done in those centers of reference we call enterprises, is that not tantamount to ordering the economic world according to the principles of analytic geometry? If rationalist thought had restricted itself to measuring the world, it would merely have represented it without ever changing anything within it. Like an anxious pedant, it would have transposed it word for word, in all its passivity. But far from being a mere transposition, rationalism became a principle of transformation by releasing energies that had been chained heretofore. Rationalism's first act was the emancipation of man; it declared him to be of age in the juridical sense of that term; it freed him from the tutelage of theology. It was not that God was denied. He suffered quite a different sort of mishap: He was proven. To have being for man, God was deduced by a process of logical reasoning. "I make God because I want to," wrote Alain, commenting on Descartes. But this intellectual God, this God who was driven from earth and exiled in a metaphysical heaven was quite simply dead, being no longer close to living man. At the same time, man's consciousness attained its majority, and that means the fullness of its mastery and its responsibility. Original sin lost its meaning. Everyone was born free, and while he was burdened with imperfection, he also had power. He became the master of his destiny.

This is the reason European *thought*, emancipated from original sin, no longer found it necessary to base itself on the myth of salvation. But this does not mean that the European *psyche* had been freed of its feeling of guilt, which is constitutive of it. But there was no further use for this feeling of guilt. It now stood ready to energize another myth that would take the place of the old one. The substitution of the myth of progress for the myth of salvation fulfilled this function. This ideological changing of the guard occurred in the eighteenth century, and the encyclopedists with their preference for concrete acts, for the crafts, the applied arts and manual labor were the apostles of this new religion. But this new religion followed the contours of the old, the already existing lines of force. The economic development of our era profited from all this mystic energy of preceding epochs, and a world based on the sacrifice of the sinner was replaced by a world that was based on man's suffering and lacked a saving redeemer.

2. Dialectics

This profound and persistent need to shake off the burden of guilt, to strive for an ultimate salvation, explains both the rise and the disintegration of the capitalist world. Our civilization has its origin in a true transfer of energy: all those psychic tensions that had been directed toward religion changed their direction and turned toward the economy, and the history of money in our society reveals the various stages of this turn. All Harpagon could do was to stop spending money. Father Grandet invented, enlarged, exploited, conquered. César Birotteau gave up his profession to immerse himself in speculation in land. But in Balzac, the fight for money still retains the form of a duel, a fight between man and man. Zola's banker Saccard already manipulates the undifferentiated masses of investment capital and creates precarious financial structures. More and more, money slipped into abstraction. It does not really represent definite and tangible wealth but rather arithmetic differences such as we see them in accounting situations. The reason for this is that in a capitalist system, success or failure of an economic activity is the function of a certain method of calculation. One can tell from a balance sheet, i.e., from the results of a certain system of computation whether individuals are rich or poor, credit-worthy or bankrupt. Abstract, general value has replaced concrete usefulness. On the day of the Wall Street crash in October, 1929, the sudden slump in the prices of shares caused the brutal impoverishment of an entire nation.

And yet, the next day the concrete wealth of the world on fields, in mines, in storage facilities, and on building sites was totally unchanged. Where was this impoverishment? It was an impoverishment that did not appear as the destruction of a thing but as a decrease in value, i.e., an arithmetic impoverishment. The capitalist economy had based itself on the wholly abstract concept of a difference in value and pursued that development to the end.

And indeed, as capitalism develops, one notices the rise and expansion of an ever-increasing number of activities whose goal it is to juggle with differences in value while abstracting from the substantive reality of the products being exchanged. This is what exchange rates and brokerage dealings are all about. They do not involve real, new creations. Those who visit the financial markets are familiar with "options," a term which summarizes this entire development. But by virtue of a natural tendency, daily differences and fluctuations extend into the future. The distinguishing characteristic of speculation is the calculation with two different moments in time, the present and the future, the certain and the probable. Every speculator gambles against all others and bases his calculation on the average opinion created by a given event. The thing itself is bracketed and serves merely as a pretext.

But it was not enough to discount value; value was determined by withholding or destroying the thing. Remarkably enough, we can observe that businessmen and the theoreticians of capitalism did not know what to do when they looked for a remedy to economic crises. Nothing occurred to them except to restrict production, to reduce the soil under cultivation, to pull out the vines, to denature wheat, to destroy supplies. At the end of its development, the capitalist system is incapable of harmonizing increased production and the maintenance of a profit margin. If this margin is to be maintained at all cost, an artificial shortage, a lack, have to be created. This system, based on the concept of difference, leads to suicide, to self-destruction. The world of money ends in absurdity: the capitalist economy can only survive if it voluntarily does less than it is capable of. It has maneuvered itself into a blind alley from which the only escape is self-denial.

Economic crises are the nightmare of bourgeois society. Even wars seem less ominous. War or, better still, preparation for war, acts as a stimulus for energies, a factor making for full employment, a firming of social ties. Economic crisis, on the other hand, appears as a generalized cancer, a putrescence which attacks the entire community. All that lives becomes lifeless: the depots and granaries, capital goods and assets, exchange and trade, and man himself. A society can only survive if there is a cementing energy which cushions the crisis. Of all declining values, human labor is the one which approaches zero most closely. Unemployment is worse than death, for death with its legal and ceremonial apparatus is still a social act, while unemployment means the dissolution of social life. But a society which disintegrates and becomes pulverized gives rise to new groupings, new political vapors which have their origin in violence. At the end of unemployment, fear and murder lurk.

If bourgeois society wants to survive, it must at all cost keep the money process going. It must create needs, invent ways of financing. It is in the midst of a permanent inflation, and can survive only at that price. The state is the great programmer of expenditures. It authorizes work, and the person who receives it thanks the state for it, for to give work has become an act of grace. Today, work no longer balances debts; it increases them. It is the state now to which one owes; it has become the supreme creditor. In the truest sense of that word, we find ourselves in an irrational economy.

This irrationality means that today, relationships between man and the state are increasingly marked by affects. Political fear has become the most tragic theme of our time. All questions of conscience which the religious life posed once upon a time, all doubts, feelings of remorse and pangs of bad conscience, all recantations have been transferred to political life. We are entering an age of civil wars which show a pronounced resemblance to the wars of religion. We are fighting a life and death struggle for political salvation, and that salvation has taken on the contours of theological salvation. The spirit of the inquisition is already in evidence. Man is no longer on good terms with the political church. He finds himself in a state of eternal sin—in his conduct, his talk, his thoughts, and the thoughts in the back of his mind.

In the course of this process, money has been lost in abstraction. Originally, it constituted material wealth; later, the symbol of that wealth. Today, it is merely a sign for evaluating production. But as it thus loses itself, it has fulfilled its historical task. It has served to raise the myth of guilt to the political plain, a myth it took from religious thought. The state has taken the place of the jealous God—a concrete, physical god of this world who daily expresses himself in his wrath. But we are lapsing into political paganism. And blood will be the price for a debt which can be paid neither by sacrifice nor by money.

Translated by Michael Shaw

Contribution 15

Psychoanalysis of Economics

Paul Schilder

At first a few words about the title. I think that there are no phenomena in human life which cannot be approached from the point of view of psychology. However, to be perfectly accurate one has to qualify such a statement when one approaches nature. As persons in nature we are acting in nature. At the same time, nature follows its own course. The way in which we adapt to nature and what we do with the problems nature puts before us belong to the realm of psychology. As we might say here is nature in the raw. When we do something to nature and the external world then the events of the outward world take a different course. This does not mean that from now on whatever may happen is the expression of our own psychology and action. We may furthermore say that many of our institutions, customs, and habits of life, which have been created as the result of the cultural process have become independent the moment we have created them. We deal here with the "objective spirit" (*Objectiver Geist*) of the German philosopher Hegel. Hegel did not think that the cultural achievements are merely the result of actions of human beings in the external world but believed in a creative spirit which manifests itself according to its own laws in the different forms of cultural achievements. One should keep these ideas of

Hegel's in mind since the dialectic materialism of Marx and Engels has been decidedly influenced by Hegel's conception. We deal here with a group of phenomena of social and cultural life which although created by human beings in action have become relatively independent, go their own way, and cannot be easily changed at will any longer. Cultural phenomena should be studied from such a point of view.

When we study psychological phenomena in the narrower sense we see that situations of life create psychological patterns. If such a purely psychological mode of reaction has once occurred and has proved its value by giving gratification, it has a tendency to become fixated and lives almost its own life. Such persisting patterns influence our actions whether we want them to do so or not. This is the basic insight underlying the first formulations of Breuer and Freud's. According to them the repressed experience retains its dynamic values. Bleuler and Jung have called complexes psychic experiences, which by dint of repression are excluded from the main stream of consciousness. Complexes live then a more or less independent life. Freud has more aptly defined complexes as ideas and thoughts of great emotional value. Bleuler finally with deep psychological insight spoke about *Gelegenheits Apparate* (opportunity apparatus) meaning by this a psychological attitude which has been created under the stress of circumstances and has crystalized into a pattern comparable to an organ which serves a definite function. When the love of a boy for his mother is very great and he is more or less dependent upon her, a pattern of filial dependence is created. It may persist independent of the individual. When similar situations occur in later life in any way related to the pattern developed in early childhood it will not provoke an action which does justice to the situation on its own merits but an action which fits the infantile apparatus which has been created by the relation of the boy to his mother, which as unconscious was not exposed to the corroding influence of criticism and experience.

Patterns although lying in the sphere of individual experience are no longer within the immediate reach of the individual. This is the realm of the so-called unconscious. In all manifestations of culture as well as in science millions of such patterns removed from further experience and criticism are evident.

When a habit has been created and developed the action based on it is obviously the expression of psychological needs and processes. However, habits and needs, lead also to actions which leave permanent changes in the outward world, which persist until they are modified by action. The results of psychological attitudes have become parts of the outward world. For instance, we live in houses which are heated and we wear clothes. It is impossible to understand why people buy the kind of clothes they wear merely from the point of view of the psychology of the individual who purchases them. The suit bought by an individual is the result of an economic process which in large parts is independent of the individual who purchases the suit. The suit which we wear has a share in the determination of our subsequent behavior. Furthermore, it also has a decided social significance. Houses, apartments, jewelry, parties, traveling may be considered from a similar point of view. Due to our psychological attitudes we change the outward world and these changes have a lasting influence upon our actions. They persist even when our psychological attitudes have changed. The product of a psychological attitude persists even when the particular attitude has long disappeared and such a product may contain in itself an admonition to return to a previous attitude. The product has not only such an influence upon the individual who created it but also on any other individual who may come in contact with it. The psychological influence of lasting objects may be considerable in the long run. This is an influence which may even reach from one generation to another.

The material culture by which we are surrounded is the product of actions which belong to a psychological sphere different from the one we actually live in. It represents the continuous influence by the cultural and civilization patterns of our ancestors. In addition, an object once created goes along on its own in a way which could not be predicted beforehand. When I have produced a gun it needs to be shot by me; a cannon needs still more men, and when I have two cannons they demand a general to supervise the men who serve the cannons. Finally, the cannons shoot whether I want them to or not. Artists always have been fascinated by the idea that the statue they have created will gain a life of its own. I refer, for instance, to the little book of Maserel, *The Work*, which depicts the adventures of a giant statue which became alive to the astonishment of its creator. Material culture although created by psychological attitudes has become a part of the world which is no longer under the direct influence of individual creator's psychology and even influences the individual whether he wants to be influenced or not.

There is no question that the houses in which we live, the clothes we wear, and the money system under which we are brought up influence our psychology even though they may have been created under very different circumstances. We have to understand everything created in economic life in terms of psychological situations and motives. We must not make the mistake of thinking that things created by psychological needs are merely psychological. They have become a part of our psychological attitudes. How far our psychological attitudes are influenced by the events in the outward world is another problem. Everything which we find in economic life which is not necessarily of our own making is connected with psychology. In a broader sense the culture of an epoch is the sum total of the history of the tribes, nations, and humanities concerning the relations of individuals to the outward world plus the result of the actions of humans in the world. We should not speak about single individuals since no single individual exists. Individuals exist merely in groups and they have similar problems and conflicts. They fight against their sexual tendencies, they fight against their own aggressiveness, and they try to love their neighbors and relatives—difficult as this may be. The cultural development of the single individual depends upon psychological and economic factors. Our work is obviously the result of our psychological attitudes. However, when the work is accomplished it goes its own way.

In the theses on Feuerbach which were written in 1845 but were not intended for publication Marx wrote: "Social life is essentially practical. All mysteries which mislead theory to mysticism find rational solution in human practice and in the comprehension of this practice.

"The chief defect of all hitherto existing materialism—that of Feuerbach included—is that the object, reality, sensuousness, is conceived only in the form of the object or contemplation but not as a human sensuousness activity, practice, not subjectively."

Marx, furthermore, draws the conclusion: "Feuerbach consequently, does not see that the 'religious sentiment' is itself a social product, and that the abstract individual whom he analyzes belongs in reality to a particular form of society."

When we talk about psychology we mean, therefore, human action, with a specific aim. Religious sentiments have to do with the practices of individuals. Religious beliefs are encouraged or discouraged according to the total social and economic situation. This is, by the way, also the opinion to which Marrett has come in his studies on primitive beliefs. There are no theoretical beliefs even if individuals pretend that they have beliefs without practical designs.

This formulation coincides with studies I have conducted for several years. There is no perception, no imagination, no thought which is not action, which does not contain in itself motility, i.e., action. When we see an object the perception is based upon the preceding and subsequent movements of the eye muscles and of the body. Without motility we would not see at all. A perception without motility is of no account. Perception and movement cannot be separated. We should not take as a unit in psychology either perception or movement but a sensori-motor unit, or still better, a sensori-motor-vegetative unit. Even this formulation is in so far incomplete as the sensori-motor-vegetative unit gets its meaning merely in a specific total situation of which the personality is a part. Whatever we may experience as individuals we live in actions and the action has its basis in the world which we perceive. Feuerbach puts into the center of his discussion desires; Marx puts actions. It is more correct to speak about actions than to speak about libido and ego instincts or desires in general.

Another problem arises immediately. For what reasons do human beings act? What are the real motives for actions? Do human beings know the motives for their actions or do they act without knowing the basis for their actions? Are they conscious of what they are doing? Marx has answered these questions in a very clear way. He states that human beings are driven by economic needs which are according to his opinion the real driving force behind actions. These economic needs are not completely understood. With remarkable insight he realized that human beings develop systems of ideas in order to hide from themselves the economic motives for their actions. Marx calls such systems of ideas ideologies. There are ideologies of the ruling classes and ideologies of the suppressed classes. Individuals pretend on the basis of their ideologies to have motives different from those which are actually behind their actions. In his way Marx has seen here the problem of the unconscious. According to his formulations the unconscious is governed by economic needs whereas Freud's unconscious is governed by libidinous needs. However, Marx emphasized that humans have to reproduce themselves not only in the sense of having children but also in the sense that individuals have to live to eat, to clothe, and to house themselves. Engels comes to a very similar conclusion in stating that the need for food cannot be postponed indefinitely and also the need for clothing and housing is urgent whereas sex urge does not demand immediate gratification.

The basic contention of Marxism is that economic drives and needs have to be fulfilled if the individual wants to continue living. The economic process is thus obviously dependent upon the basic necessities of the worker to reproduce himself, i.e., to eat sufficiently in order to be able to work efficiently and to supply his family with food if the other members of the family are not capable of working. One must admit that psychoanalysis has neglected this viewpoint to a great extent. Only in its latest development psychoanalysis has spoken more about the Ego and Ego instincts. However, Freud has blurred the issue and devaluated the Ego instincts by saying that they drive the individual to its preordained destruction. In psychoanalysis the necessity for food and for the satisfaction of hunger appears as oral libido. When one looks over large parts of the psychoanalytic literature one would not conceive the idea that one eats because one is hungry and wants food for sustaining one's life but one would rather suppose that eating is a sly way of satisfying oral libido. There is no reason to doubt that the mouth fullfills libidinous functions. However, its basic function is the preservation and increase of the life of the individual. The overextension of the libido theory into the oral sphere is the beginning of the downfall of the psychoanalytic theory of instincts. It finally leads, indeed, to a pansexualism since according to Freud the death instincts are not immediately experienced. When Freud started his studies he had taken it for granted that individuals needed to preserve themselves. It did not come prominently into his mind that there might be problems behind their will to life, but he devoted himself more especially to the study of the sexual problems of humanity. Individuals seem to have reasons to hide their sexual urges from themselves and from others. However, Marx is correct when he says that human beings are not clear about their economic motives. Freud might be inclined at the present time to explain the wish of human beings for economic survival, not to the Ego instincts but to the Ego as organization which strives to find some middle way between the various libidinous drives and their complications.

A rather famous theory has explained the right of the capitalist to get interest for the capital which he has invested by saying that the capitalist could use all his capital at once and thus get maximum pleasure and satisfaction. However, the capitalist denies himself this immediate pleasure and is rewarded for his abstinence by getting interest on his capital which he does not consume at once. However, such a theory is an ideology invented by the ruling economic classes which may cover up the motives which lie behind the accumulation of capital. The man responsible for this theory was obviously not fully aware of his own motives and many who believed him were also not aware of the motives which lead to the acceptance of such a theory. The capitalist obviously does not only want the pleasure and the power but he wants to appear to others and to himself as a kind and just person. Furthermore, whoever opposes him does something which is against the principles of justice. He succeeds therefore in justifying himself before his ideals. Dreams which emerge in our preconscious mind at first in disconnected form, undergo a secondary elaboration which not only covers up the logical flaws in the sequence of the dream but veil still more the latent dream thought which is disapproved by one's moral personality. Whoever profits by the present economic situation does not want to know what is implied in his profiting and develops an ideology which allows him to cover his real motives and the motives of his class. One capitalist thinks similarly to another—a class develops a specific ideology. Ruling classes have specific ideologies, so have the classes which are in an inferior position. Ruling classes will inevitably develop ideologies which stress great differences between human beings. Sometimes races think themselves vastly superior to others without justification of facts. Race and class ideologies mix very often with each other and form a rather dangerous mixture. It is difficult for persons belonging to lower economic strata to develop an ideology which gives superiority to their class. People belonging to a race which is not ruling will probably assert that all human beings are equal. Races, classes, and individuals pushed into the background and into an inferior political or economic situation will always seek equality. Among the psychiatrists and psychologists some will stress the variation of human types. Jewish psychiatrists and psychologists as a group are more inclined to believe that there are no fundamental differences between human beings. Jung, who was so interested in the difference between introverts and extraverts, is not Jewish, and in his later formulations has come very near to the Nazi ideology and has enlarged his concepts by stressing that Jewish and Aryan psychotherapies are different. He adheres obviously to the ideology of the superiority of his race. The complicated and sometimes abstruse type psychology of Jaensch's is again very closely related to his belief in the greatness of the German race. Ideologies are not merely the background but also the driving force in so-called objective scientific pursuits. Generally, one would not suspect the influence of class and race ideologies on a psychology of types.

The psychologies of Marx and Freud have a deep inner connection. Curiously enough both are Jews. One might think that the similarities in their psychologies are due to specific qualities in the thinking of the Jewish race. I am inclined to think that much of the so-called differential psychology of races belongs in the realm of a myth. However, Marx and Freud both belong to a race which is not a ruling race, and it might be advisable for the members of such a race to understand other human beings. They may have a better chance to find out something about the motives of human beings and become psychologists. Marx and Freud both found out that individuals live up to demands of which they are not conscious. However, Marx's ideologies comprise the economic and social forces as well as the sexual behavior. The accent is on the former. Freud had introduced the important connotations of the Super Ego, the forces of conscience in ourselves. The Super Ego is built upon identifications and prescribes to a great deal unconsciously the social and sexual behavior of the individual, the accent lying on the latter. Marx put the emphasis on the economic forces, self-preservation and reproduction in the widest sense; Freud on the libidinous (sexual) forces. Marx was more interested in material which psychoanalysis would call preconscious—that means that it follows the same rule as conscious thinking without having the quality of awareness. Freud stresses the unconscious part of the Super Ego (conscience) which follows laws of thinking different from the laws of conscious thinking.

I would like to refer here to what psychoanalysis has to say about money and about work. Unfortunately, psychoanalytic literature has not paid very much attention to this fundamental problem. Freud has made a few remarks concerning this in his book *Civilization and Its Discontents* and Winterstein has written a small article on the subject. It has not been sufficiently acknowledged that by working something is done in the outward world which is changed. This done, we have no longer complete power over work. It has become independent. Work is a real "projection." When the work is once completed we have freed ourselves from the strivings which lead to action. It has become a part of the external world. It is perhaps the only true projection. Individual strivings have become a part of the object. Silberer once said, in substance, that one should not think, according to psychoanalytic conceptions, that the Danube exists as such but is merely a projection of urine and birthwater. However, the Danube exists, its course can be changed by work and action. Marx, Engels, and Lenin have put work and action in the center of their philosophy. The system of economics is such an independent part of the reality which has come there by "true projection." We did not ourselves create the economic system. Perhaps our ancestors did. But the economic system, like the statue alluded to, walks around and does not care what we want or do not want unless we change it by new action.

Charlotte Bühler has written a book, *Der Menschlische Lebeslauf*, which compares many biographies and stresses the history of work and achievement in the diverse biographies.

This is a very important step forward. The psychological analysis of any individual without the analysis of his work is incomplete. Does the child work? I am inclined to believe so. We speak about work when we want to change the outer world. The child does. It does not mind its effort. However, it would be wrong to speak about work only if we mind the effort necessary to produce the change. It is a fundamental human trend to choose one's surroundings and to change them according to one's needs and desires. The world resists any change. Sometimes the resistance is slight and sometimes it is severe. We may have to fight and to force the world. We have to destroy and to dissolve structures in order to rearrange them. If the structure resists, one may destroy more than is necessary and advantageous for the subsequent structure. In order to do something we have to be active and sometimes aggressive. Activity and aggression are the basis of work which implies by its very nature a change in the outer world. It is interesting to study the causes and consequences of increased aggression. Patients with an obsessional neurosis show an increase in their aggressive tendencies. The aggression is tinged with sexual conflicts. Increased aggressiveness coming out or transgressing into the sexual sphere is called sadism. The obsessive patient is sadistic. He starts to work, he cannot complete it, or he pays too much attention to details. Finally, he cannot do anything at all. He is more or less inhibited in activity, in aggression, and his work. Even when he should have finally done something he may undo it or may do the opposite, in order to undo it symbolically. His drives and energies toward the world, fed by strong sadistic impulses in connection with childhood situations, attempt a destructive change in the world. Since they are suppressed by a powerful and cruel Super Ego, the action started is stopped, undone, or contradicted. The work remains so; incomplete or undone. Still more outspoken is the inhibition in the work of the depressive case. Here we find that the individual does not dare to move lest he may kill. He has powerful drives of aggression consisting of killing and devouring which the Super Ego resists. Work becomes a symbol of ruthless aggression and is therefore inhibited. Every action becomes as forbidden as cannibalism. In inhibitions of work of any type we find sadism and aggression which the Super Ego of the individual does not tolerate. Primitives work only in order to live. Carnivorous as man is, he has to kill in order to eat. Aggression also plays its part in primitive agriculture and in the collection of food stuffs. If the sex energy is not used up it is carried over to the work, especially the aggressive component of sex. When civilization suppresses direct aggression and sexual aggression it also tries to harness the unused energy into work. The question immediately arises how much should an individual work. This is a question of great interest for economists and for psychologists. At the present time there is no great necessity for people working very hard. However, in earlier stages of economic development the individual and the community could survive only by hard work. An ideal coming from the past forces us to work "overtime." Our Super Ego demands that we should work. This was perhaps very necessary once, two or three centuries ago. It is not anymore. The old book of Bebel's elaborates the idea that in a socialistic state no more than two or three hours of work a day will be necessary. This is probably true if one considers merely the necessity for physical work, and it is more true today than it was in Bebel's time. However, we are burdened with the old patterns; the past has left us not only material cultures but also ideologies difficult to dislodge. The increase of interest in work and the extolling of work in modern civilization may be due to the deflection of libido and direct impulses in work. This would be the psychoanalytic interpretation. This is, however, arbitrary. It neglects the general interest of humanity in changing the world so that it can be utilized. Maybe the primitive deflects genuine work energy into sexual and aggressive channels since he has not learned yet to utilize them. Even in the obsessional neurotic and depressive case, the individual may find himself with a greater amount of work energy at hand than he can handle. This may have to be deflected into primitive channels which in turn are blocked by the Super Ego.

Our culture as every other culture contains besides its useful aspects system of ideas, rites, and material structures which do not apply to the present. Generally the ideologies which by their very nature are protected from corroding ciriticism are more antiquated than the material goods and the material culture in general. Useless tools are pretty soon eliminated. Unfortunately this is not true concerning useless ideas. It is easier to deceive oneself about an ideology than about a suit of clothes. Men's clothes although ugly fulfill some useful purpose. The ugliness of men's clothes is historically and ideologically determined. It is difficult to get rid of useless religious ideologies. We might call these phenomena ideological lags. Problems like this cannot be understood by merely studying what is going on in a specific individual. We have to see the relation of this individual and his strivings and ideologies in relation to the economic and political situation of the times. Ideologies are almost a part of the outside world in the same way as houses, streets, and sewers. They have arisen out of specific needs in relation to specific cultural conditions.

We have to get food from somewhere. We have to destroy animals or the continuity of plant life in order to get the food we need. When we hoard more than we need we look into the future. Children and primitives have a very limited time horizon. (Compare Róheim.) Possession means to have something for future use. However, even the primitive tribes in central Australia have their spears, their houses, and their ceremonial appliances. Psychoanalysis has shown that in our unconscious thinking feces are very often treated as valuable property. This reaction is seen in children in dreams, and in neurotic symptoms. Feces very often substituted for money and money for feces. One can see this connection very clearly in obsessive neurotic cases and I have not the least doubt that these psychoanalytic findings are correct. The interpretation of this connection is a more complicated problem. From its very beginning psychoanalysis has felt that human beings are chiefly interested in their own bodies and consider every part of their bodies and whatever may be in connection with them as extremely valuable. Feces are therefore considered as primary value. I have doubts concerning these formulations. Individuals are not more interested in their own body than in the bodies of others and in the outer world. If there is any difference their interest in the external world is prior to the interest in their own bodies. If one wants to keep something it is safer to put it in one's own body. From this viewpoint things inside of the body are symbols of value. However, what has been in the body has previously been in the outer world. My own investigations have shown me that children believe that the insides of their bodies consist of food. Feces might have a value from a similar point of view. Psychoanalysis feels that what is going on in the outer world is a symbol of what is going on in the body. However, one might say just as well that we experience the outside and inside of our bodies as a symbol of what is going on in the outer world. One should not neglect the colossal urge of human beings toward the world.

Many years ago I published a case history which contains material pertaining to the above topic. This woman had her uterus removed several years before she became sick. She quarreled continually with her husband who was impotent but had sex play of some semblence of intercourse with other women. This naturally angered the patient very much. After a tonsillitis she developed an hallucinatory psychosis. She had hallucinations in which her husband was castrated. She pretended to be very worried about the castration but in her innermost heart she felt jubilant. She also visualized the castration of other men—one does not stop so very easily once one has started to castrate in one's fantasy. She blamed herself severely for her sexuality. She heard voices saying that horses and dogs were found in her feces. The implication was that she had introduced these animals into her anus. She gave in to these accusations and had tremendous feelings of guilt. When she approached recovery she heard other voices which blamed her for her premarital relations with her husband. When her condition improved she became one of the best workers on the ward. She had such intense feelings of guilt that she was compelled to work in order to relieve them. Finally she felt she was so bad that work alone was not an adequate expiation and she felt that she would have to be sold to an eskimo and thus would have to work the entire day exposed to the intense cold temperature. She thought that she would lose her sexuality in a cold climate. On the other hand unconsciously she anticipated sexual gratifications since she believed that eskimos were rather immoderate in their sexual demands. In the meantime, she cleaned the ward with great energy. Thanks to her psychological processes the ward gained cleaner aspects.

Feelings of sexual guilt and sexual dirt may have close relation to the origin of hygiene. Work which is aggressive in nature is self-punishment for aggressiveness. There is obviously also a relation of feelings of guilt to anal satisfaction and the urge for cleanliness is again a self-punishment by working. By work also the patient tried to relieve her poverty which was very oppressive. The evaluation of work is therefore continually dependent upon psychological factors among which sadism, aggression, and feelings of guilt in connection with sex in general and anality in particular are outstanding. This, however, does not prove that work in an economic sense has no other roots. There is the urge of mastering the world. The wish for possessions, the experience of power, and the increase of the time horizon have to be considered. Furthermore, once the hoarding process has started it increases by the psychological factors mentioned. The feces were a part of one's own body. One has some power over them and they retain some value as relics of food and as a part of one's own body. However, they are valuable only when the time horizon is very limited. The book of Osborn on Freud and Marx treats the problems from a similar aspect as ours.

We turn now to the analysis of some basic concepts of political economy. Those who have studied economics know the terms "use-value" and "exchange-value." An example of use-value is water. Water is very important. We cannot live without it and in one form or other everybody has to use it. In spite of the fact that the use-value of water is so great it is not very expensive. Indeed it is one of the few things we can get for nothing. This is a use-value of great importance which still has no exchange value. Many other use-values of this type exist which are of a very low exchange-value. The use-value is in very close relation to immediate psychophysiological needs. The exchange-value is not.

We measure the exchange-value of an object by gold. One cannot do very much with gold. It is nice, it is durable, it can be divided into parts and into the small units which we demand for measurement of exchange-values. In spite of this gold fulfills no urgent need. It serves merely as ornament. What makes a use-value an exchange-value? Marx writes: "As use-values, commodities are, above all, of different qualities, but as exchange-values they are merely different quantities, and consequently do not contain an atom of use-value." All exchange-values are to some extent in relation to use-values, but not all use-values can become the basis of exchange-value, labor. Labor is obviously psychophysiological. It means that the individual has to given first by Ricardo and later on by Marx. Use-value becomes exchange-value by labor, i.e., by work. By adding a sufficient amount of work to the substance found in nature the use-value becomes an exchange-value. Nature's raw material has to be worked upon, has to be changed in its form or at least has to be taken from one place to another.

There is only one true exchange-value and this is work. One might also call work which tends to produce exchange-value, labor. Labor is obviously psychophysiological. It means that the individual has to work as a psychophysiological organism. The individual has to reproduce himself; has to get food and the protection of clothes and housing.

According to Marx the proper way to distribute goods would be to let the individual who has produced the exchange-value by work have the value. This does not occur. The individual who works seven, eight, ten or fifteen hours does not get the entire amount of value he has produced. Value is frozen or crystallized labor. The capitalist gives to the worker only a part of the value produced; enough to maintain the life of the worker and his family. However, such may be the case after seven or eight hours of work. If the worker works seven hours more he does surplus labor and produces a surplus-value which is taken over by the capitalist. The riches of this world are produced by work and those who have produced them get only a part of it. It is not necessary to discuss this Marxian formulation in detail.

I want to draw attention to the fact that the reproduction of the worker is a psychophysiological function. If he does not get sufficient pay he cannot maintain the necessary strength for work and life and cannot maintain his family. Sooner or later there will be no worker. This has occurred at times during the history of humanity. Even in our present civilization the amount of exchange-value the worker gets is not sufficient, if one considers reproduction as living to one's full span of life. There are obviously a great number of people who do not get enough food even if they only starve by slow degree. The medical care which they get may not be sufficient. They are, furthermore, more exposed to disease by their living conditions.

When somebody works for you, you have to support him so that he can live. What he does with the money is of no importance for the man who uses the worker to produce values. It is of importance to realize that the capitalist is in no way conscious of the processes involved here. He does not realize that he gets surplus-values. He feels that since he risks the capital he is entitled to a reward and he does not feel that the worker who works for him is entitled to a large reward. He might even feel that it is not good for the worker himself if he works only short hours and gets good compensation. This principle has found expression in economic literature and it has been stated that the worker might not work unless he is continually threatened with hunger and has to be kept at a minimum subsistence level in order to be induced to work. Similar ideologies under a thin disguise might even be preferred today.

The capitalist is indeed himself exposed to danger. He does not know whether he can sell the product and whether the surplus-value created will not lose by competition or otherwise its exchange-value. He may even lose a part or the whole of his capital. His dangers and fears in turn will influence his psychological attitude toward the worker and he might feel entitled to an extra compensation for his worries. He must necessarily develop an ideology very different from the ideology of the worker and they will not understand each other.

The concepts of use-value, exchange-value, and surplus-value are concepts which are closely interrelated with psychological concepts. However, they describe objective factors of the outward world, and the data to which they refer belong to the "objective mind" of

Hegel's. In private discussions I have been blamed for using Hegel's terms. However, the term has not only historical value but points also to the fact that psychological processes have a creative share in institutions. It is good to keep in mind that the use of the term does not mean that one has to follow the philosophical implications which the term has for Hegel.

One should try to analyze the connotations of the classical economists and of Marx from a similar point of view. The problem of marginal utility is a psychological problem. As long as we have, for instance, thousands of dollars, ten dollars do not mean very much. However, when all is spent besides ten dollars, the ten dollars have the importance of marginal utility. The human problem of need in a given situation becomes paramount, and every value appears dependent upon the total situation.

The problem of so-called "differential rent" is again a problem of economics best understood from a psychological point of view. If an individual lives on a piece of land which is of little value, rent cannot be expensive. The individual must be capable to reproduce himself while working the land. If this is not possible anymore the land is not worth the work invested in it. The problem of subsistence presents itself once more.

The theories concerning the basis for interest paid on capital have to be considered from a similar point of view. An individual who gets interest receives exchange-values without working. The person who gives the capital lends an instrument of production and gives a tool for which he demands work. If he would demand for his tool so much that the worker could not reproduce himself there would obviously be no sense in the worker's giving his work for the tool. The capitalist therefore gets a surplus-value for letting the other individual use the instruments of production.

Each one of these basic concepts of economics have been discussed in numerous volumes. The problems cannot be followed in detail but the same psychological principle underlies all phases of the economic process;

the individual wants to wrest from the outer world means of subsistence and wants to secure this subsistence also for the future. However, he is continually in danger that the results of the work which could secure for him subsistence at a future date might be taken away from him either by force or by an economic situation which takes away the surplus-value of his work.

The economic process cannot be understood merely by the analysis of the present but the analysis has to be extended into the past. A theory of economics sooner or later therefore expands into the theory of the history of the economic process. Hegel tried to solve this problem by "dialectics." He developed the theory that there exists first the absolute (concept) which is assumed as existent. The absolute alienates itself from itself, whatever that may mean, and becomes nature without self-consciousness, which does not understand itself. Finally, this world which has alienated itself from the absolute regains self-consciousness in man which in historical development becomes clear self-consciousness in Hegel's philosophy. The world is for Hegel the result of a self-alienation of the spirit. Real existence, therefore, is primarily the existence of the mind, and the world is a derivate of processes in the mind. There is an inner movement in the development of the mind. This philosophy has had an enormous fascination for the contemporaries of Hegel, and the history of the post-Kantian philosophy is to a great extent dominated by Hegel's conceptions. The world is not conceived as static. There are processes going on and there is a development which progresses in spirals. This progress is described as a change from the positive to the negative which is followed by a position on a higher level. Hegel's philosophy is dominated by the assumption of true opposites. This philosophy made a great impression on Marx, and he found in these dialectics a valuable tool for the understanding of the development of economic laws. According to Marx, economics start with the ownership of property by the community. Then on a basis of individual endeavor private ownership occurred. Private ownership hires labor for capitalist enterprises. Sooner or later capitalistic ownership will have to be substituted by communal ownership of the masses. This is again a change from a situation to its opposite and the return of this situation on a higher level. Marx is convinced of the general validity of these principles: of "dialectics."

There is, however, a great difference between the dialectics of Hegel and the dialectics of Marx. Hegel's dialectics start with the spirit, with the mind, the absolute concept. Marxian dialectics are materialistic. They start with the real world. Engels says very aptly that Hegelian dialectics had the world on its head but Marx put it on its feet. However, the dialectics of Hegel as well as Marx are based on a fundamental misunderstanding of logic. Human beings like to think in opposites. Freud, for instance, has pointed out that dreams express very often a thing by its opposite. Dreams of fire, for instance, stand very often for the interest in water, i.e., urine. He has written an article in which he emphasizes one word may mean two facts or two relations opposite to each other, for instance, high and low. In the hands of his former pupil, Stekel, this idea of opposites blossomed out in the idea of polarities which are considered as a fundamental factor in psychological processes. There seems to be, therefore, some fascination and seductiveness in the thinking in opposites. Before we discuss the value of dialectics in general we think it advisable to quote directly from Engels (*Anti-Dühring*):

> Let us take any algebraical magnitude whatever: for example, a. If this is negated, we get $-a$ (minus a). If we negate that negation, by multiplying $-a$ by $-a$, we get a^2, i.e., the original positive magnitude, but at a higher degree, raised to its second power. In this case also it makes no difference that we can reach the same a^2 by multiplying the positive a by itself, thus also getting a^2. For the negated negation is so securely entrenched in a^2 that the latter always has two square roots, namely a and $-a$. And the fact that it is impossible to get rid of the

> negated negation, the negative root of the square, acquires very obvious significance as soon as we get as far as quadratic equations.
>
> It is the same, also, in history. All civilized peoples began with the common ownership of the land. With all peoples who have passed a certain primitive stage, in the course of the development of agriculture, this common ownership became a fetter on production. It was abolished, negated, and after a longer or shorter series of intermediate stages was transformed into private property. But at a higher stage of agricultural development, brought about by private property in land itself, private property in turn became a fetter on production as is the case today, both with small and large land ownership. The demand that it also should be negated, that it should once again be transformed into common property, necessarily arose. But this demand does not mean the restoration of the old original common ownership, but the institution of a far higher and more developed form of possession in common which, far from being a hindrance to production, on the contrary for the first time frees production from all fetters and gives it the possibility of making full use of modern chemical discoveries and mechanical inventions.
>
> What therefore is the negation of the negation? An extremely general—and for this reason extremely comprehensive and important—law of development of Nature, history and thought; a law which, as we have seen, holds good in the animal and plant kingdoms, in geology, in mathematics, in history and in philosophy.

It is true that there are other passages especially in the book on Feuerbach in which Engels shows a better insight into the problem and retains merely the idea that the world consists not of ready-made things but of processes. Furthermore, it states that the antitheses have only a relative validity. However, what is the use then of stressing the importance of antithesis and to substitute for the varieties met in experience a rigid and empty formula? Instead of seeing true and false, good and bad, necessary and accidental, as opposite entities one should look at the things themselves and their meaning.

One will find then thesis and antithesis are very crude expressions of rejection or acceptance which do not help one to come to a deeper insight into the structure of things. In dialectics the variations of reality are over-simplified and dialectic materialism not only is not a reliable tool, as Marx and Engels supposed, but a useless one. Fire is not the opposite of water and the whole theory of opposites has to be changed if one wants to approach objects in their variety. Some Marxists wish to retain the term but wish merely to indicate that economics is not static but a continuous process. This latter statement is obviously true but it has nothing to do with dialectics. In literature we are suspicious about characterizations in which persons appear either as perfect heroes or as out and out villains. We justly suspect that such characterizations neglect important sides of human experience. I might conclude: beware of antitheses in philosophy, in psychoanalysis, and in economics. We have to study the process of economics by more subtle methods. Thinking in opposites is a primitive way of thinking and it implies that one accepts or rejects a thought or an object without having fully investigated the thought or object.

Psychoanalysis likes to emphasize that the unconscious attitudes of individuals determine their fate. However, Freud has acknowledged that there is a fate which lies in the anatomy and in the outward circumstances. However, he himself and most of the psychoanalysts of the older generation have obviously underrated the forces of the social and economic process toward which the individual is rather helpless. The rules of bourgeois society seemed to be rather well established when Freud started with his discoveries. The difficulties of the working classes were considerably underrated. It is obvious that especially at the beginning of the psychoanalytic movement, only the wealthy could profit from the procedure. Even at the present time the amount of psychoanalytic work done for the economically lower strata is inconsiderable and insufficient. Physicians are very often captured in a class ideology themselves. Even if they are not they cannot change the fundamentals of the economic process and its political consequences. Psychotherapy has only a meaning when more than a minimum of subsistence is guaranteed to the individual. Only when we may ask whether it wouldn't be possible to bring individuals to a better insight into themselves and to a better adaptation to the social situation. However, psychotherapy cannot help the persecuted Jew or the attacked Chinese and is helpless in the great catastrophe of humanity—war. However, this problem would need a deeper discussion since it comprises the fundamental problem of the relation of the single individual to the masses and to the social, political, and economic processes. Even Marx and Lenin rely upon the insight of single individuals which may help in the final solution of the economic process. Neither of these men obviously has felt that their individual actions were unnecessary and useless in furthering the economic process.

It would be very interesting to determine in a socio-psychiatric study how human beings behave on a borderline-minimum-subsistence. What do individuals do who have been on Home Relief for a long time? What are the problems of adaptation? What does the person who has been unemployed for a long time do to amuse himself? Economic and psychological problems cannot be completely separated. When we deal with economic questions we are concerned with work which has been crystallized and this has to be contrasted with working conditions and psychological factors which in the definition of our terms is work going on, work in action. Important psychological problems arise when we consider the relation between crystallized work and work in action. Thus we can see immediately that the final understanding of economic problems can only be reached when we first understand the work from the viewpoint of human needs and the psychology of action.

References

It is, of course, not possible to give even a half-way complete bibliography. *The Handbook of Marxism* edited by Emile Burns, (International Publishers, New York City) contains most of the passages which have been directly quoted in this paper. The book by Reuben Osborn, *Freud and Marx*, (Equinox Cooperative Press) deals with problems similar to this lecture. Compare further, Charlotte Bühler *Der Menschliche Lebenslauf*, (Leipzig, Hirzel, 1933). The psychoanalytic literature can be found quoted in my book *Psychotherapy* (Norton, New York, 1938). Furthermore, compare Géza Róheim, "Psychoanalysis of Primitive Cultural Types," *International Journal of Psychoanalysis*, 13: ½, Jan.-April, 1932, 1-224. Bleuler, Eugen, "Uber Gelegenheitsapparate and Abreagieren." *Zeitschr. f. Psychiatrie*, 76, 1920. R. R. Marett, *Faith, Hope and Charity in Primitive Religion*, (New York, Macmillan, 1932). W. A. Winterstein, "Zur Psychologie der Arbeit," *Imago*, 18, No. 2, 1932, 137-150. P. Schilder: "Psychologie einer Psychose bein Corticaler Encephalitis": Z. *Neur.*, 118, 3, 1929, 327-346.

Postscript: The Midas Complex

If there is to be a psychoanalysis of money, it must start from the hypothesis that the money complex has the essential structure of religion—or, if you will, the negation of religion, the demonic. The psychoanalytical theory of money must start by establishing the proposition that money is, in Shakespeare's words, the "visible god"; in Luther's words, "the God of this world."

—*N. O. Brown*

I

When Norman O. Brown published his catalytic study *Life against Death* in 1959, this most important psychoanalytic study of our generation not only paved the way for a new chapter in the history of psychoanalysis, it also opened up entirely new perspectives for the anal theory of money. His point of departure was that Freud's "Character and Anal Erotism" (Bibliography 1) and all research stemming from it (Bibliography 2-8) were false, or at least inadequate. Only Róheim (Bibliography 13-15) and Harnik (Bibliography 9), he felt, had come close to an adequate interpretation of anality. The effort to derive anal erotism, the anal character, and anal neurosis from toilet training was vulgar and naive. A correct view of all three phenomena would have to be looked for in the connection between anality and the phenomena of displacement, the Oedipus and castration complexes, and especially the death instinct. Anality was not merely sadistic but fundamentally destructive and therefore also masochistic, and contained a socially destructive element in the form of money. The key figure of the anal paradox had to be searched for in the religious and its antithesis, the demonic, especially in the figure of the devil. While we come across this notion in Freud (cf., Contribution 1, paragraph 7), Brown gave it new substance in his character analysis of Martin Luther and his interpretation of Protestantism. "The painters paint the devil black and filthy," Luther said, and Brown adds that the color of the devil had always been black, not because of his abode, but because of the association between black and filth, and filth and feces. He goes on to say that the sulfurous odor of the devil is also an attribute of his anality. The climax of the witches' sabbath is kissing the devil's posterior. During black mass (black again as an equation of filth and feces), a mixture of feces and other disgusting substances was always kneaded on the buttocks of a naked woman. Dante pointed to Satan's anus as the "still point" of the world, Bosch painted the devil on the latrine where damned souls fall out of his anus. Luther, who experienced the devil with greater immediacy, force, and persuasiveness than any other person of his time was for that reason the most significant representative of his age. In his *Table Talks*, he repeatedly described his encounters with the devil—never as encounters with a symbol, but always with a living being which stank and farted. The ink Luther hurled at him is anality, thinly disguised. He repeatedly enjoined the devil to kiss his arse, to shit into his pants and to wear them around his neck; he threatened that he would empty his bowels into his (i.e., the devil's) face or put him inside his (i.e., Luther's) arse where he belonged. And finally he drove the devil away by farting.

Brown infers from all this that Luther recognized the devil as the incarnation of his own anality. It is therefore hardly surprising that his great illumination occurred on a toilet. In the devil, he hated and despised what he feared in himself: his dependence on the material. The sequence of the chthonic gods from the mother religions of prehistory by way of the Greek Hermes down to the Christian devil corresponds to the sequences of material productive capacities and trade. Just as Baudelaire and Blake had later stressed the essentially satanic character of trade, Luther had already identified the devil with both the merchant and death: "Thus Luther stresses the busy restlessness of the devil, and his mastery of all techniques. Conversely, Luther's concept of the devil as the personified death instinct sustains his vision of the usurer as a murderer, and usury as a plague killing Germany" (Brown, *Life against Death*, p. 220). Luther's most profound statement on capitalism is therefore the sentence that "money is the word of the Devil through which he creates all things, the way God created through the true word" (op. cit. p. 221). The structure of Luther's kingdom of Satan is "essentially capitalistic: we are the devil's property" (op. cit. p. 221). Troeltsch, Tawney, Sombart, Weber, and Fromm were therefore incorrect when they held that the psychological nexus between

Protestantism and capitalism was the figure of God as the God of order. Rather, that nexus is the devil, for he is "Lord of this world." The world cannot get along without him: it cannot do without usury, avarice, miserliness, the desire to amass wealth, or theft. The world is the devil's hostelry and we are his bondsmen. Whoever wants to walk peacefully in this world must be money's guest. But while our flesh is in bondage to the devil, our spirit is not. Consequently the spirit remains free, while the flesh pays homage to the devil. Luther's critique of monasticism as an escape from inescapable reality pointed to this world as the only place where salvation can be won. As Christ surrendered to the cross, so the Protestant surrenders to life in this world, and particularly to the acquisition of money. To take up the cross does not mean doing penitence or good works, as the Catholics think, but to assume the sin and burden of earning money. The dedication of the Protestant to his calling is thus a means of surrendering both to the devlil and to death. The decadence of Protestantism did not begin until the "liberals" within the church had misinterpreted dedication to one's calling as obedience to God's word: "From the psychoanalytical point of view, if the Devil is Death, and if capitalism is the Devil, then modern Protestantism's alliance with capitalism means its complete surrender to the death instinct" (op. cit. p. 224).

"The money complex is the demonic, and the demonic is God's ape; the money complex is therefore the heir to and substitute for the religious complex, an attempt to find God in Things. In psychoanalytical terms, modern secularism is no release from the Oedipus complex, from which Freud said religion was derived; it is only the transfer of the projections originating in the Oedipus complex from the world of spirits to the world of things" (op. cit. p. 240). All attempts, including the Marxist, to explain money rationally are therefore doomed from the start, and this for three reasons: first, because rationality is the opposite of what bourgeois society and Marxism mean by it; everything they consider rational thinking and rational behavior is irrational according to the insights of psychoanalysis. Secondly, because money is fundamentally meaningless, useless, and pointless. It is this senselessness and meaninglessness that are money's distinguishing characteristics. It can therefore never serve the rational, purposive exploitation of the worker by the capitalist, but instead creates a purely neurotic tie between the two which is destructive for both. Thirdly, because money can never bring real, material satisfaction. For the adult, satisfaction is the fulfillment of an infantile longing, but money is no infantile wish.

In somewhat greater detail, Brown argues as follows:

1. Reason, a product of repression, is precisely that aspect of the psyche which is least capable of "rational" activity. Every form of thought, but especially "economizing calculation," is anally motivated and therefore especially unreliable as a yardstick of rational conduct and guide to useful activity.

2. All currencies, from the prehistoric dog teeth, the shell and stone money of the primitives (particularly the large stone cart wheels of the island of Yap which—although sunk into the sea—yet symbolize value) down to gold, paper money, and the "drawing rights" of our time are not rationally comprehensible and have no use value. The fact that some, such as shells, gold, and silver, could be worked into ornaments underlines the finding that they are not useful objects but always represent a surplus, i.e., a waste product and only appeared as surplus-producing societies developed. But surplus-producing societies are intrinsically paradoxical because they have lost the criterion of what is necessary and instead perform surplus, unnecessary labor: "There is something in the human psyche which commits man to non-enjoyment, to work (*negotium*, non-leisure) . . . . There is something in the structure of the human animal which compels him to produce superfluously, but obviously the compulsion will apply only so

long as the human animal draws no distinction between the necessary and the superfluous. It is an integral part of the money complex and the compulsion to work to confuse the superfluous with the necessary; the confusion still reigns in the vague talk about 'economic necessity.' But the core of the necessary is the need for food. We may therefore say that it is inherent in the money complex to attribute to what is not food the virtue that belongs to food. In Freud's succinct formula: 'excrement becomes aliment' " (op. cit. pp. 256-257).

3. Surplus can only be achieved through the division of labor, and the division of labor kills all those human satisfactions which originate in a balanced use of all his capacities. Every specialization means the neglect of other capacities of mind and body. Just as certainly as organs wither when they are not used, so the specialization and neglect inherent in the division of labor drive men into physical and psychic illness. Marx also arrived at the "gloomy conclusion" that "some crippling of body and mind is inseparable even from the division of labor as a whole" (op. cit. p. 260), so that we cannot expect complete liberation from illness and neurosis even from a classless society as long as the division of labor remains in force.

The fact that we consider the division of labor rational is part of our general illusion that the materially useful is also rational, but actually this is "demonolatry." Instead of giving the surplus to God as in archaic societies, we have begun to worship as a god the process of production which creates surplus. But neither capitalist nor socialist rationality eliminates irrational impulses. It merely allows them to get out of hand by removing the restraints of sacred tradition. This alienation has its analogue in the money economy. Its root is the compulsion to work, which subjects man to things, confuses their utilization, and at the same time produces the devaluation of the human body. This compulsion reduces man's drives to greed and competition, to aggression and the need to own, as in the anal character. The desire for money replaces all original human needs. The illusory amassing of wealth is actually an impoverishment of the human being. What results is that concrete, total man is replaced by the abstraction of the *homo economicus*: human nature is dehumanized; "and this dehumanized human nature produces an inhuman consciousness, whose only currency is abstractions divorced from real life—the industrious, coolly rational, economic, prosaic mind" (op. cit. p. 238). Capitalism has made us so dull and one-sided that objects only exist for us if they give us the naive illusion that they are materially useful. And this illusion derives in turn from the erroneous assumption that the appropriation of the products of the work of others can give us satisfaction.

Of course, some of these ideas are reminiscent of Marx's concepts of alienated compulsory labor and the fetishist character of goods, but as Brown questions the entire trend of human development from the division of labor and surplus production down to industry, he casts doubt on the possibility of progress and rational knowledge, the pillars of everything that seemed indispensable to Marx if man was to be liberated. According to Brown, socialism cannot do away with the fundamental evil of capitalism but only make it more rational. This fundamental evil is the notion that material possessions can give satisfaction and that the more rational use of the means of production is progress. On the contrary, the attempt to dominate nature is the root of all discontent, which cannot be eradicated by any material progress but will merely increase the burden of human guilt. This concept of guilt is the core of Brown's thought.

He begins his explanation of the problem of guilt with Nietzsche's definition of man as the "animal that can promise." It can promise because it is conscious of its ancestors. Man's ability to promise something to others is the connecting link between past and future. But it also "involves an unhealthy constipation with the past," the anal character "can 'get rid of' nothing." The ability to promise is therefore also the ability to calculate and to be calculable, to owe and to pay one's debts. In all languages, the concepts "guilt" and "debts" are closely connected, as in English, for example, "ought" and "owe." Contract and duty, price and retaliation go hand in hand. Both spheres—the economy (the relation between creditors and debtors) and morality (the relation between guilt and expiation) radiate cruelty. Culture is thus the debt to one's ancestors. As culture grows, the feeling of indebtedness to them increases. In Christian theology, it culminates in the notion of an unpayable debt.

Guilt is repressed hatred of someone who has been good to us, and arises from the inseparable intermingling of love and hatred. Every child that is told by its loving parents that to be "good," i.e., to be accepted by the society of adults, it must renounce this or that satisfaction dams up a lifelong guilt, for unconsciously it hates the parents that demand so much renunciation from it. But at the same time, it loves them because it is aware of the sacrifices the parents made for it. The suppression of a complete enjoyment of life in the present thus unavoidably releases aggression against those ancestors for whose sake repression occurred. But aggression against those who are also loved is guilt. And the more the debt toward the past is paid, the more aggressive become its interventions in the enjoyment of life in the present. Each new aggression against the past triggers new feelings of guilt: the avalanche of the past constantly threatens to bury the present.

One of man's oldest methods to decrease this burden of guilt is the giving of gifts. Man gives because he wants to lose. The psychological motive is not economic but simple sacrifice of self. For this reason, money is much more closely tied to religion than to economics. The reciprocal gift is a profane form of the sacred gift to the gods. Just as it is the function of the gods to decrease guilt when one sacrifices to them, it is the function of the fellow human being to take on guilt when one brings him a sacrifice, i.e., a gift. Thus human society did not develop for the improvement of the material conditions of life of the individual through collective measures but in order to share individual guilt through the process of reciprocity. While it is true that one does not rid oneself of guilt in this fashion, the illusion of expiation is consoling. Human society can only be understood as an institution for the sharing of guilt. But because unconscious ideas can only become conscious as external perceptions projected onto the real world, only social organization can raise to consciousness and thus mitigate repressed guilt. Social organization is thus a symbolic, shared confession of guilt.

Of course, this entire line of reasoning goes back to Freud's thesis of the primal crime, the killing and devouring of the Primal Father, which also plays a central role in Róheim's work. But while Róheim views this Freudian metaphor as a historical fact, Brown is much more ingenious. He explicitly rejects Freud's notion of an archaic heritage consisting of memory traces of the experiences of former generations, and posits instead a primal guilt which everyone invents for himself: a fantasy, created ex nihilo by the infantile Ego in order to "sequester its own unmanageable vitality—the Id, by repression." Just as the sexual organization is created by the infantile Ego to repress its bodily vitality, the life of the adult remains tied to this world of infantile fantasy until the adult Ego is strong enough to free itself of this primal repression and to enter the "kingdom of enjoyment."

Just as these infantile sexual fantasies do not mirror a real event, money also has no reality, for nothing exists in reality that corresponds to its symbolic value. It is nothing more than the product of unconscious feelings of guilt, and such feelings do not have their roots in any particular infantile misdeed toward its parents but are the necessary sediment of every relationship between generations. But this insight must not lead one into committing the error of underestimating the reality value of these guilt feelings simply because they appear to be baseless, for one has the obligation to use the currency of the country in which one finds oneself, and in the country of neuroses, this is the neurotic currency. In this sense, money is always the material form of the neurosis, but all forms of money are not always the material form of a neurosis, but all forms of money are not equally neurotic. In the archaic consciousness, for example, the feeling of indebtedness coexisted with the illusion that the debt could be paid by sacrificing to the gods and giving gifts to one's neighbor. In the bourgeois consciousness of our time, feelings of guilt are much more pronounced: the unconscious tells us that the burden of guilt cannot be repaid. This has been particularly clear since the time of Luther, who was the first to have recognized the bankruptcy of the bourgeois world.

The history of bourgeois society is consequently the emancipation of the economic process from divine control. The increased guilt feeling created the secularization of the economy, and that secularization destroyed the comforting illusion that work saves. In Luther's words: man is not justified by works. But at the same time, the bourgeoisie insists on the compulsion to work. Protestantism as the religion of the bourgeoisie even intensifies the need to work by referring to work as the necessary surrender to the cross. What results is an economy propelled by nothing but feelings of guilt which are not mitigated by any hope for salvation. The illusion that Christ could save us has been lost, but not the illusion that Adam fell. This is the reason why man in bourgeois society believes he has to punish himself by working. It is characteristic that the bourgeoisie only considers genuine work those activities which are not enjoyed. The more difficult work of the artist and scientist, which often demands much more time and energy, is not accepted as "real" work because it brings pleasure and satisfaction. The economy consequently does not obey economic logic, but the logic of guilt. It is driven uncontrollably by guilt feelings because not only liberal Protestantism but also bourgeois rationalism and the anti-bourgeois workers' movement deny the existence of the problem of guilt, which is repressed more and more as a result of this denial.

To shed light on interest—one of the darkest aspects of money—Brown establishes a connection between guilt and expiation and a psychoanalytical concept of time he took over from Harnik and developed in a very intelligent manner. Since the idea of expiation is the expression of the belief that what has happened can be undone, it is also always an expression of time. The idea of time could consequently only come from an animal that feels guilt and looks for expiation. What mankind understands by time is a product of the repression of instincts, for in the unconscious—that part of the psyche which man shares with other animals—time does not exist. Unconscious psychic processes are always atemporal. There is nothing in them of any notion of time. To put the matter the other way around: like money, time is neurotic and belongs to those fundamental structures of the distortion of reality which are necessary to create and bear repression, i.e., culture.

Time is indeed part of the self, but of that unconscious part which consists of the Super-Ego, the character structure, and the defense mechanisms. According to Brown who here adopts Freud's late theories, the Super-Ego is the shadow of a lost past and arose through the internalization of the ancestors. It represents the cultural past and originates in the infantile wish for identification with the ancestors and the desire to be its own father. Functionally, it operates with the aid of that defensive technique Freud called isolation. Isolation protects the ego from being overwhelmed by the force of the instincts through fragmenting the burden of experience into parts in order to deal with them more easily. Such fragmentation, however, is always also a division into temporal sequences which can then be *counted* and *saved* because they are *valuable*: "Time is money." Thus we have not only a transformation of experiences into time, but also a transformation of time into merchandise, and this transformation supports the abstract, alienated, and reified character of the bourgeois world.

According to Brown, archaic society used another means of defense: a yearly expiation ceremony based on the idea of rebirth. Man expiated his guilt by a symbolic death and was born a second time, free of guilt. This is, of course, a technique of denial, but since, according to Freud, the contents of a repressed idea can enter consciousness through denial, the archaic technique actually represents a practicable form of therapy. In the bourgeois world, on the other hand, the unconscious burden of guilt has increased to such an extent that it is no longer possible to reduce it through religious rites. This is primarily due to the fact that all of us have a historical consciousness which archaic society was fortunate enough to be without. The archaic concept of time was cyclical—from rebirth to rebirth, while the bourgeois concept of time is cumulative. The consciousness of the past therefore burdens bourgeois society with a historical fate: the sins of the fathers are visited upon the children down to the third and fourth generation. This means: the schemata of cumulative debt and of cumulative time work together in producing an economy of compound interest.

Here, Brown believes he has discovered a similarity with Marx's theory of labor value since Marx measures the value of products by units of labor which have both a temporal and a spatial dimension. The value of every human product is measured by the time required to make it. The cost of this time includes the living and educational expenses of all those who have participated in its production. And since this also includes the living- and educational expenses of the parents, the theoretical cost of every product must be computed by going back to the beginnings of mankind. Capital also is nothing other than the expropriated, accumulated labor of the millennia. As a result, time is everything, man nothing. He becomes a fleshless skeleton of time. Capital, the hand that stretches from the grave of the dead past, appropriates labor, the living power of the present. Just like guilt, interest is thus a tribute paid by the present to the past. Differently expressed, the rate of interest is the price of time and of guilt burdened by time. Since the dynamics of bourgeois society rests on postponing enjoyment to an ever-more remote future, the rate of interest may be defined as the market price of crystallized impatience. In the same sense, goods must be viewed as crystallized time, for otherwise they could never be owned as property.

According to Brown, the exploitation of the proletariat is thus not pursued in the concrete, material interest of the ruling class but represents a transformation of the archaic act of expiation (gifts to fellow human beings, sacrifices to the gods) into the modern process of expiation which is the surrender to the cross. It is the result of the psychic process of denial. Brown does not think that there is a significant difference between that form of surrender which enriches itself through the exploitation of others and the one which suffers from exploitation. At least he does not mention it. Instead, he writes: ". . . in accumulating possessions the individual shoulders his own burden of guilt and thus negates the first solution (i.e., giving instead of taking)" (op. cit. pp. 278-279). The place of this transformation of giving into taking was the city. According to Brown, the city proclaims that man no longer wanted to live with and from nature as in the village, but proposed to rebel against it. With the city, there began the irreversible destruction of human life on earth, both physically through pollution and somatic illness and psychically through incurable neurosis. Unlike most Marxists, Brown does not understand the ecological problem as a proliferation of what are fundamentally healthy institutions caused by the profit motive but as a wrong turn that was taken in earliest history and that cannot be made good by socialist measures. The city is not the walled feudal settlement, the bourgeois city, or the socialist metropolis, but the *urbs per se* which is the "deposit" of accumulated guilt and therefore incurable in principle. It owes a debt, he says, "to be paid by further accumulation of monuments. Through the city the sins of the fathers are visited upon the children; every city has a history and a rate of interest" (op. cit. p. 283).

The institution of interest not only presupposes cumulative time but also a shift of that loyalty which was once felt toward one's fellow man. A new form of loyalty is born which is seen in the value of the gift which was once given without an awareness of its value. Thus gifts are transformed into goods, and presents into money: "Thus money in the civilized economy comes to have a psychic value it never had in the archaic economy" (op. cit. p. 279). Money inherits the infantile magic of excrement. It can therefore breed and have children: interest is increment, as the etymological roots demonstrate (Greek *tokos* and Latin *faenus* mean, according to Brown, both "increment" and "interest").

II

Brown's theses are a fascinating intellectual game which will bring considerable intellectual pleasure to any receptive reader. But like so many of the nontherapeutic writings of the great analysts, it really doesn't mean anything. It is an accumulation of epigrams, metaphors, and allegories where the thought processes of one academic discipline are expressed in the vocabulary of another—in the case of Brown, it is usually theological thought that is expressed in the vocabulary of psychoanalysis. His work, therefore, can be properly appreciated only if it is seen as a theology in psychoanalytic disguise. But there is no arguing with theologians because the superstructure of their intellectual framework, however logical it may be, rests on unverifiable premises that are articles of faith. What Brown says about money applies to his entire book: it is a theoretical model to which nothing in reality corresponds. All it reflects are the thoughts of its author.

Wherever one can come to grips with him, Brown can be refuted easily enough. But since the major portion of his study is purely speculative, this is possible only where he abandons the language of parable and momentarily steps onto the ground of reality. He criticizes the Marxist development of the doctrine of the anal character as elaborated—more or less in accord—by Reich, Fenichel, Fromm, and Adorno, for example. He reproaches them with having turned Freud's analytical categories into watered-down sociology, and claims that in the process they sacrificed Freud's most important insight, the bodily origin of the anal symptoms of orderliness, thrift, and obstinacy, to a social abstraction. In their work, he says, the idea of the authoritarian character, a concept without somatic importance, largely replaced the anal character: "With the loss of the Freudian materialism of the body, psychology becomes, in neo-Freudian hands, as also in Jungian hands, once more what it was before the Freudian revolution, a psychology of the autonomous soul. This is the 'advance' celebrated in neo-Freudian circles as overcoming Freud's 'biological orientation' " (op. cit. p. 204).

This criticism may have merit as regards Fromm, but certainly does not hold for Wilhelm Reich, whose truly fanatical insistence on looking for the roots of all psychic suffering in the somatic went far beyond Freud's. Fenichel is a more appropriate target, for he understood the anal character as a fixation on a trauma which develops during the child's toilet training. This is the thesis I advocated in my own contribution at the beginning of this book. Brown employs the following argument against all of us who take this stand: suppose our capitalist civilization really does show anally erotic traits. In that case, we Marxist analysts can offer nothing better toward the abolition of capitalism than permissive toilet training. But that is neither revolution nor socialism nor psychotherapy, for instead of dealing with the real problem, the anal neurotic, we turn our entire attention on his parents, which means that "this whole approach . . . betrays the classic Freudian axiom that the child is father of the man. While apparently deriving the adult anal character from infantile anal erotism, it is really deriving infantile anal erotism from the adult anal character . . ." (op. cit. p. 205). The argument is therefore circular: "adult anal character is derived from adult anal character" (loc. cit.).

That's perfectly correct, for in contrast to Freud and Brown, I trace both the somatic and the psychic structure of man to his social condition and not to the isolated experience of the child in the home of its parents. All I know about is that the parents in their infancy were molded as they now mold their children. But who molded the parents' parents? Or, in Freudian terminology: who molded the primal father? Freud attributes precisely defined character traits to him; where do they come from if the child is the father of the adult and does not need a father to create itself? If Brown reproaches me with deriving the anal character of the adult from the anal character of the adult, I can only reply that he himself merely derives the anal character of the child from the anal character of the child.

My central question stands: why does one culture introduce excessive toilet training and thereby raise an entire generation of anal neurotics, while another is indifferent or permissive in matters of anal weaning and produces a character type which is neither anal erotic nor anal neurotic? It seems to me that this question cannot be answered by any psychological method but only through the study of the productive forces and their development. Those who make the best use of the means of production and who most effectively unfold the latent productive forces will also determine kind and form of education. If a class requires orderliness, thrift, industriousness, and the ability to make one's way in order to come to power, the entire society including the exploited classes will adopt these pedagogic methods, at least temporarily. To speak of a death instinct in this connection instead of looking at the realities means lending support to the ruling class by keeping silent about the methods through which it retains power.

Brown refers to this as a pre-Freudian mode of thought "decorated with unessential (and confusing) psychologistic patter" (op. cit. p. 206). He thinks that psychoanalysis is neither causal and scientific nor understandable by "ordinary common sense." This may be true of Brown's kind of analysis but does not apply to what I advocate here. The attempt to do rational analysis he calls "morbid" since it stems from a greedy, anal desire for domination, the desire for mastering knowledge. To want knowledge, to want a rational understanding of the world is, in his vocabulary, a sublimated offshoot of the desire for possession, a striving for power transposed from the anal to the spiritual. He quotes Ferenczi's famous phrase: "Thinking is after all only a means of preventing a squandering through action," and interprets this as proof that the desire for rational knowledge is merely "a special expression of the tendency to economize," i.e., irrational. As an alternative, he postulates a non-neurotic science which would have to be "more erotic than sadistic" in its goal. That goal would not be domination but union with nature. Not the anal instincts but the entire polymorphously sensitive body would be its base. This corresponds more or less to what we Marxist analysts mean by the psychology of a classless society, but I fail to see how we can ever create such a society if we begin by desisting from the effort to acquire whatever rational knowledge may be necessary to defeat our adversaries.

III

The irreality of Brown's thought becomes especially conspicuous when he deals with verifiable questions of early and prehistory. He believes, as we have seen, that the reciprocal giving of gifts which he mistakenly attributes to primitive society (actually it only appears in the hunting cultures of our time) is devoid of economic significance but derives from the sacred sphere and can only be understood as a secular counterpart of the sacrifice to the gods. But in one of his best books, *Der Einbruch der Sexualmoral* (*The Imposition of Sexual Morality*) (Berlin,

1932), Reich described in an absolutely persuasive and irrefutable fashion how reciprocal giving invariably leads to the enrichment of the chief and the beginnings of a ruling class. This argument is retained in the revised version, published under the title *Der Einbruch der sexuellen Zwangsmoral* (Cologne, 1972) (Translated as *The Invasion of Compulsory Sex Morality*, Farrar, Straus & Giroux, New York, 1971. Transl. note). Whether giving creates the class society or class society gives rise to giving may be a matter of dispute, but one thing is certain: it has a specific, material effect on the development of classes and cannot be interpreted as a purely sacral, wholly noneconomic phenomenon.

A central tenet of Brown's thesis is the shift from this "archaic" culture of giving to the "modern" culture of taking. When and where this change with its negative effect on the entire history of mankind actually occurred, Brown does not tell us. He merely associates it vaguely with the "rise of the cities." But no such change can be discovered anywhere in the world during the history of urbanization. It is as unknown in early and prehistory as is the death of the primal father in ethnology. Brown could only maintain his thesis if he viewed it as he does Freud's thesis of the primal crime: a fantasy created by the infantile ego whose only purpose is to tame the infantile Id through repression. But even then it lacks logic, for if archaic society was able to effectively eradicate guilt feelings through giving there is no reason, according to Brown's criteria, why it should ever have died out. But the fact that the archaic world did die out proves that it is impossible to argue that cultures perish when the burden of repressed guilt feelings becomes unsupportable and that they survive only when they succeed in making conscious the unconscious or prevent the rise and subsequent repression of such feelings in the first place.

IV

Brown believes that the differences in character and behavior resulting from changing toilet training are minimal: profound differences are effected only by the death instinct. I do not share that view, especially because it entirely disregards the collapse of the illusion of fecal omnipotence which has a traumatic effect on some, though not on all children. If the infantile Ego is to develop sufficient strength so that the character of the adult will be marked neither by hesitancy and indecisiveness nor by dogmatism and aggressiveness, the transition from the anal-sadistic phase to the latency period must occur through a gradual overcoming of the illusion of fecal omnipotence. There must be neither a shock toward the end of the anal phase, for then the adult always regresses to this trauma, nor must it be carried over into adult life.

The girl's discovery that the boy has a penis, and the boy's that the girl has none became the core of all of Freud's theories, as is well known. He was right in viewing the trauma of this discovery as fundamental. But there is also a secondary trauma that occurs during the period of maturation which has almost as much importance, and that is the child's discovery that its power is limited, that it is not the only one in the world that can defecate, that others do the same, that one is consequently not unique but just one among many. Unless this discovery is gradual and mitigated by the love of the parents, it casts a shadow over much of adult life and becomes the origin of all those symptoms which we associate with a certain weakness of the Ego, with overcompensation for that weakness, aggressiveness, and especially with a vanity that is easily hurt. In most cases, this syndrome manifests itself in the fear of being demoted, robbed, insufficiently respected. Such an individual frequently will try to compensate for the loss of fecal omnipotence by insisting that he and his achievements are unique.

When a creative person—a scientist, artist, composer, writer—complains that others want to steal his ideas, this syndrome is often involved. Even among analysts who might be expected to have a stronger Ego and a more profound self-knowledge, such cases are not rare. Let us take the case of colleague A who reproaches colleague B with having plagiarized his work—both its basic idea, and the relevant documentation. But if B truthfully states that his work was not his own idea but a project proposed by his training analyst and if, in addition, the documentary material is folklore and therefore neither A's nor B's work, what does "plagiarized" intellectual property mean here?

If we measure property by Marx's theory of value, B's book has as much value as the time he spent working on it. If this comes to ten or twelve years, the value of the work is considerable, whatever its exchange value may be. If we define property by the civil code (theft), no one has been robbed. On the contrary, the publicity of such a quarrel between prominent colleagues usually results in increased income for both. But if we bring psychological criteria to bear, we see immediately what has happened: the infantile illusion of one's omnipotence is destroyed when the adult discovers regressively or too late that he is not unique; that what he considered his very own—the laboriously accomplished sublimate of infantile feces—can also be produced by others.

What would a more balanced, less compulsively aggressive behavior look like in such a case? Freud wrote a number of pioneering studies on art, including some of folk art. Later, Ernst Kris took up the same subject and expanded it significantly. Let us assume that I am now writing a psychoanalytic study on folk art and ten years later a book written by my colleague B comes out. It deals with the same topic. B is a disciple of Kris, and the subject was proposed to him as a doctoral dissertation. One-third of the works of art analyzed by him was previously analyzed by me. If I am asked to review B's book, I cannot confine myself to describing what his book has in common with mine but must also consider what distinguishes it. However much my vanity may suffer, I have to take it for granted that he used similar material, for the quantity of folk art is limited. I have no right to imagine that he stole from me, nor can I impute theft to him. If he mentions Kris as the father of his work, I cannot reproach him by saying that the idea of the book wasn't his. We notice that what applies to material also applies to intellectual property. The development of anality causes significant differences between A and B and they cannot be explained by the death instinct, as Brown believes, but only by the pathogenesis of the anal syndrome.

V

Brown repeatedly calls attention to the affinity between his own and Géza Róheim's work, and this is no accident. Both subscribe to the idea that causality is a nineteenth-century notion, that logic implies a kind of popularized materialism, and that the use of scientific categories other than psychoanalysis constitutes a betrayal of that discipline. Both reject the economic motives of mankind as irrelevant, both question the power of rational thought, and both conceive of analytic thinking as André Breton did. They did it as an intuitive breakthrough to the sources of the Id which yields poetic rather than rational knowledge.

In the theoretical parts of his studies, Róheim confesses repeatedly that he acknowledges hunger as the determinant of the reality principle and that he views the libido only in its relation to the object world on the one hand and the sense of reality on the other, the libido being the source of unconscious and often unrealistic behavior. But when an ethnological problem is to be solved, he always decides in favor of the unconscious, antirealistic explanation and either presents a causal interpretation as an anachronistic error due to the rationalism of the eighteenth and nineteenth centuries, or ignores the possibility of a causal explanation based on facts as if such a thing did not exist. When confronted with a social hierarchy in Australia, for example, where the clan and tribe elders monopolize the best food (Contribution 9), he does not attribute this to the real power of this ruling group but to the influence of "surviving infantile memory traces" among the younger who "voluntarily" renounce this food because from earliest childhood on they were accustomed to having their nourishment served by their parents and now cannot rid themselves of the self-imposed compulsion to eat only what the elders portion out to them. The question why this compulsive dependence is present only in a few cultures while in others the young soon emancipate themselves from their elders' influence does not occur to Róheim because it is a sociological problem and thus lies outside the area of competency of psychoanalysis (in this same case, Brown would have argued that to voluntarily eat inferior food is a form of paying one's debt).

While Freud always saw human behavior as the result of the interaction of inherited and external influences (where the parents constitute both the genetic and the most important outside influence), Róheim's world is almost exclusively the plaything of unconscious psychic factors. He says, for example, that "functionally interpreted," the gods are the projections of socially caused inhibitions, "but ontogenetically, the projection of the father imago." Having thus paid his purely formal respect to the reality principle in the form of socially caused inhibitions, he immediately turns to the influence of the father imago and ignores everything else. Since it is his view that the unconscious processes of the psyche express themselves most clearly in the magico-mythical and considers it a characteristic of the magico-mythical that it inverts the relationship between cause and effect, he actually turns the world upside down: where both a causal primary and an anti-causal secondary explanation for a process can be given, he invariably prefers the latter and fails to mention the former.

When he discovers that during the rites of passage

among the Australian Yaraikana the young males have a tooth knocked out and the name of a tribal region is called at every blow, he sees in this the psychic origin of property, for the region whose mention coincides with the accidental falling out of the tooth "belongs" to the young man. For Róheim as for Brown, property has no economic but only psychic significance: it is the introjection into the ego of part of the external world through the mediation of a severed part of the body. The primary economic interpretation of property is ignored and replaced by a secondary and speculative one which permits important inferences concerning the origin of the rite but has nothing whatever to do with the origin of property. The sequence of cause and effect is perverted.

Yet even this would be pardonable, had it not led Róheim to "interpret" the motives of those not sharing his opinions according to the same schema. In footnote 129 of his Contribution 9, he states, for example, that the mother right theory advocated by Bachofen, Morgan, Marx, and Engels (in Róheim's terminology "the chain of hypotheses promiscuity-primitive communism-monogamy") had been shaped psychologically by the more or less conscious tendency of these thinkers to "communize women" and that this unconscious desire for polygamy represented "the real, unconscious mainspring of the entire movement." In other words, and more clearly: science obeys the same dominion of the unconscious as the magico-mythical. Scientific theses, particularly when they pretend to be logical, are forms of self-delusion caused by unsatisfied sexual desires and serve the purpose of hiding these wishes from consciousness.

That scientists also have a libido and were molded by it like the rest of mankind has never been disputed by anyone with the barest inkling of psychoanalysis. But that scientific theses must be false because scientists transform libido into thought, like everyone else, and that investigators who cannot ignore the documented material concerning prehistorical promiscuity should obey the unconscious desire to reintroduce such promiscuity no one ever dared maintain before Róheim. We can only hope that after Róheim no one will have the impudence to suggest it. With a candor envied by a number of analysts of our time and considered naive or even somewhat embarrassing by others, Róheim uncovers the ticklish contradiction between the sociological and the analytical view of progress: "From the analytical point of view . . . progress means an adaptation of the Ego and the libido to reality." From the sociological point of view, however, progress can never be the adaptation to the external world but only the adaptation of the external world to man. This is the Achilles' heel of Freudian doctrine and also the vulnerable point of Róheim's ethnology. Róheim thinks of Freud's metaphor of the primal father who is murdered and devoured by his sons as a historical event and uses it in an etiological explanation of certain Australian and Melanesian rites (Contribution 9). If this is to be taken seriously, it implies one of two axioms: either the phylogenetic memory of the Melanesians and Australians extends to the origin of mankind, or the primal murder did not take place just once but repeatedly and in identical form. This is like assuming that one is being visited by Jocasta's son himself whenever one discovers an Oedipus complex in a person.

It is a fact, Róheim states, "that during the period after the death of the primal father an inhibition of the genital and a predominance of the anal and the closely connected oral instincts set in." Why is this a fact? Who proved it? Who was there? It is this kind of improvising and improvised analysis which affirms everything and proves nothing that has prompted many once-orthodox analysts to look for a cathexis in the clear, hard, unmistakable categories of Marxism in order to escape in their work the daily slide into the amorphous.

VI

In contrast to Róheim and those analysts whose essays I selected for the second part of this book (Contributions 6-10), in contrast also to Norman O. Brown whose views I used as an antithetical motto at the head of this postscript, I question that the psychoanalysis of money can be derived from the allegedly sacral natural of primitive currency. In contrast to Freud and the great pioneers of psychoanalysis whose studies on money I collected in part I (Contributions 1-5), I also do not believe that the character of money can be derived from the structure of the anal character. I think the opposite is the case: the structure of the anal character can only be understood as the mirror image of those social structures which created it. Being not only determines consciousness, but also the unconscious; not only the structure of the psyche but also its contents and dynamics. Through the studies of Reimut Reiche, W. F. Haug, and Michael Schneider, this insight has been newly confirmed in recent years. In what follows, I shall make extensive use of this material.

Everywhere and always, Freud begins with what was for him a self-evident presupposition: the structure of the psyche he discovered in his patients is the psychic structure of all mankind. The tripartition of the psyche into the Id, the Ego, and Super-Ego was, for him, a discovery of absolute biological significance. What he saw as the specific Ego function, consciousness, has the task of reality testing. But in its characteristic, abstract, and reified form, it is "not primarily an intrapsychological . . . achievement of the ego but rather a reflex of the abstract relation of exchange and money in the mind of economic subjects" (Michael Schneider, *Neurosis and Civilization*, Seabury Press, 1975, p. 142). The capacity to reason, abstract, and think which Freud viewed as the specifically human aspect of the Ego is in reality a phenomenon limited to the Occident and simply reflects the abstract, desensualized character of money.

To understand what is involved here we must first

deal with the concept of repression which Brown also considers fundamental: "There is one word which, if we only understand it, is the key to Freud's thought. The word is 'repression.' The whole edifice of psychoanalysis, Freud said, is based upon the theory of repression. Freud's entire life was devoted to the study of the phenomenon he called repression. . . . In the new Freudian perspective, the essence of society is repression of the individual, and the essence of the individual is repression of himself" (Brown, op. cit. p. 3).

If social existence determines psychic being, psychic repression represents a social form of repression, the repression of the sensuous, useful, and concrete by the abstract and useless. Viewed historically, this process is the repression of use value by exchange value. The seed of this repression is the exchange of goods where that transubstantiation occurs by which the products of labor become merchandise. The personal, sensuous, concrete qualities of both the labor which makes the object and of the function the object is to serve are wiped out and metamorphosed into an abstract, impersonal, desensualized something: exchange value. The daily, unavoidable, ineluctable transformation of all tangible values into intangible, exchangeable categories such as merchandise, money, prices, and wages utterly changed the psychic life of man in capitalism as compared to the feudal period. The natural, sensuous needs of man have been largely repressed. The earning of money, the discipline of the work place, and the renunciation of instinctual gratification have taken their place.

The assimilation of use value to exchange value, of the concrete to the abstract, of the personal to the impersonal necessitated certain psychic adaptations which Freud called defense mechanisms: repression, regression, reaction formation, isolation, undoing, projection, introjection, turning against one's own self, turning into the opposite, sublimation. The motor of these psychic processes, however, is always money which is both abstract and unbounded—unbounded because it does not satisfy any concrete, sensuous need and is therefore not subject to the natural limitation imposed on all other needs. A person who has eaten is full; one who has drunk is no longer thirsty. The satisfaction of sexual desires also has physical limits. Only the greed for money has none. In the case of food and drink or a pathological degeneration of sexuality, addiction may lead to a transgression of these natural limits, but this always happens in the case of money. It is "the eternally dissatisfied, boundless, ill, lustful instinct as such" (Schneider, op. cit. p. 130).

Many years ago, I called the psychic precipitate of this social phenomenon the "Midas Complex." The Midas legend has come down to us through Herodotus, Hyginus, Cicero, Strabo, Ovid, Valerius Maximus, Plutarch, Pausanias, Aelianus, and Maximus of Tyrus. Midas, king of Phrygia, requested from Dionysus whom he had entertained as his guest that everything he touched might turn into gold, and discovered too late that he could now neither eat nor drink, make love or keep warm, for food and drink, women and clothing all turned into cold, unyielding gold at his touch.

Nowhere in the mythology of the Occident has the senselessness, the destructive effect of money that negates all that lives been described in a more compressed form. And nowhere has there been as persuasive a demonstration of the unbounded, neurotic, insatiable aspect of money. Here, the repression of use value by exchange value has not only negated the usefulness of beings and objects but already threatens to negate its owner: he dies of money, he starves, dies of thirst, freezes to death. In this sense, the anal character destroys himself, for he also is a product of the same repression.

Use value is a qualitative value; it expresses itself in concepts such as "good" or "bad," "useful" or "useless," "satisfactory" or "unsatisfactory." Exchange value, on the other hand, cannot be expressed qualitatively but only quantitatively. Only the quantification of all things, their "total calculability" (Lukacs) which finds expression in accounting, the "greatest invention of the bourgeoisie," made possible the bourgeois age, and it is only the bourgeois age that put its definitive stamp on the anal character, the calculating and calculable individual: "An anal-retentive character whose overt form of illness is the compulsive neurotic thus compensates for the loss of qualitative relationships with instinctual objects by compulsively quantifying them and formalizing them. It formalizes the material of its repressed instinctual wishes in its compulsion for order, cleanliness, and punctuality; and it quantifies them in its obsession with avarice, thriftiness, and hoarding and in calculating" (Schneider, op. cit. p. 135).

What Freud viewed as the human ego is actually merely the bourgeois ego. It is the psychic precipitate of those specifically bourgeois virtues which cluster around such concepts as "control, dominion, decision, delimitation, summary, overview, subordination, vigilance" (Helmut Reiche, "*Ist der Odipuskomplex universell?*" in *Kursbuch* 29, Berlin, 1926, p. 169). What Freud called ego weakness, on the other hand, is often what only bourgeois society calls "weak": the healthy satisfaction of natural desires, the refusal to perform hated labor daily, and, at the same time, doubt in the mission of the bourgeoisie and its leadership; everything, in short, that Freud would have considered the disintegration of control, rebellion of the instincts, dissolution of the character structure. Freud's definition of the structure of the ego "only reveals its secret meaning when one sees it in the context of a social group based on competition; it is tied to the market-oriented, merchandise-selling bourgeois who must eliminate his deadly competitors, but has to do so by affectively neutral means, i.e., without killing them outright" (Reich, op. cit. pp. 169-170).

That the ego structure Freud calls "normal," "healthy," "mature," or "non-neurotic" is specific to a class and not universal in origin becomes clear from the history of the proletariat, among other things. Before the working class was driven into the bourgeois process of production, it was characterized by a pronounced ego weakness if judged by psychoanalytical criteria. It "did not at first have to interiorize the consumption and instinctual abstinence of the accumulating bourgeois since, lacking all means of production, it could not itself accumulate, and thus had nothing to abstain from. It lived from hand to mouth. For centuries on end the bourgeoisie also sought vainly to impose its Protestant ideology and its psychology of 'anal-retentive' achievement on wage laborers who in the sixteenth, seventeenth, and eighteenth centuries frequently worked only a three-day week, that is, just long enough to earn as much as they needed to subsist on. . . . Only when the bourgeoisie acquired the power of the state and enacted the six-day week and twelve-hour day, Sunday and night shifts, child and woman labor, were the capitalist work morality and its corresponding 'social character' also imposed on the wage laborers" (Schneider, op. cit. p. 139).

It was the family that imposed it. The barracks discipline of the factory system "must be pre-molded and guaranteed technically through the socialization and education of the worker child according to rigid conceptions of order, cleanliness, and authority. The suppression of the polymorphously perverse sexuality of childhood by 'cultural sexual morality' is a social-technical means of repression that is part and parcel of the logic of capital and anchors the psychic disposition to wage labor at an early age in the instinctual structure of the growing wage laborer. The 'cultural sexual morality' which Freud made responsible for the massive creation of neurosis is therefore the historical twin of a developing capitalist Protestant 'work morality' (Schneider, op. cit. p. 140). The production line, automation, piecework, the ever-progressing suppression of thought at the work place, the ever-increasing opaqueness of the process of production as a whole makes the machine the systematic "instrument of regression" (P. Schneider, "*Die Frauen bei Bosch*," *Kursbuch* 21, Berlin 1970, p. 100). Since the worker is refused an insight into the process of production in its organic totality, he regresses into the past:

"The regressive and pathogenetic effect of work at a half-automated machine thus refutes all psychoanalytic, that is, psychotherapeutic, illusions about 'ego reinforcement' and 'ego strengthening' and 'ego autonomy' for wage-dependent 'patients.' The classic objective of psychoanalytic therapy—'Where there was id should become ego' (Freud)—remains illusory as long as work on capitalist regression machines maintains mental activity in a 'twilight state' between consciousness and unconsciousness and drives it constantly back into the ever-present past of 'endless work agony' (Engels)" (Schneider, op. cit. p. 177). At the same time, the segmentation of the production process into assembly line units, piecework groups, branches, creates a segmentation of the psyche. This Freud also saw as a universally human phenomenon, for he was unaware of both the social origin and the relative newness of the symptom. What he called "partial instincts" was, for him, simply the segmentation of the psyche into oral, anal, genital, voyeuristic, exhibitionistic, sadistic, and masochistic territories. If the integration of the component instincts under the primacy of genitality failed, he used the term "neurosis" and viewed it as a case of individual pathology. But here also we are dealing with nothing more than a psychic reflection of the worker's inability to recognize his social existence as a unity, and to internalize it as such:

> In the same degree as the "organic unity" of the process of life and work is destroyed, so is the "organic unity" of the working individual destroyed: he himself is "divided." As little as individual acts of detail work—in the consciousness of the detail worker—still come together into the "organic unity" of the product, that little do his "fragmented and partialized" capacities and qualities still fit together into an "organic unity" of the person. Thus it is no longer possible to create an integration of partial psychic functions, of "partial drives," into an "organic unity" of the "structure of genital instincts and character." There reproduces itself in the psychic ap-

> paratus a "similar rational-inhuman division of labor as was found in the factory" (Lukacs), namely, the dissection of the psychosexual totality (that is, genitality) into individual partial psychic functions, into their "partialized" instinctual aspects. The rationalization and isolation of (industrial and bureaucratic) partial functions, which become autonomous with regard to the entire process of production and administration, necessarily goes hand in hand with the fact that the accompanying emotional and cognitive functions also become autonomous (Schneider, op. cit. p. 173).

It is the result of this condition that the individual egos, isolated and atomized by exchange relationships and the process of production only have social relations with each other "When they eliminate their 'personal' feelings in the process, according to the motto: 'No sentiment in money matters!' " (Schneider, op. cit. p. 142). What was to Freud an absolute, eternal and universal characteristic of the human psyche, the dialectics of the Id and the Ego, is actually a relatively recent split in it:

> One part of his psychic activity, the ego, must subject itself to the "formal equality" of commodity traffic and the logic of the exchange (of accumulation, of profit), that is, to make calculating reason its own so as to be socially "adjusted." The other half of psychic activity, the "passions," "sensuousness," and the "instinctual nature" of man is shunted off into the incalculable (and therefore rebellious) psychological remnant of the private sphere, that is, into the underground of the "personality," into the "Id." . . . The "sentiments," the "heart," or in Freud's terminology the "functions of the id" have to be eliminated as incalculable emotional ballast from this exchange. . . . The pathic gap, the dysfunction between "ego" and "id," which is the basis of neurosis, therefore comes into existence only in the course of the development of a capitalist mode of production which compels a progressive subsumption of any kind of spontaneity, emotion, or instinct under the rationalism of capital. (Schneider, op. cit. pp. 141-144).

What Freud saw as axiomatic, the unified structure of the consciousness of mankind, is thus a completely new phenomenon that only had its inception as the bourgeois system expanded. According to Lukacs, "it was capitalism that first of all produced with its uniform economic structure for the entire society a structure of consciousness at once formal and uniform for the whole. But it has also— one could amplify Lukacs' insight—produced a psychological structure both formal and uniform, namely, the tendential dissociation of 'ego' and 'id,' of reason and passion, of a '*ratio*' molded by a calculating and quantifying exchange principle, and a remnant of feeling that is still attached to use value (from the standpoint of capital)" (Schneider, op. cit. p. 144).

What Freud called the "censor," the filter between the unconscious and the preconscious which monitors our dreams, among other things, is also only secondarily a psychic force. Primarily, it is the psychic analogue of the social control organs of the bourgeoisie: "The psyche was represented as a kind of three-story apartment house. In the third story lived the respectable members of the conscious family. Below them lived preconscious individuals, calm, reserved people who were permitted to visit their neighbors on the floor above. It is true that a policeman stood on the stairs between the two, but he was quite good-natured and let almost anyone pass. But those living on the ground floor were a noisy, uncivilized bunch which screamed and shouted as they tried to push their way past the overworked policeman between their floor and the preconscious people. But occasionally one of them, usually disguised as a harmless person, succeeded in slipping by at night when the policeman was less alert" (R. Osborn, *Marxismus und Psychoanalyse*, Frankfurt/Main, 1970, p. 29). In the psychic structure of the individual, the class structure of capitalist society thus appears as though "refracted by a prism: 'policemen' represent the 'censor,' that is, the 'forces of repression'; the 'inhabitants of the ground floor' represent what has to be repressed, that is, what *is* repressed. The latter seek to penetrate to the top floor where the members of the conscious family live, so as to become conscious themselves. Freud's dynamic model of neurosis—regarded in this way—is a disguised political model, the model of an impeded revolution. According to this model, the qualitative and quantitative extent of the neurosis is directly proportional to the strength of the 'censor,' that is, the social and political 'repressive forces' " (Schneider, op. cit. p. 162).

It is similar with one of the central tenets of Freudian doctrine, the castration complex. What Freud view-ed as the castration complex, the separation of man from his potency, also is no universally human phenomenon but the psychic reflection of the separation of human labor power from the personality of the worker, "its transformation into a thing, an object, which he sells on the market place" (Lukacs, *History and Class Consciousness*). The castration complex arises from the "castrating" (Marx) characteristics of wage labor. One's own activity "appears as suffering, power as impotence, procreation as castration, the worker's physical and spiritual energy, his personal life . . . as a capacity which is turned against him, is independent of him and does not belong to him" (Marx, MEW, *Ergänzungsband*, I. Teil, p. 515). "Fear of castration is certainly not a primal, so to speak 'biological' fear, but rather the reflex of that social 'castration' which permeates the 'preservation' of the family, which consists in the fact that the wage laborer with his product is simultaneously 'separated' from his genital qualities and potency which now confront him as an alien power" (Schneider, op. cit. p. 172).

Almost everything Freud believed to be permanent, universal human aspects of the psychic structure are thus relatively recent deformations of the psyche which manifest themselves only in the bourgeois world and reflect concrete social situations. The conviction of earlier Freudians that they could derive the relationship of man to money from his psychic structure has proven illusory. Only by proceeding in the opposite direction, from the psychic mirror images of social relations, can one explain how money is understood in the bourgeois world. Without a knowledge of social history there can be no reliable psychoanalysis. The genesis of money, derived from the putative structure of the individual psyche, such as we find it in most of the contributions of the first and second part of this book reveals an alarming ignorance of the real history of money. Psychoanalysis can maintain its claim to be considered a scientific discipline only if it first becomes knowledgeable concerning the real events of history. Without a precise knowledge of history, sociology, and economics, every psychoanalytic attempt to interpret monetary problems becomes charlatanry.

VII

The permanent, increasingly acute currency crisis of capitalism cannot be explained as the result of the irresponsibility of the "oil sheiks," "speculators," or of some other scapegoat. It is an everyday phenomenon in monopolistic capital which has emancipated itself from its creator, the capitalist, and, having become an autonomous force, now threatens to destroy him. But in the meantime, those having least to do with the causes of the crisis suffer the most from its effects. Prices always rise more rapidly than wages and salaries. However "aggressively" unions may conduct themselves, their wage demands will never be met if they threaten to catch up with price increases. The better off wage earners are, the greater becomes the distance between wage and price. The richer the rich, the more they make from inflation. The poorer the poor, the more they lose through it.

At the same time, capital also devours its owners; the small ones first, the big ones later. According to the law that profits increase in relation to the risk, the risk of loss increases for all except the very big owners of capital. Since the market is no longer transparent to anyone except to those who are big enough to be able to partly manipulate it, the probability of loss increases. Freud thought that the child is the father of the man. Now capital is devouring its children who were once its fathers. On the black Friday of the German Federal Republic, the 9th of February, 1973, the Federal Bank had to purchase about two billion dollars, the largest sum which up to that day had ever been spent by a single country on a single day to support a currency. But by the time this book is in print that depressing record already may have been beaten, for the crisis becomes more acute with each countermeasure. Those who think it a "disgrace" that the European nations cannot unite and reject "the attempt of the Americans to pass the cost of the Vietnam war onto others" still live under the illusion that the abstract, impersonal, supra-national power of capital can be broken by personal or national effort. But this is precisely what is impossible.

The hopelessness of man in bourgeois society has begun to spread from the exploited proletarian to the exploiting capitalist. The escapist addiction to purchaseable amusements which allegedly console and make one forget reality for a short while is no longer the pathetic privilege of the proletarian drunk, but has taken hold of the ruling class itself. The ever-present sense of impotence vis-à-vis the workings of anonymous, intangible forces which manipulate our destiny has spread from the manipulated to yesterday's manipulator. Capital, which only a short time back was the "most rational" of all means of exploitation has lost its rationality even for the exploiter: it no longer obeys. The psychic impoverishment, until recently the most effective of secret weapons to get the proletariat to work, to obey, and not to resist, has begun to affect the ruling class.

If a psychoanalysis of money today is to accomplish more than the run-of-the-mill academic publication, it cannot just be reading and discussion material for intellectuals. It will have to make a political issue of the nexus between the social effects of unbridled capital and the psychic impoverishment of all classes. What Wilhelm Reich attempted during the 1930s with partly incorrect means based on partly incorrect analyses must be tried again with better means and more lucid analyses:

> Besides tradiditonal political-economic arguments, which elucidate capital's economic exploitation mechanism, political-psychological arguments elucidating the pathogenetic effects of capital domination must be given increasing importance for revolutionary mass agitation and propaganda: not only rising profits, prices, rents, taxes, armaments outlays, but also the rising rate of psychoneurotic and psychotic illnesses, functional and addictive illnesses, potency and communicatory disturbances, and the like must be made the object of political agitation and propaganda. . . . Only when capital's "Janus-face" of increasing material affluence and mental impoverishment is seen simultaneously from both sides will capitalist exploitation be perceived not only objectively, but also subjectively as the scandal which it has always been. Only when the wage-dependent masses become aware at what economic *and* mental cost their relationship with capitalist production can be maintained—at the price of an increasing economic exhaustion *and* psychic derangement of their labor power, even of the increasing mental, intellectual, and psychic crippling of the entire Western "affluent society"—will the few shares, the personally owned home, the color television, the stereo set, the vacation lose their mystifying, that is, conciliatory effect. When the mental balance of the so-called affluent society is placed next to the profit and exploitation balance—in the Federal Republic alone there are 7,000,000 neurotics requiring treatment, roughly 2,000,000 alcoholics, 600,000 psychotics of the schizophrenic type, 250,000 youthful drug addicts, and so on (to mention only those who are statistically ascertainable)—then the ideology of affluence and consumption will become suspect once and for all (Schneider, op. cit. pp. 257-258).

A psychoanalysis such as Michael Schneider provides in these words can do much to help us understand how things came to be what they are. But even it cannot help us construct an alternative world. What we need is not only a mobilization of those who are threatened by psychic disarray but also an action therapy of those already ruined, for they also are our comrades in the fight against the elimination of what has made them ill. Beginnings of this kind can be found in the documents of the Socialist patient collective in Heidelberg. It is true that Schneider is right when he says: "If SPK Heidelberg declares the 'patient' *eo ipso* into a 'revolutionary class,' then the 'revolutionary subject' is no longer—as in Marxist revolutionary theory—derived from its objective position in the process of production. This attitude also simply ignores the class character of 'illness,' that is, the class differences between individual 'groups of patients' " (Schneider, op. cit. p. 259). But if psychoanalysis is ever to be taken from the study of the bourgeois analyst to the arena of political struggle, it must become more than a therapy of adaptation to a sick bourgeois society for those the bourgeoisie has made ill. Having been passive, it must become active and move from therapy to mobilization, from soothing prescriptions to techniques of combat. "Superannuated models of political organization, such as the Bolshevik one, should also be rethought, that is, questioned from this perspective. In view of the historically new level of mental impoverishment, the structure of organizations for political struggle can no longer be determined by the sole criterion of political efficiency and organizational ability. The therapeutic viewpoint must enter and determine the structure of revolutionary organizations in the sense of creating qualitatively new, non-alienated, non-reified forms of communication. The political 'self-organization' must simultaneously be a therapeutic 'self-organization' in which atomized, psychically depleted, 'ill' individuals, whose ability to communicate has been inhibited, acquire together with their political consciousness also a collective ego consciousness, a cooperative 'ego strength' " (Schneider, op. cit. p. 260).

What we need is an analytic technique which moves from the analysis of money to the analysis of what is not money, a technique for the retraining of those who have despaired of society into those who hope for its future, of a hopeless person into a participant, a passive into an active individual, an apolitical into a revolutionary one. Everything this study has taught us about the pathogenous characteristics of money and the interest in it must be reminted into a psychotechnique for overcoming money, for overcoming the tyranny of capital, for teaching participation in a society free of the dictatorship of money.

There is no such thing as "reforms," "improvements" of capitalism. There is only the alternative between destruction in a totally dehumanized, opaque chaos governed by demonic forces, and the rise into a humane, rational, and comprehensible world of the gratification of useful desires. What Norman O. Brown calls the social order of polymorphousness is what we mean by a classless society: an order which is dominated neither by the oral nor the anal, the phallic or the genital, a nonhierarchical, decentralized society of free individuals whose voluntary association serves the unhampered development of their individual personalities. Such a society must have a psycho-technique which stimulates rather than adapts, serves constant vigilance rather than "reassurance and pacification," permanent revolution, not the inculcation of submissiveness.

The psychoanalysis of capital must become a psycho-technique for the prevention of capitalism. The analysis of money must develop into a therapy that will cure us of the interest in it.

Translated by Michael Shaw

BIBLIOGRAPHIES

Acknowledgments and Bibliography of Psychiatric and Psychological Writings on the Theory of Money

1. K. Abraham: "*Ergaenzungen zur Lehre vom Analcharakter*" in: *Psychoanalytische Studien zur Charakterbildung*, Frankfurt am Main, 1969

2. K. Abraham: "The Spending of Money in Anxiety States," Contribution 5 of this volume. Originally in: *Internationale Zeitschrift fuer aerztliche Psychoanalyse*, 4, 1917, 252-253. Chapter XIV, "The Spending of Money in Anxiety States," from *Selected Papers of Karl Abraham, M.D.*, with an Introductory Memoir by Ernest Jones, translated by Douglas Bryan and Alix Strachey, Basic Books, Inc., Publishers, New York

3. R. F. Allendy: *Capitalism et sexuality*, Paris, 1932

4. André Amar: "A Psychoanalytic Study of Money," Contribution 15 of this volume. Translation by Michael Shaw from the French "*Essai psychanalytique sur l'argent.*" Appeared originally in: *Revue Francaise de Psychanalyse* 20, 1956, 332-344, reprinted with permission of Presses Universitaires de France, Paris

5. E. Bergler: "Are you a Money Neurotic?" Appeared in *Harper's Bazaar*, May, 1958, 94-95, 140

6. E. Bergler: *Money and Emotional Conflicts*, New York, 1951

7. E. Bergler: "The Psychopathology of Bargain Hunters," Contribution 13, originally appeared in the *Journal of Clinical Psychology*, 8, 1947, 623-627, reprinted with kind permission of The Psychiatric Digest/ Medical Digest, Inc.

8. E. Bergler: "*Zur Psychologie des Hasardspielers,*" in *Imago* 22, 1936

9. S. Blanton: "The Hidden Faces of Money," from: Blanton and A. Gordon: *Now or Never, The Promise of the Middle Years*, New York, 1959, Contribution 12 of this volume, reprinted with the permission of Prentice Hall, Inc., Englewood Cliffs, New Jersey

10. G. Bose: "Business and Psychoanalysis," from: *Englishman*, 1925

11. I. H. Coriat: "Anal-erotic Traits in Shylock," from: *International Journal of Psycho-Analysis*

12. I. H. Coriat: "A Note on the Anal Character Traits of the Capitalist Instinct," Contribution 3 of this volume, from: *Psychoanalytic Review*, 11, 1924, 435-437, reprinted with friendly permission of Psychoanalytic Review, New York
13. B. Dattner: "*Gold und Kot*," from: *Internationale Zeitschrift fuer aerztliche Psychoanalyse*, 1, 1913, 495-496
14. W. H. Desmonde: *Magic, Myth and Money*, Glencoe, 1962
15. W. H. Desmonde: "On the Anal Origins of Money," Contribution 7 of this volume, appeared originally in *Imago*, reprinted with friendly permission of the Wayne State University Press
16. W. H. Desmonde: "The Origins of Money in the Animal Sacrifice," Contribution 8 of this volume, originally appeared in the *Journal of Hillside Hospital*, 6, 1957, 7-23, reprinted with friendly permission of this journal
17. O. Fenichel: "The Drive to Accumulate Money," an essay given on January 5, 1935, before the Czech Psychoanalytic Society, translated by David Brunswick under the title: "The Drive to Amass Wealth" in *Psychoanalytic Quarterly*, 7, 1938, 69-95
18. S. Ferenzci: "Pecunia-olet," Contribution 4 of this volume, originally appeared in *Internationale Zeitschrift fuer aerztliche Psychoanalyse*, 4, 1916, 327, Chapter LXIX, "Pecunia Olet," from *Further Contributions to the theory and Technique of Psychoanalysis* (Selected Papers of Sandor Ferenczi, M.D., Volume II), by Sandor Ferenczi, published by The Hogarth Press, Ltd., and The Institute of Psycho-Analysis, London, and Basic Books, Inc., Publishers, New York.
19. S. Ferenczi: "*Reizungen der analen erogenen Zone als ausloesende Ursache der Paranoia*," from: *Zentralblatt fuer Psychoanalyse und Psychotherapy* 1, 1911, 557-559
20. S. Ferenczi: "*Sonntagsneurosen*," from: *Schriften zur Psychoanalyse*, Volume 1, Frankfurt am Main, 1970, 260-264
21. S. Ferenczi: "*Zur Ontogenie des Geldinteresses*," Contribution 2 of this volume, appeared originally in: *Internationale Zeitschrift fuer aerztliche Psychoanalyse*, 2, 1914, 506-513, reprinted with friendly permission of the Hogarth Press, Ltd., the Institute of Psychoanalysis, London, and Basic Books, Inc., New York
22. S. Freud: " Character and Anal Eroticism, "Contribution 1 of this volume from: *Psychiatrisch-neurologische Wochenschrift* 9, 1908, Heft 52, 465–467, reprinted with the friendly permission of Basic Books, Inc., Chapter IV, "Character and Anal Erotism," from *Collected Papers of Sigmund Freud*, Volume 2, authorized translation under the supervision of Joan Riviere, published by Basic Books, Inc., by arrangement with The Hogarth Press, Ltd., and The Institute of Psycho-Analysis, London
23. S. Freud: "*Ueber Triebumsetzung insbesondere der Analerotik*," from: *Internationale Zeitschrift fuer Psychoanalyse*, 4, 1917, 125-130
24. E. Fromm: "Individual and social Origins of Neurosis," in: *American Sociology Review* 9, 1944, 380-384
25. E. Fromm: "Social Origins of Neurosis," in: A.M. Rose (Ed.): *Mental Health and Mental Disorder*, New York, 1955
26. E. Fromm: "*Probeerhebungen ueber die seelische Einstellung Arbeitsloser zur Unterstuetzung in USA*," in: *Studien ueber Autoritaet und Familie*, Volume 1, 463-469, Paris, 1936

27. M. Ginsberg: "Property and Possessiveness," originally appeared in S. Isaacs (Ed.) *Childhood and After*, London, 1948, 63-69
28. Graumann/Froehlich: "*Ansaetze zu einer psychologischen Analyse des sogenannten Steuerwiderstandes*," in: *Finanzarchiv*, N.F. volume 15, 1957
29. J. Harnik: "*Kulturgeschichtliches zum Thema Geldkomplex und Analerotik*," Contribution 6 of this volume, "Some Data from Cultural History Relating to the Subject of the Money Complex and Anal Erotism," originally appeared in *Internationale Zeitschrift fuer aerztliche Psychoanalyse*, 5, 1919, 121-122
30. K. G. Holtgrewe: "*Der Steuerwiderstand. Das Verhalten des Steuerpflichtigen im Lichte der modernen Psychologie*," in: *Finanzwissenschaftliche Forschungsarbeiten*, N.F. volume 5, 1954
31. S. Isaacs: "Property and Possessiveness," originally appeared in: *Childhood and After*, London, 1948, 69-78
32. E. Jones: "*Haarschneiden und Geiz*," appeared originally in *Internationale Zeitschrift fuer aerztliche Psychoanalyse*, 2, 1914, 383.
33. E. Jones: "*Hass und Analerotik in der Zwangsneurose*," in: *Internationale Zeitschrift fuer aerztliche Psychoanalyse*, 1, 1913, 425-430
34. E. Jones: "*Ueber Analerotische Charakterzuege*," in: *Internationale Zeitschrift fuer aerztliche Psychoanalyse*, 5, 1919, 69-92
35. W. Kaufmann: "Some Emotional Uses of Money," Contribution 11 of this volume, originally appeared in *Acta Psychotherapeutica*, 4, 1956, 20-41, reprinted with kind permission from S. Karger AG, Basel
36. R. Laforgue: "*Gold und Kapital. Psychoanalytische Bemerkungen*," in: *Psychoanalytische Bewegung*, 3, 1931, 481-492
37. A. Lauterbach: *Man, Motives and Money. Psychological Frontiers of Economics*, Ithaca, 1954
38. A. Lauterbach: *Psychologie des Wirtschaftslebens*, Reinbek, 1962
39. H. Lierz: *Psyche und Eigentum*, dissertation, Cologne, 1956
40. T. H. Marshall: "Property and Possessiveness," originally appeared in S. Isaacs (Ed.) *Childhood and After*, London, 1948, 78-83
41. P. Matussek: "*Zur Psychodynamik des Gluecksspielers*," in *Jahrbuch fuer Psychologie und Psychotherapie*, 1955
42. R. P. Morris: "Personality Characteristics of Gamblers," in: *Journal of Clinical Psychology*, 13, 1957
43. E. G. Neisser: "Emotional and social Values Attached to Money," in: *Marriage and Family Living*, 22, 1960, 132-138
44. Ch. Odier: "*L'argent et les neuroses*," in: *Revue Francaise de Psychanalyse*, 2-4, 1928-1930
45. Ch. Odier: "*Le complexe du petit profit*," in: *Revue Francaise de Psychanalyse* 5, 1932, 402-423
46. B. Parker: *Therapie und Honorar*, Frankfurt am Main, 1970, 196-214
47. O. Pfister: *Der seelische Aufbau des klassischen Kapitalismus und des Geldgeistes*, Bern, 1923
48. S. H. Posinsky: "Yurok Shell Money and 'Pains,' " Contribution 10 of this volume, originally appeared in *Psychiatric Quarterly*, 30, 1956, 598-632, reprinted with kind permission from Psychiatric Quarterly
49. Th. Reik: *Geld und Kot*," originally appeared in: *Internationale Zeitschrift fuer aerztliche Psychoanalyse*, 3, 1915, 183
50. J. Riviere: "Hate, Greed and Aggression," in: M. Klein and J. Riviere: *Love, Hate and Reparation*, London, 1953, 3-53

51. G. Róheim: "*Heiliges Geld in Melanesien,*" originally appeared in: *Internationale Zeitschrift fuer Psychoanalyse*, 9, 1923, 384-401, and also available in the *Selected Essays of Géza Róheim,*
52. G. Róheim: "*La psychologie raciale et les origines du capitalisme chez les primitifs*, originally appeared in: *Revue Francaise de Psychanalyse*, 3, 1929, 122-149, but also available in the *Selected Essays of Géza Róheim*
53. G. Róheim: "*Die Urformen und der Ursprung des Eigentums,*" Contribution 9 in *International Archives of Ethnology*, 28, 1927, 1-28, reprinted with friendly permission of Warner Muensterberger.
54. J. Sadger: "*Analerotik und Analcharakter,*" in: *Die Heilkunde*, 1910
55. P. Schilder: "The Psychoanalysis of Economics," Contribution 15 of this volume, originally appeared in *Psychoanalytic Review*, 27, 1940, 401-420, reprinted with friendly permission of Psychoanalytic Review
56. G. Schmoelders: *Psychologie des Geldes*, Reinbek, 1966
57. G. Schmoelders: "*Psychologische Aspekte der europaeischen Waehrungspolitik*" in Riber/Koellner: *Waehrungspolitik in der europaeischen Integration*, Baden-Baden, 1965
58. E. Servadio: "*Il denaro nelle considerazioni di un psicoanalista,*" in: *Meridiano di Roma*, 7, 1936, 18, 25
59. K. Singer: *Das Geld als Zeichen*, Jena, 1920
60. I.D. Suttie: "Property and Possessiveness," in S. Isaacs (Ed.) *Childhood and After*, London, 1948, 51-62
61. W. Taeuber: "*Psychologie des Geldes,*" in: *Jahrbuch fuer Psychologie und Psychotherapy*, 1, 1952, Volume 1
62. F. Vonessen: "*Sich selbst bestehlen. Von der symbolischen Natur des Eigentums,*" in: *Symbolon*, 5, 1966, 25-38
63. F. Wilken: "*Phaenomenologie des Geldwertbewusstseins,*" in: *Archiv fuer Sozialwissenschaft und Sozialpolitik*, 1926, 420 ff.
64. E. Zolla: "*Gola, invidia ed avariza,*" in Zolla: *La Psicoanalisa*, Milan, 1960, 196-197

Bibliography of the Origin and History of Money

65. L. Brentano: *Das Wirtschaftsleben der antiken Welt*, Jena, 1929
66. B. Büchsenschütz: *Besitz und Erwerb im griechischen Alterthume*, Halle, 1869
67. K. Bücher: *Die Entstehung der Volkswirtschaft*, Tübingen, 1901
68. A. R. Burns: *Money and Monetary Policy in Early Times*, London, 1927
69. J. G. D. Clark: *Prehistoric Europe. The economic Basis.* London, 1952
70. Ch. Comte: *Traité de la propriété*, Paris, 1834
71. E. Curtius: "*Uber den religiösen Charakter der griechischen Münzen*," in: *Monatsschrift der Preussischen Akademie der Wissenschaften*, 1869, 466 ff.
72. L. Dargun: "*Ursprung und Entwicklungsgeschichte des Eigentums*, in: *Zeitschrift für vergleichende Rechtswissenshaft*, 5, 1884, I ff.
73. Fr. Delekat: "*Vom Wesen des Geldes. Eine theologische Marxanalyse*," in: *Marxismusstudien*, Volume I, Tübingen, 1953
74. A. Deloume: *Les manieurs d'argent à Rome jusqu'à l'empire*, Paris, 1889
75. M. Dobb: "*Marx on Pre-Capitalist Economic Formations*," in: *Science and Society*, 30, 1966, 319-325
76. J. R. Ederer: *The Evolution of Money*, Washington D. C., 1964
77. P. Einzig: *Primitive Money*, London, 1948
78. Fr. Engels: *Der Ursprung der Familie, des Privateigentums und des Staats*, MEW, Volume 21, Berlin, 1962
79. L. Felix: *Entwicklungsgeschichte des Eigentums*, 1883-1903. Reprinted Aalen, 1963
80. B. Fritsch: *Die Geld- und Kredittheorie von Karl Marx*, Frankfurt am Main, 1968
81. H. Gebhard: *Numismatik und Geldgeschichte*, Heidelberg, 1949
82. W. Gerloff: *Die Entstehung des Geldes und die Anfänge des Geldwesens*, Frankfurt am Main, 1947
83. H. Grossmann: *Das Akkumulations- und Zusammenbruchsgesetz des kapitalistischen Systems*, 1929. Reprinted Frankfurt am Main, 1968
84. B. V. Head: *Historia Numerorum*, Oxford, 1911
85. Fr. M. Heichelheim: *Wirtschaftsgeschichte des Altertums*, Leiden, 1938
86. R. Hilferding, *Das Finanzkapital*, Frankfurt am Main, 1968
87. E. Hobsbawm, *Introduction to Pre-Capitalist Economic Formations*, New York, 1965
88. M. Kaser: *Eigentum und Besitz im älteren römischen Recht*, Weimar, 1943
89. R. Kaulla: *Beiträge zur Entstehungsgeschichte des Geldes*, Bern, 1945
90. M. Kovalevski: *Tableau des origines et de l'évolution de la famille et de la propriété*, Stockholm, 1890
91. S. J. Kowaljew (Ed.): *Karl Marx und Friedrich Engels über die Antike*, in Russian, Leningrad, 1932
92. J. A. Kronrod: *Das Geld in der sozialistischen Gesellschaft*, in Russian, 1960, in German, 1963

93. J. Kuczynki: *Allgemeine Wirtschaftsgeschichte von der Urzeit bis zur sozialistischen Gesellschaft*, Berlin, 1951
94. B. Laum: *Heiliges Geld*, Tübingen, 1924
95. B. Laum: *Uber das Wesen des Münzgeldes*, Halle, 1929
96. A. Lemnitz: *Das Geld und die Funktion des Geldes im Sozialismus und in der Ubergangsperiode vom Kapitalismus zum Sozialismus*, Berlin, 1955
97. A. Luschin von Ebengreuth: *Allgemeine Münzkunde und Geldgeschichte*, 1926
98. G. Macdonald: *Coin Types. Their Origin and Development*, Glasgow, 1905
99. B. Malinowski: "*Kula. The circulating Exchange of Valuables in the Archipelagos of Eastern New Guinea*," in: *Man*, 20, 1920, 97-105.
100. F. K. Mann: "*Die Finanzkomponente der Revolution*," in: *Finanztheorie und Finanzsoziologie*, Göttingen, 1959
101. N. Marr and A. G. Prijuzin: *Probleme der Geschichte der vorkapitalistischen Gesellschaftsordnungen*, in Russian, Moskow—Leningrad, 1934
102. K. Marx: *Das Kapital*, MEW, Volume 23, 24, 25, Berlin, 1968/69
103. K. Marx: *Lohn, Preis und Profit*, MEW, Volume 16, Berlin, 1968
104. K. Marx: *Lohnarbeit und Kapital*, MEW, Volume 6, Berlin, 1968
105. E. Meyer: "*Die wirtschaftliche Entwicklung des Altertums*," in: *Jahrbuch für Nationalökonomie und Statistik*, 3rd series, 9th Volume, 1895
106. M. Meyer-Holzapfel: *Die Bedeutung des Besitzes bei Tier und Mensch, Ein psychologischer Vergleich*, Biel, n.d.
107. C. Miller: *Studien zur Geschichte der Geldehre*, Stuttgart-Berlin, 1925
108. F. Negro: *Das Eigentum. Geschichte und Zukunft*, München, 1963
109. B. Nelson: *The Idea of Usury*, Princeton, 1949
110. W. Nippold: *Die Anfänge des Eigentums bei den Naturvölkern und die Entstehung des Privateigentums*, Den Haag, 1954
111. N. Oresmius: *De mutatione monetarum tractatus*, E. Schorer, Jena, 1937
112. R. Petrucci: "*Les origines naturelles de la propriété*," in: *Institut Solvay*, 3, 1005, 14
113. P.-J. Proudhon: *Qu'est ce que la propriété?* Paris, 1840-1841
114. A. H. Quiggin: *A Survey of Primitive Money. The Beginning of Currency.* London, 1949
115. J. Salvioli: *Der Kapitalismus im Altertum*, Stuttgart, 1912
116. R. Sannwald: "*Marx und die Antike*," in: *Staatswissenschaftiche Studien*, N. F. 27, 1957
117. J. Schacht: *Die Totenmaske Gottes. Kulturanthropologie des Geldes*, Schweinfurt, 1964
118. R. Schlatter: *Private Property. The History of an Idea*, London, 1951
119. A. Sègre: *An Essay on the Nature of Real Property in the Classical World*, New York, 1943
120. G. Simmel: *Die Philosophie des Geldes*, München, 1922
121. F. Somlo: *Der Güterverkehr in der Urgesellschaft*, Brussels—Leipzig, 1909
122. F. Somlo: "*Der wirtschaftliche Urzustand*," in: *Monatsschrift für Soziologie*, März, 1909
123. C. R. Temple: "*Beginnings of Currency*," in: *Journal of the Royal Anthropological Institute*, 29, 1899, 102 ff.